ARCHITECTURE

THE NATURAL AND THE MANMADE

Other books by Vincent Scully

The Architectural Heritage of Newport, Rhode Island
(with Antoinette Downing)

The Shingle Style

Frank Lloyd Wright

Modern Architecture

Louis I. Kahn

The Earth, the Temple, and the Gods

Arquitectura Actual

American Architecture and Urbanism

The Shingle Style Today

Pueblo Architecture of the Southwest
(with William Current)

Pueblo: Mountain, Village, Dance

The Villas of Palladio
(with Philip Trager)

New World Visions of Household Gods and Sacred Places

The Architecture of the American Summer

ARCHIT

ECTURE

THE NATURAL AND THE MANMADE

VINCENT SCULLY

ST. MARTIN'S PRESS

NEW YORK

Cover image: Delphi, Temple of Apollo.

Full title page: fig. 413. Bensançon. Tour Bastionnée Vauban.

Photo opposite Contents: fig. 276. Reims. Cathedral. West facade, with equestrian statue of Joan of Arc.

Photo opposite Preface: fig. 159. Athens. Parthenon from the east.

ARCHITECTURE: THE NATURAL AND THE MANMADE.

Copyright © 1991 by Vincent Scully. All rights reserved. Printed in the United States of America. No part of this book may be used or reproduced in any manner whatsoever without written permission except in the case of brief quotations embodied in critical articles or reviews. For information, address St. Martin's Press, 175 Fifth Avenue, New York, N.Y. 10010.

Library of Congress Cataloging-in-Publication Data
Scully, Vincent Joseph.
    Architecture : the natural and the manmade / Vincent Scully.
        p.   cm.
    ISBN 0-312-06292-3 (hc.)
    ISBN 0-312-09742-5 (pbk.)
    1. Architecture.   2. Nature (Aesthetics)   I. Title.
    NA2520.S37   1991
    720—dc20   91-21550
                                                         CIP

First Edition: November 1991
First Paperback Edition: October 1993
10 9 8 7 6 5 4 3 2 1

For Tappy

In memory of Frank Brown
and Eugene Vanderpool

CONTENTS

PREFACE

This book grows out of the research and teaching of some forty-five years. For this reason, and perhaps for others unrecognized by me, the treatment of its theme varies in density and detail from place to place and time to time. I have written extensively in the past about Greek and Pueblo architecture, so that those and related chapters are perhaps more summary in treatment than others dealing, for example, with Gothic architecture and the French classic garden. The latter especially, in my opinion, has never been written about properly or its greatness appreciated. I therefore argue the issues related to it in greater detail than is normally employed elsewhere. However, all the chapters in this book have in common the fact that they are conceived visually, as part of an extended visual experience, shaping an argument that can be carried on throughout the history of architecture entire.

Indeed, the relationship of manmade structures to the natural world offers, in my view at least, the richest and most valuable physical and intellectual experience that architecture can show, and it is the one that has been most neglected by Western architectural critics and historians.[1] There are many reasons for this. Foremost among them, perhaps, is the blindness of the contemporary urban world to everything that is not itself, to nature most of all. That highly dangerous condition is beginning to change for the better at the present time. My life's work, like that of other scholars in many disciplines, has been largely devoted to dispelling it. But the visual and conceptual reorientation involved in seeing things whole and as they are in nature is not easy to accomplish on the printed page. It is never possible, for example, to illustrate the whole vast landscape clearly enough with the kind of illustrations that are normally available in books. Nor is it always possible to persuade the reader to consult the visual evidence in a book at those moments in the visual/verbal discourse when looking is most necessary.

For these reasons, a book, which in terms of scholarship is most easily produced in a library employing a library's tools, is not a wholly satisfactory medium through which to explore the most fundamental architectural themes. Here film is in fact the best available answer to the problem, or ought to be, despite its various failures in the architectural field so far. Therefore a series of some eight films to complement this book is now in preparation. Its completion will, however, take several years.

Meanwhile, I hope that this book can stand by itself. In its coordination of text and illustrations, it at least tries to deal with what I believe to be the essential fact of architecture and, indeed, of human life on earth: the relation of mankind to the natural order. That it rarely can be as successful in that attempt as I would like it to be is the fault of its author, not of its theme. It is illustrated in large part with my own slides and photographs, some of them old friends of long standing, veterans of many teaching years. If sometimes technically primitive and battered by time, they at least illustrate what I have seen myself, and so supplement my text as others, however accomplished, cannot normally do. But a word should be said in conclusion about my previous work in this field. From 1955 until 1963 I studied the relationship between temples and landscape in Greece, resulting in *The Earth, the Temple, and the Gods,* of 1962, and in its various later editions,[2] while from 1964 until 1973 I concentrated on similar problems in the American Southwest and Mesoamerica, resulting in *Pueblo: Mountain, Village, Dance,* of 1975 and, after further work in 1987–1988, in its new edition of 1989.[3] In 1975 I began to study French gardens and fortifications of the seventeenth century from a similar point of view and was led by them into further interpretations of modern urbanism and the architecture of the nation-state and of war. These topics came to be associated in my mind with work on French Gothic cathedrals which I had begun in 1946–1952 and picked up again in 1975, and the topic as a whole resulted in the Mellon Lectures of 1982 at the National Gallery of Art in Washington, D.C., and the William Clyde DeVane Lectures of 1988–1989 at Yale. This book represents an extensive rewriting of the latter series.[4]

I am grateful to Caroline Astrid Bruzelius, who read an early version of the Gothic chapters some years ago and made many excellent suggestions; to Ann Friedman, who read the chapters on the French garden at the same time; to my colleague Mary Miller, who has helped me in pre-Columbian studies in many substantive ways; and to James Wilson, whose conversations with me about Louis XIV were always a delight. At this time, too, one thinks of friends now gone from whom one learned so much, especially of Eugene Vanderpool of the American School of Classical Studies in Athens, with whom I tramped the mountains of Greece and Turkey and whose love of landscape was another spur to my own, and of Frank E. Brown of Yale University and the American Academy in Rome, in my view the greatest teacher of classical architecture of our time and the very embodiment of the soul, and the authority, of Rome.

I think as well not only of architects I have known whose work helped me see— Frank Lloyd Wright, Le Corbusier, Mies van der Rohe, Philip Johnson, Louis I. Kahn, Robert Venturi, Aldo Rossi, Leon Krier, and, in special ways, Robert A. M. Stern and Allan Greenberg—but also of the thousands of students, among them architects, art historians, and the undergraduates of Yale, with whom I have discussed these issues, to my great benefit over the years. I owe a special debt to Christopher Maclehose, who asked for this book, to all the editors of Collins Harvill and St. Martin's Press for their diligence and good will in producing it, and especially to Thomas McCormack, James Bugslag, Karen Gillis, Amélie Littell, Eric Meyer, Blake Spraggins, and Robert

Weil. Other colleagues, students, and friends have helped this work along: Helen Chillman in every way as usual, Barbara Adams with her continuing support, Amy Weisser and Andrew Myers with the illustrations, Elizabeth Peyton with the notes, and Susan Emerson and Glen Bailey with the typing. I am deeply grateful to Kris Ellam for her generous help in England, to Isabelle Gournay and her parents

for their hospitality and many kindnesses in France, and to my dear wife, Catherine Lynn, for her unfailing comradeship and support. I also think, among others, of my children, Daniel, Stephen, John, and Katherine, my daughters-in-law, Carol and Rosanna, and my grandchildren, Michael, Benjamin, Eleanor, and Chiara, some of whom love architecture as much as I do.

NOTES

[1] With the exception of America, this book deals only with European architecture and its precursors around the Mediterranean. India and the Far East are not included. I am deeply sorry for this lack but cannot remedy it at present, since this topic precludes writing about sites not visited in person. On the other hand, fundamental themes such as that of the Sacred Mountain are common to American, Mediterranean, Indian, and Far Eastern architecture alike and have previously been much better explored in relation to Asiatic developments. A glance at a Jungian potpourri like Joseph Campbell's *The Mythic Image,* Princeton, 1974, shows the weight given to Asian examples. More directly visual and art-historical approaches, like that of Nelson Wu in his short but trenchant book, *Chinese and Indian Architecture,* New York, 1963, tell the same story, and Chinese and Japanese gardens, too, have been especially well studied, as recently by Maggie Keswick, *The Chinese Garden,* London, 1978. In that

sense, therefore, the architecture of India, China, Japan, and Southeast Asia has already been at least partially explored along these lines.

[2] Yale University Press, New Haven and London, 1962. New enlarged eds. 1969, 1979.

[3] Viking Press, New York, 1975. 2nd enlarged ed. Chicago University Press, Chicago, 1989.

[4] I also wrote an article, "Architecture: The Natural and the Manmade," for a symposium on landscape in modern architecture, of 1988, at the Museum of Modern Art in New York (not yet published), and another, "Mankind and the Earth in America and Europe," for the catalogue of an exhibition of Mesoamerican sites organized by Richard Townsend for the Chicago Art Institute, scheduled for 1991.

1
AMERICA:
THE SACRED MOUNTAIN

THE SHAPE OF ARCHITECTURE is the shape of the earth as it is modified by the structures of mankind. Out of that relationship, human beings fashion an environment for themselves, a space to live in, suggested by their patterns of life and constructed around whatever symbols of reality seem important to them. Most of all, that environment and those structures invest the vast indifference of nature with meanings intelligible to, indeed imagined by, mankind, and they involve in the end all those complex relationships of human buildings with each other that shape within nature a new manmade topography: the human city entire. At present, most human beings of the developed nations live in an environment that is almost entirely manmade, or think they do so. Hence the major contextual questions of contemporary architecture have come to be those having to do with the modification of existing manmade environments by new structures. But underneath all the complexity of those urban situations the larger reality still ex-

21. Puye. Buffalo dance.

ists: the fact of nature, and of humanity's response to the challenge—the threat, the opportunity—that nature seems to offer in any given place. It follows, therefore, that the first fact of architecture is the topography of a place and the way human beings respond to it with their own constructed forms. Do they attempt, for example, to echo the shapes of the landscape or to contrast with them? In a rather too large generalization, it might be said that all pre-Greek or non-Greek cultures chose the first alternative and the Greeks more or less invented the second.

Yet the changes played by human cultures upon those two major alternatives have not been simple ones. Each culture has worked special qualities of its own into them, and the results can be read in all urban groupings, most spectacularly, for example, in New York (fig. 1). There the skyscrapers seem to rush forward to populate the tip of the island as it sails out to sea, each one clamoring to be seen from afar, as if floating on the water. Behind the skyscrapers the man-

27. Tikal. Temple I with clouds.

1. Manhattan. Before 1939. Air view.

3. New York, N.Y. Park Avenue. Before 1950. General view.

made grid stretches the length of the island, dramatizing its length as the great avenues rush uninterrupted to the north. Between them, far uptown, the city breathes its fresh green breath in Central Park, whereby nature is brought into the city, urbanized as garden, here in Olmsted's synthesis of Classic and Romantic modes (fig. 2). Of all the avenues running through the island, Park Avenue was once the outstanding example of what architecture could accomplish in that line (fig. 3). The buildings along it were contiguous and all much the same. They formed a wall shaping the environment as a whole, which was that of the avenue's flow. Its

continuous movement was once enormously dramatized by the spire of the New York Central Building by Whitney Warren, so narrow that the space of the avenue could be perceived as rushing freely past it on both sides, as indeed the traffic itself was made to do around Grand Central Terminal down below.

At present, that movement is visually blocked by the Pan Am Building, a destructive example of Bauhaus design, turned sideways like a table ornament for maximum visibility from the street, thus smothering its flow (fig. 4). Even before that, the wall of buildings shaping the avenue had been breached by Lever House,

2. New York, N.Y. Central Park. 1980s. Air view.

with its slab turned sideways (fig. 313), cutting a big hole in the street facade and actively leading the eye laterally out of it to undesigned chaos beyond. "Look at me, look at me," it cried, the product of an International Style designer who thought in the manner shaped by Bauhaus architectural education: at small, tabletop scale, and of his building alone, and with complete contempt for the existing urban fabric as a whole. That fabric had indeed been Western architecture's climactic achievement, hard won over the centuries, enveloping and complex but fragile, requiring, like everything worthwhile in human culture, continuing civilized care from generation to generation. In New York the rising spires of the skyscrapers of lower Manhattan were finally invaded by the flat slabs of the International Style, of which Chase Manhattan Bank was the

first. These instantly reduced the scale and quelled the wonderfully competitive action of the earlier towers. The whole pyramidal grouping of spires began to die. The tall but inert twin chunks of the World Trade Center seemed to kill the whole thing off at last (fig. 5). So big and dead were they that all the dynamic interrelationships of the earlier buildings came to seem lilliputian, inconsequential in scale. By the late 1980s, however, the lonely dominance of those towers was challenged by a new group of skyscrapers at Battery Park City, which began to pull them into a new, much vaster pyramidal relationship. The new buildings themselves showed a renewed respect for urban principles, casting aside as they did the abstract slab of International Style design. Though much too thin in their surfaces— that itself a legacy from the aesthetics of

4. New York, N.Y. Park Avenue, looking south to the Pan Am Building. 1960s.

5. New York, N.Y. World Trade Center with World Financial Center of Battery Park City, 1982–1989. Cesar Pelli and Associates.

the International Style—they at least began to rise like mountains again, recalling the grand old skyscrapers behind them and creating new canyons between them, calling up the past, standing on the water (fig. 6).

From them, in fact, we can legitimately turn to the canyons of the continent itself, most particularly to the Grand Canyon of the Colorado (fig. 7). Modern Americans are especially fortunate because of the fact that a non-European indigenous

into this Fourth World of earth out of the depths of the Grand Canyon itself. They thus regarded themselves as an integral part of this particular landscape, and their early buildings tended to echo its shapes and evoke its depths.

The little Basket Maker Pit Houses were partly dug into the earth with a *sipapu* in the floor to record the emergence from below, while their low roof profiles echoed the shapes of the mesas around them (fig. 8). The same is true of the in-

6. New York, N.Y. World Financial Center.

culture is still wholly alive on their continent and a pre-Hellenistic attitude toward nature can still be read clearly in its architectural forms. Here one thinks especially of the Pueblo people of the Southwest, who believe that their ancestors—the Anasazi, the Ancient Ones—emerged

dividual house type that was introduced into the area around A.D. 1500 by nomads from the north. The Navajo hogan, polygonal and domed over with earth, picks up the profiles and the colors of the lovely painted mesas that shape its horizons. The same was equally true of earlier types, like the forked-stick hogan. Examples standing in ruin below the incomparable buttes of Monument Valley show a conical shape, once covered with earth to form a little hollow mound evoking the big shapes around it (fig. 9). The entrance doorway faces east into the rising sun. The tiny, lonely family dwelling is thus locked into the patterns of the sky as well as the shapes of the earth, and its circular plan is an image of the enormous desert horizon brought down literally to individual scale. Here, around the periphery of the circle, there is, with great dignity of being, plenty of room for everyone, while the father, standing upright, fills the dome to its apex. When one of the family dies, the hogan is abandoned, and a hole is cut through its western side to release the soul.

The architectural principle at work in these individual dwellings, therefore, is that of the imitation of natural forms by human beings who seek thereby to fit themselves safely into nature's order. When the resources of large populations made it possible to build monumental architectural forms of communal function and at the landscape's scale, exactly the same principle was brought to bear. We can see it at work in Teotihuacán (figs. 10,

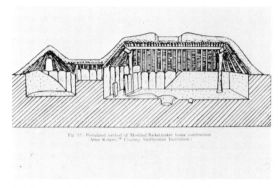

8. Mesa Verde, Colorado. Pit House, Modified Basket Maker. Section.

9. Monument Valley. Navaho hogan.

11), which was in all likelihood the most important ceremonial center the North American continent ever produced. There, the long axis of the site is traversed by an avenue called "of the Dead" by the Aztecs and, in all likelihood, by its original builders. Elsewhere, as among the Hopi, the god of death is the god of the city, because it is in the city that the living are closest to the dead. They build it together. It is a conversation between generations, the closest state to immortality that living human beings can know. At Teotihuacán the Avenue of the Dead runs straight toward the pyramidal notched mountain, the Cerro Gordo, but more properly called Tenan, Our Lady of Stone, running with springs, which closes the site on the north side.* Directly below it lies the Temple of the Moon—that name probably pre-Aztec as well—at once repeating and compacting its profiles. The shape of the mountain is echoed but intensified by human symmetry and geometry; its power is thus harnessed and abetted. Men,

*So named in Stephen Tobriner, "The Fertile Mountain: An Investigation of Cerro Gordo's Importance to the Town Plan and Iconography of Teotihuacán," in *Teotihuacán,* XI Mesa Redonda, Sociedad Mexicana de Antropologia, Mexico, 1972.

10. Teotihuacán. Valley of Mexico. Temple of the Moon with the notched mountain, Tenan, "Our Lady of Stone." 3rd century A.D.

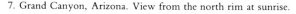

7. Grand Canyon, Arizona. View from the north rim at sunrise.

12. Teotihuacán. Water goddess. Basalt. Before A.D. 300.

13. Teotihuacán. Temple of Quetzalcoatl. Feathered serpent and Tlaloc, detail.

as in human sacrifice, are helping nature along, forcing it to function, just as they fed it with their blood. So the pyramid of the temple is compacted, with strong horizontal shadow lines as of internal fracture. The water in the mountain is being actively squeezed from it and brought down to the valley floor.

11. Teotihuacán. Temple of the Moon and the Avenue of the Dead. With Tenan.

That this interpretation is a valid one is corroborated by the shape of the water goddess from Teotihuacán which is now in the Archaeological Museum in the capital (fig. 12). A great mass presses down upon her head. Like the cleft heads of Olmec gods, it is notched in the center, as is Tenan itself. Its weight compresses her body, fracturing it in compression, so that water flows under pressure out of her hands. Below them, her kilt is compressed into strong horizontal fractures like those suggested by the *tablero* construction that especially distinguished the Temple of Quetzalcoatl at Teotihuacán. This stands to the right of the Avenue of the Dead just at the entrance to the ceremonial heart of the site. Here the pressure expressed in the horizontal fractures literally forces the gods of water, Tlaloc and Quetzalcoatl, out of the mountain in jets like springs (fig. 13). Tlaloc is god of the rain, but Quetzalcoatl, in his guise as feathered serpent, seems to embody at once the water from the ground and that from the sky. He is the major divinity of the American land, and his great, fanged, horned and feathered head, bursting with power, stands out on the stairway of his temple, with the pyramids and the sacred moun-

14. Teotihuacán. Temple of Quetzalcoatl with the horned and feathered serpent, with the Temple of the Sun and the Temple of the Moon in the distance.

tain deployed beyond it (fig. 14).

In that view, the Pyramid of the Sun, larger than that of the Moon and equally evocative of the mountain's form, is, nevertheless, not on the central axis. It faces across it toward the sunset of the day of the summer solstice, so fixing the site into the celestial as well as the terrestrial order, but when it is viewed from the Temple of the Moon itself it is seen to be backed by its own mountain mass to the south, just as the central axis of the Avenue of the Dead is also locked into its own set of cones on the southern horizon. In this way the buildings of the site are adjusted to the landscape on all major

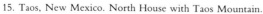

15. Taos, New Mexico. North House with Taos Mountain.

bearings, but the clearly operative line of sight is that along the ceremonial avenue toward the sacred mountain, Tenan, pressing down upon the Temple of the Moon, set like a glowing jewel or a man-made pacemaker in its heart.

The settings of the pueblos of the Southwest, as we can see them now in modern times, are essentially the same. Taos remains the most traditional and complete of them all (fig. 15). North House echoes the forms of Taos Mountain but clarifies and abstracts them; South House rises as a pyramid in the folds of the Sangre de Cristo behind it, and a never-failing stream runs down between the two, drawn out of the mountain's fastnesses, where sacred Blue Lake lies cupped below horned peaks.

North House is a communal dwelling. Hence its sacred function is not purely specialized, like the pyramids of Mexico. But its profiles, though asymmetrical, are fundamentally pyramidal. In the typical Pueblo way its statement is unemphatic and partly concealed. It is also packed with people, hence egalitarian in the Pueblo manner. But it is wholly sacred too, and, much more than the solid, symmetrical pyramids of Mexico, its syncopated masses clearly dance before the mountain's face. They are active themselves. At the same time, seen from the west, North House rises straight into the sky, and the step-backs of its south face shape the typical Pueblo sky-altar, abstracting the shapes of the clouds (fig. 16). The building itself is once again the god of sky and mountain alike, no less wholly embodied in it than at Teotihuacán.

The sacred dances that can be seen at Taos—miraculous that Stone Age rituals are still alive in the modern world—all culminate before the face of North House, and they cement that union of natural and

16. Taos Pueblo. The sky-altar.

17. Taos. "Justice Day." 1968.

manmade which mountain and building establish (fig. 17). Spectators look down upon the dancers from the roofs; their own bodies crown the flat cornice lines like a Classical frieze. Below them the dog dancers may sniff, questing for the scalp sticks in the Comanche dances of spring. In deep winter the buffalo come tramping along before the building in a blind herd, each dancer wearing the whole buffalo head, some without eyes (fig. 399). Each carries an arrow and so is prey and hunter as well. Catlin painted such a dance among the Mandans of the Northern Plains. It cannot be photographed at Taos. Sometimes between the buffalo a were-deer walks entranced, the dancer wearing the whole deer skin, the tongue lolling out in death, the foresticks, which are the forelegs, carried dangling in his hands—he blank-eyed, neither wholly man nor animal, a ghost of the dead prey loved and desired.

Southward along the Rio Grande, the camera can be brought into play. Photography is allowed under certain, not too stringent, conditions at the Tewa pueblos that are settled in the great bowl of landscape just north of Santa Fe. At Tesuque the long lines of the corn dancers, the army of the pueblo, stretch out in front of the low sand hills to the west of the town and, most of all, before the climactic ranges of the Sangre de Cristo to the east of it (fig. 18). There, the profiles of the governor's house on the plaza subtly repeat the profiles of Lake Peak, which is the Sacred Mountain of the East for the Tewa in this area. Between its horns, too, a deep, quiet lake lies open to the sky.

Beside the governor's house, the facade of the Christian church, the European intruder, is the only vertical plane in the pueblo, and it alone is painted white— that, too, an intrusive, ultimately Hellenic color (fig. 19). But the towers, so important in Mexico and, as at Ranchos de Taos, in all the Hispanic towns of New Mexico, have been sheared off, so that the parapet of the church not only suggests a sky-altar but also picks up the gently mounded profile of the mountain—Old Baldy—that rises behind it. In this way, European religion has been gentled into the Pueblo pantheon, and the beat of the dancers before its face declares the unity of church and landscape as well. The natural, the

18. Tesuque Pueblo, New Mexico. Corn dance with Sangre de Cristo.

manmade, and the human act of ritual in the dance all become one.

The feet of the male dancers in the corn dance pound the earth while the turtle-shell rattles shiver with rain sounds behind their knees and the bells on their moccasins jingle like showers. Behind each of the men, a woman dances, sometimes more than one, their feet never leaving the earth but caressing it. The sky-altars on their heads pick up the shapes of the clouds. The men are warriors, forcing the earth to open and produce life; the women gently assist in that birth, and the long lines of men and women together touch the mountain profiles no less than those of the buildings near at hand. They affirm in this way that nature's indifferent machine may well be kept in motion by human beings, who are, within it, a thinking, scheming, caring part. Humanity throws the weight of its numbers into the scale of things, so that the city seems to take on a power to affect nature's rhythms, perhaps even to shape natural events. From time immemorial, the nomads of the Southwest—Apache, Kiowa, Navajo—have flocked to the Pueblo dances for exactly that reason. As the king of the Scythians was drawn to the rites of Dionysos in a Greek colony on the Black Sea, so here the wanderers come, hoping to tap into a power more effective than their own. It is a power that only the city

19. Tesuque Pueblo. Corn dance with "Old Baldy" and Lake Peak, Sacred Mountain of the East.

can seem to wield, because only there are enough human beings able to work together so that a critical mass able to sway nature may perhaps be attained.

In the Southwest, that power has traditionally been directed largely toward rectifying nature's greatest shortcoming in the region: its inability, all too often, to rain. Desiccation has been increasing in the Pueblo area for several thousand years. From the beginning human beings fought it with the public works of irrigation ditches, canals, and so on, and with magic. They are still doing so. The buffalo dance of winter, for example, is intended to help bring the snow. The greatest of such dances today are those of the Keres people to the south of Santa Fe at the pueblos of Cochiti, Santo Domingo, and San Felipe; they cannot be photographed. But at Puye, a prehistoric Tewa pueblo west of Tesuque (fig. 20), situated on land owned by the modern pueblo of Santa Clara, fragments of such dances can be recorded.

The plaza of Puye is set on the summit of a long *potrero,* sailing like a ship above the Pajarito Plateau below the heights of the Jemez Range, where the Tewa Sacred

20. Puye. The plaza. July 1968.

22. Walpi. San Francisco. Peaks right, horned buttes left.

Mountain of the West rises. It is Tsi-como, cloud gatherer, and every summer, when the dances are held at Puye, the storm clouds assemble around the summit by noontime, and lightning sometimes strikes among the spectators who crowd the tops of the ruins as once they stood on the roofs of the houses that shaped the plaza of the town. The long axis of the plaza runs from east to west with its major entrance at the southeast, from which a strong line of sight runs diagonally across the plaza toward the summit of Tsi-como itself. In this charged space the buffalo come stamping forward wearing the magnificently abstracted buffalo headdress of the Tewa and Keres, not the whole blind head as at Taos (fig. 21). In the winter dances they bring the snow clouds with their stamping. They are heroes, dancing

upright, believing themselves to be the hunters but doomed in the end to be the prey. Sometimes, late in the afternoons of the greatest dances, like those at San Felipe and Santo Domingo, they come to realize that fact and may seek to escape from the plaza. They are then run down and brought back by the chorus of hunters, but sometimes, as at Santo Domingo, it may be the buffalo maiden herself, the Amerindian Artemis, Mother of the Beasts, who reaches out to touch their foreheads with her medicine bundle, so bringing them back to the rhythm of the dance, wherein they, with all the other animals, embrace the common fate. Most of all, the dancers are building up power in the pueblo through the long day. The white breast feathers of eagles, tied to the buffalo horns, fly like wild birds under the black clouds. Energy, electric and dangerous, is flowing down through them into the pueblo from the sky. They stamp it into the earth, releasing the sky's waters and driving them into the plaza.

So in the great buffalo dances of the Tewa and Keres pueblos, the buffalo normally wear the plumed water serpent on their kilts. He is surely Quetzalcoatl; the Anasazi called him Avanyu and pecked his image on the rocks. The Hopi call him Palulukang. They catch him as bull snake, whip snake, and rattler down near the water holes in the desert below their mesas, and they dance with him in late-summer dances to call up the rain. In the recent past, the snake dances at Walpi have been perhaps the most moving. They take place by Snake Rock, high up at the tip of First Mesa, under the pyramid of the pueblo that crowns the prow of the mesa there (fig. 22). Out in space, the horns of the sacred buttes march along the south-eastern horizon and the distant masses of the San Francisco peaks, home of the Kachinas, stand out to the southwest. In the face of that tremendous, that dry and fatal landscape, the dancers stamp decisively around the plaza with the serpent in their jaws, its head free to weave and strike if it cares to do so (fig. 23). Its attention is attracted by the eagle feathers with which a second dancer caresses it, turning its poor earth-wriggling self into Quetzalcoatl, at least partly of the sky. Soon it is allowed to undulate through the plaza's dust, inscribing the patterns of rain washes in it, like those to be seen far down in the desert below. Finally, ennobled and befriended, it is released to the open desert itself to bring the rain.

So the pattern has remained much the same in the pueblos and in Mexico since pre-Columbian times. Manmade pyramids echo those of the sacred mountains

23. Walpi. Snake dance. 1911. Carrier and assistant.

still and help them along, whether at Walpi on First Mesa or Monte Albán in Oaxaca (fig. 24). In return, the human structures themselves take on enormous power; they resonate to the horizon. The vast landscape, the whole structure of the world, which human beings from the dawn of their consciousness probably have feared might mean nothing at all, is made to mean something. Human beings—angry, determined—will it to be so, will the "idle gods" of nature to concentrate for once and do their duty to the world. So the Hopi speak sternly to the Kachinas, messengers to the gods, making sure their dim wits grasp the urgency of mortal needs. So human buildings reinforce the landscape's forms, focus them, wind them up to work as they damn well ought to do.

25. Tikal, Guatemala. Temple I, Ah Cacao, and Temple II, Lady Twelve Macaw, at the main plaza.

When, nevertheless, we visit the major Classic Maya site of Tikal, well to the south in modern Guatemala, it appears at first to diverge from that pattern of form and meaning. The temple bases are very tall; there are no mountains on the horizon. The temples ride high above the rain forest as once they rode above the houses of their town. Temple I at Tikal, the highest, contained the tomb of Ah Cacao, a Maya king, and it looks like a human king, tall, imperious, high-crowned (fig. 25). It strongly suggests the embodiment of a human image in an architectural form, and so seems to be the reverse of the landscape image in force elsewhere. Moreover, facing Ah Cacao across the plaza of his acropolis sits his queen, Lady Twelve Macaw, short and broad, husky, as she is carved in relief on the lintel of the temple

24. Monte Albán. Oaxaca. General view looking south.

26. Tikal. Entrance to Temple I.

27. Tikal. Temple I with clouds.

itself. Though no tomb has been found in it, her temple is as much an embodiment of the human figure as is that of the king. The two become the exemplary royal couple; their monumental union is kept in view by the other high temples that were built on the site later. As in Greece, there is some sense that human beings are now confronting nature with forms evocative of their own bodies rather than of nature's topographic shapes. But is there only that? Is the natural analogy wholly absent? I think not. Ah Cacao's temple base rises high. The temple on its summit—unlike those of Mexico, which were made of less permanent materials and are therefore long gone—is still there, a solid concrete mass with very small corbel-vaulted

chambers within it. We mount toward it in the heat, and when we arrive before its doorway, it breathes out a dank, wet breath upon us, the very breath of the clouds, the chill of rain (fig. 26). The roof comb of the temple itself is like a cloud, touching the real clouds above it; the mountain lifts it there (fig. 27).

Hence, the temples at Tikal are at once persons, mountains, and clouds. They rise in stages from earth to heaven, linking the Maya to the sun of life, as well as to the dark afterworld below. They are in fact the first skyscrapers of the North American continent. It is no wonder that when the architects of New York set out in the 1920s to create a set-back image that would at once respond to the new zoning laws to let light into the street and at the same time rise higher than buildings had ever risen before, the shapes they created suggested, and were indeed in part suggested to them by, the Mayan forms. The Paramount Building is a fine early example, rising to a roof comb that is at once Mayan and Art Deco (fig. 28). The Empire State Building climaxes the impulse, leaping to the sky gods like the tallest of all Mayan temple bases and lifting

28. New York, N.Y. Paramount Building. 1925. Rapp & Rapp.

29. New York, N.Y. Empire State Building. Colored postcard. 1939.

its mooring mast to the cloud-floating dirigibles of the time (fig. 29). That relationship to pre-Columbian forms was conscious enough. It surely was to Hugh Ferriss, who was the most influential image maker of the set-back skyscraper type. His major book, *The Metropolis of Tomorrow* (of 1929), was prefaced by a drawing entitled "Buildings Like Mountains," showing a skyscraper emerging out of mountain forms. And when Ferriss shows his skyscrapers rising up mountainously out of the city below them (fig. 30), it is Tikal to the life, as its temples deploy in space to keep those of Ah Cacao and Lady Twelve Macaw in view (fig. 31).

The architects of New York surely entertained some instinct for the building as human image, as well. Indeed, they wore their buildings as costumes and so became

30. Hugh Ferriss, *The Metropolis of Tomorrow*, 1929. General view.

31. Tikal. View of Temple II from Temple I.

them at one famous party in 1931. Hence, the skyscrapers of New York, mentioned at the beginning of this chapter, are specifically American in more than one way, and today, in the grand new stands of skyscrapers, such as that of Battery Park City, which are reviving that tradition, they are in fact much more Mayan than they were a generation ago (fig. 32). The flat, inert slabs of the International Style have been given up. The masses of the buildings are now articulated, as much as economics seem to allow them to be, into stepped-back masses, and they shine out across the waters of the Hudson and New York Harbor like the temples of Tenochtitlán, described by Bernal Díaz at the time of the conquest, rising out of the water and shining in the sun. Díaz is the best of men to quote here, because he tried, with desperate urgency and long after the event, to remember and describe something that was wholly foreign to him but whose grandeur he somehow perceived, allowing it, beyond everything, to fill him with wonder:

> During the morning we arrived at a broad causeway and continued our march toward Iztapalapa, and when we saw so many cities and villages built in the water and other great towns on dry land and that straight and level causeway going toward Mexico, we were amazed and said that it was like the enchantments they tell of in the legend of Amadis, on account of the great towers and cues and buildings rising from the water, and all built of masonry. And some of our soldiers even asked whether the things that we saw were not a dream. It is not to be wondered at that I here write

34. Popocatepetl and Ixtaccihuatl, Valley of Mexico. General view from the southeast.

32. New York, N.Y. World Financial Center.

it down in this manner, for there is so much to think over that I do not know how to describe it, seeing things as we did that had never been heard of or seen before, not even dreamed about.*

Perhaps F. Scott Fitzgerald had Díaz in mind when he wrote his greatest lines, coming all unexpected at the end of *The Great Gatsby* and saying of the discovery of America that "for a transitory enchanted moment man must have held his breath in the presence of this continent, compelled into an aesthetic contemplation he neither understood nor desired, face to face for the last time in history with something commensurate to his capacity for wonder."*

*Bernal Díaz del Castillo, *The Discovery and Conquest of Mexico,* ed. Genaro Garcia, trans. A.P. Maudslay, New York, 1970, pp. 190–191.

*F. Scott Fitzgerald, *The Great Gatsby,* New York, 1925, p. 182.

In the center of Aztec Tenochtitlán the very heart of that wonder lay. There, under the present zocalo and the cathedral, the great Temple Major spread its ample mountain mass (fig. 33). Two temples shared its summit: that of Tlaloc on the left, that of Huitzilopochtli on the right. Across the plaza in front of them, the temple of Quetzalcoatl sat, constructed to look for all the world like a throned figure, with a distinct head, facing directly at the notch between the two temples that their roof combs formed. We know that the Aztec kings paid ritual visits to Teotihuacán throughout the year. Here, they reconstructed the basic ritual view down the Avenue of the Dead toward the notch in the mountain's crest above the Temple of the Moon: Quetzalcoatl's view. Moreover, the sun rose at the equinox in the notch between the slanting temple roofs, and when it passed northward behind the Temple of Tlaloc, God of Rain, it was the season of agriculture in the Valley of Mexico, the season of rain. When it passed to the south, behind the Temple of Huitzilopochtli, God of War, it was the dry season of hunting and war, which was the hunting of men for sacrifice on these altars. Outraged, the Spaniards massacred their worshipers and pulled them all down. Díaz wrote: "I say again that I stood looking at it and thought that never in the world would there be discovered other lands such as these . . . of all these wonders that I then beheld today all is overthrown and lost, nothing left standing."*

But the Spaniards could not pull down the mountains themselves; sixteenth-century technology did not as yet permit them to do so. And out on that bearing from the temple of Quetzalcoatl, far beyond the two temples of rain and of war, the two highest mountains around the valley of Mexico still emblazon the horizon (fig. 34): Popocatepetl to the right, "White Lady," with a sound like boulders being shot off; Ixtaccihuatl to the left, "Smoking Mirror," with a name like hot lava flooding down. Today the valley has filled up within the mountains with people, machines, and deadly smog. All the life-giving relationships are obscured in the yellowish haze over a natural environment in process of destruction by man. It is the very earth which the first men on this continent—no conservationists otherwise—had the wit to worship as divine.

33. Tenochtitlán. Aztec sacred precinct in the 16th century A.D. Great Temple: Tlaloc left and Huitzilopochtli right, with Temple of Quetzalcoatl. Reconstruction.

*Díaz, *The Discovery and Conquest of Mexico,* p. 191.

2
THE SACRED MOUNTAIN IN MESOPOTAMIA, EGYPT, AND THE AEGEAN

WHEN HUGH FERRISS CONCEIVED of his skyscraper masses as riding high over the Metropolis of Tomorrow, he clearly had more kinds of sacred mountains in mind than those of Mesoamerica alone. He might have thought of his buildings equally well as ziggurats, like those that once towered over the cities of Mesopotamia, which were the very first cities of all constructed by mankind. Their ziggurats are several millennia older than the American pyramids and, in the complex interaction of human civilizations over the centuries, just conceivably may be the originals of a common, indeed worldwide, development. The ziggurat of Ur, a vast mass of brick moldering in the

57. Phaistos. Central court. Circa 1500 B.C. Entrance to Royal Apartments.

plain, is still the best preserved of them all and has been the most spectacularly reconstructed in model form (fig. 35). Like the temples of Tikal, but unlike those of Teotihuacán, the ziggurat of Ur, along with those of the other Mesopotamian cities, was built with no natural mountains in view on the flat sea-level land of the lower Tigris-Euphrates valley. It, too,

was intended to connect the earth and the sky, which, in Mesopotamian myth, had been forcibly separated long before.

Like the Mesoamerican temples, the ziggurats were climbed by a priest-king, who sacrificed to his people's gods on the summit. The king was the protector of the city and the builder of its walls. Those walls were everything; they were the city's major protection against all the other cities, with which it was more or less perennially at war. So the wall was honored in Sumerian architecture, its mass exaggerated, its face embellished. Ur's ziggurat still shows those qualities. Its walls are all organized in vertical planes; the mass *lifts* hugely; it is not compressed like the pyramids of Teotihuacán or springy like Ah Cacao's at Tikal. There is no sense whatever of a human body, only of the mountain. The walls advance to buttresses and recede into deep niches in multiple planes; their surfaces are enlivened by pilasters, accentuating the mountainous, thrusting bulk of the mighty brick masses in every possible way.

36. Saqqâra, Egypt. Stepped pyramid of King Zoser. Pyramid and entrance gate, boundary wall.

23

35. Ur. Ziggurat. 3rd millennium B.C. Reconstruction.

The stairway rises as if ascending a high, broad mountain, wide-shouldered, blotting out the sky. It is a heroic stair, and with it the concept of the epic hero arises. He is the king, and is identified in particular with Gilgamesh, a king of Uruk, whose incomparable epic dominates the literature of the ancient East until the destruction of Assurbanipal's library at Nineveh in the late seventh century B.C. Gilgamesh builds the walls of Uruk and scales the heights of the Lebanon to obtain cedars for his temple doors. He finds a friend and loses him to the captious gods, seeks immortality and sees it stolen by a serpent—ubiquitous symbol of the earth's power—and finds at the end that only his work in the city remains. In its latest version, as engraved on the clay tablets at Nineveh, the poem both begins and concludes with the king's work at Uruk:

He ordered built the walls of Uruk
  of the sheepfold, the walls of holy
  Eanna, stainless sanctuary.
Observe its walls, whose upper hem
  is like bronze,
behold its inner wall, which no
  work can equal.
Touch the stone threshold which is
  ancient;

draw near the Eanna, dwelling-place
  of the goddess Ishtar,
A work no king among later kings
  can match.
Ascend the walls of Uruk, walk
  around the top,
inspect the base, view the brick-
  work.
Is not the very core made of oven-
  fired brick?
As for its foundation, was it not laid
  down by the seven sages?
One part is city, one part orchard,
  and one part claypits.
Three parts including the claypits
  make up Uruk.*

The city thus affords all the immortality that human beings can attain, and the king is the most qualified of humankind to achieve long-lasting works within it. It is he who ascends the sacred mountain, like Gilgamesh or Naram-Sin on his stele, the king who climbs the ultimate conical peak, rising to the sun and the moon, and wears the regal, godlike crown, conical and bull-horned itself. The king must do this because nothing is to be hoped for from the gods. They are heartless and wholly irresponsible. Unlike Jehovah, who, dangerously unbalanced though he abundantly shows himself to be, nevertheless signs a covenant with his people guaranteeing his relatively sane behavior under certain conditions, they, the Mesopotamian gods, never sign anything. Their flood is brought about for no particular reason. They are mad and have no justice in them.

*John Gardner and John Maier, eds., *Gilgamesh,* translated from the Sin-legi-uninni version, New York, 1984, p. 57.

Not so in Egypt. There, gods and men alike are governed by the concept of ma'at, which is justice itself. The king, Narmer, more or less contemporary with Naram-Sin, need only act out the idea of power; he need not struggle to achieve it. His relief carving is flat rather than cylindrical and muscular like that of the Sumerian king. He is not an epic hero but the very embodiment of cosmic justice. He rules over an ordered land. There are no warring cities in it; in Narmer's day, really no cities at all. It is one great agricultural structure, watered by the never-failing periodicity of the Nile's flood. The land is always fertile. It must be ruled by a single centralized authority to ensure the proper irrigation of all its fields.

The afterlife will naturally be just the same, for how else could existence be? There, too, the farmers will lead the animals out along the narrow paths between the rectangular fields and settle them down with their fodder for the day as they tend the always-productive land. They are workers on an agricultural assembly line, and they can rest at ease only during the flood, hunt and fish and think about the life to come. Then, however, they have their other great task, which is to build the Pharaoh's permanent habitation, his pyramid tomb. We may assume, I think, that despite the view of the matter held in later ages, they did so willingly, since the Pharaoh's immortality clearly had something central to do with the quality of their lives on earth and, in their view, hereafter. The reliefs and paintings in Egyptian tombs show the whole structure: the Nile flowing through the ordered fields with their people; the hawk, Horus, unblinking, looking toward the east, riding across the whole of Egypt in the Sun Boat of Ra.

The tombs are laid out in the sand on the west bank of the Nile, on the higher desert at the side of the setting sun. By the early third millennium King Zoser of the Third Dynasty decides that his tomb should be a mountain, visible to all those working in the fields below it. So his architect, Imhotep, who was to be honored as a sage throughout Egyptian history, steps the tomb up and back to shape a mountainous mass, not of brick, as in Mesopotamia, but of cut stone. Still, the influence of Mesopotamia is obvious at Saqqâra, but there is no stairway, no temple on the top, no drama (fig. 36). Once again, heroic action is not required. The image of the Pharaoh, his *ka,* resides down below. He himself is probably with the sun, and the emblem of his immortality, his mountain, dominates the skyline where the sun goes down.

Nevertheless, the wall around the sacred precinct at Saqqâra is Mesopotamian

37. Saqqâra, Egypt. Stepped pyramid of King Zoser. Axial view.

enough, with setbacks and pilasters on the Mesopotamian model, though linearized and flattened by the smooth certainties of Egyptian sensitivity. The plan, too, shows the Egyptian difference. While the manmade mountain rises within a walled enclosure, as at Ur, everything else is totally unlike Mesopotamia. The plan is utterly abstract, static, and fixed; there is no struggle embodied in it. The entire Mesopotamian plan is pushed in and out, embodying every kind of change over time and endless competition between various sacred precincts for building room. The Mesopotamian plan is thus urban, center-city in every fundamental way, responding to pressures from every side; the Egyptian is the unstrained emblem of a permanent conceptual order imprinted on the open desert and oriented precisely north–south.

But entry into Zoser's precinct shows that the principle of imitation is also at work there. It involves the impermanent architecture of vegetable materials. The engaged columns along the entrance passageway are carvings in stone of reeds bound together and capped with clay, a technique of building still to be seen in Egyptian villages today. The buildings representing the Pharaoh's *heb-sed* festival (they have no interiors) imitate the kind of vaulted swamp architecture of reeds that can still be seen in the community houses of the marsh Arabs of Iraq. In the North Building, near the Pharaoh's tomb

38. Gizeh, Egypt. Pyramid of Khafre (Chephren). Circa 2500 B.C.

chamber, the walls are set with engaged papyrus stalks; their buds open in a bell. From these, the stepped pyramid hulks massively near at hand, a manmade mountain right enough.

But directly opposite the entrance passage to the sacred enclosure and on axis with the pyramid itself, there is a wall crowned by cobras, recalling the snake heads of Quetzalcoatl at Teotihuacán, from which, it will be recalled, the whole range of pyramids and mountain could be seen most fully (fig. 37). At Saqqâra, too, the serpents mark a critical point of vantage. From their wall, the pyramid shows exactly on axis, therefore in pure profile. In this view, its mass wholly dematerializes, since nothing about it causes the mind's eye to supply it with any other sides, let alone the other three it actually possesses. It seems instead to step back like a weightless stairway, mounting to the heavens. It is a flat folded plane, and it is climbing into the sky itself, carrying Zoser with it, one supposes. Effortlessly, it avoids the springy upward thrusts of Tikal and the muscular drama of Ur. Its magic conquers gravity and enforces belief in transcendence.

That triumph over matter, with its escape from every terrestrial limitation and even from earthly weight, seems to have dominated Egyptian thinking about the pyramid from that time onward. Its mass is progressively smoothed over. The setbacks disappear. At Dashhur, a stepped pyramid is bent upward to a point, and soon the true pyramid emerges. It achieves its climactic grouping at Gizeh, where, at enormous scale, the avoidance of the appearance of weight is almost entirely achieved from every viewpoint, not only from an axial one (fig. 38). The four planes of the pyramids' faces slant back and re-

cede, disappearing to a point in the sky. In a perspective view, the mind of the observer will supply only one other side rather than two. One thus "sees" the pyramid as a tetrahedron. Already some of the reality of the mass is disappearing. On closer approach to a single face, the entire plane slants weightlessly away (fig. 39).

Originally, all the faces of the pyramids at Gizeh were sheathed in gleaming white limestone, blindingly bright, sending out reflections far across the plain. The cult was of Ra, the sun, and the pyramids were indeed transformed into pure sun's rays, pure light. Louis Kahn perceived this beautifully when he painted his pastels of Gizeh in 1951 (fig. 40).* Sometimes he shows one pyramid pure white, another pure black, another the color of desert sand. He hailed the group as the "Sanctuary of Art / The Treasury of the Shadows," built of "Silence and Light," and when he received the commission for the

*From the notebooks of Louis I. Kahn, 1973, in *The Travel Sketches of Louis I. Kahn,* Philadelphia, Pennsylvania Academy of Fine Art, 1978, p. 49.

39. Gizeh, Egypt. Pyramid of Khufu (Cheops). Circa 2530 B.C.

40. Gizeh, Egypt. The Great Pyramids, pastel. 1950. Louis Kahn.

Yale Art Gallery in that same year, he managed to condense the pyramids as tetrahedrons with his knowledge of Buckminster Fuller's tetrahedronal space frames and to use them as containers of light.

It was into light itself that the Pharaoh was, at least symbolically, loaded. One thinks of the obelisk, Ra's major symbol, capped with a pyramidion: It is as if the pyramids at Gizeh capped mighty obelisks, buried, directed toward the sun. Indeed, the entire group can be seen as a battery of missiles aimed at the sun, taking position at just the right spot for a clear shot at it, on the great bank of desert that rises above the Nile plain at the point where it begins to widen out to the delta

(fig. 41). And what must have seemed to the Egyptians to be the special magic of the site supplied that battery with a gunner. An outcropping of rock suggested the form of the Sphinx, the lion-bodied Pharaoh. He bears Chephren's face and rises above Chephren's valley temple below his pyramid (fig. 42). It is the critical position in relation to the whole group, which deploys in echelon behind the Sphinx while he gazes unblinking into the eastern sun, rising across the Nile.

Below him, Chephren sat in his temple in multiple effigies, all alike, his head supported by the unblinking hawk, so that he too became a Horus capable of staring at the sun. There is no decoration in the temple, nor in any of the pyramids at Gizeh—

42. Gizeh, Egypt. Circa 1910. Sphinx before excavation.

41. Gizeh, Egypt. Great Pyramids. Circa 2530–2460 B.C. Air view from the west.

no imitation whatever of natural forms. It is all abstract, as unadorned as a rocket motor; its magic is mechanical, perfect; its only imagery is of light. Later, in the next dynasty, the fifth, when confidence in the mechanics of human magic had waned, the new pyramids, like that of Unas, were filled with magical texts, in the hope of getting the Pharaoh to the sun through incantation, the power of the word. Poor

Unas himself rants and rages, boasts and weeps, threatens his brothers the gods and grovels before them.

There is none of that at Gizeh. Menkare and his queen, of the third pyramid, await the moment of transcendence with absolute confidence. There is nothing in the history of art so wholly at peace with the triumphant self as their faces are, unless it is the face of Chephren with his totemic hawk, which was too godlike for later times. During the Middle Ages, a puritanical emir turned his cannon on the face of the Sphinx; its expression of total assurance filled him with holy rage. Menkare and his wife share the Sphinx's calm. Why should they not? They had conquered death, laying their battery of human intelligence unerringly on the sun.

Mankind has never felt so confident again. The mood faded in Egypt itself almost at once, with the end of the Fourth Dynasty, and the single most consistent movement in Egyptian architecture thereafter was a kind of regressive return to the security of the earth and the imitation of its forms. A sail up the Nile to the site of the New Empire city of Thebes on the east bank brings us to a point where the western cliffs across the river opposite the city open into a vast shape, today called Qurnain, "horned," which is capped by a roughly pyramidal mound on the cliff's summit between the horns (fig. 43). The whole formation strongly suggests the horned-disk headdress that is worn by the cow goddess, Hathor, the earth goddess, herself. The horns also resemble an inverted pyramid, and directly below them the Middle Kingdom Pharaoh Mentuhotep IV placed his tomb. In it, the pyramid had dwindled markedly in size and was surrounded by deep colonnades. The manmade pyramid was now content

43. Deir-el-Bahari, Egypt. "Qurnain" with Tomb Temple of Queen Hatshepsut. Circa 1480–1450 B.C.

to reflect the natural form in the earth.

In the tomb of Queen Hatshepsut of the Eighteenth Dynasty, placed right next to Mentuhotep's, the pyramid disappeared completely, and the tomb was cut deep back into the cliff itself. Hatshepsut would seem to have positioned herself as closely as she could to the magical shape in the cliff, but, not placed to reflect the inverted pyramid and perhaps not caring to do so, returned to the earth entirely instead. Before her chamber, she laid out broad garden parterres, prefiguring in plan those of seventeenth-century France but probably planted thick with trees. So

Hatshepsut's tomb is in one sense entirely natural in its manmade correlatives of tomb as cavern and garden grove as orchard and forest.

Finally, the mound on the summit of the cliffs, when it is approached from the other side, marks the Valley of the Kings, where later Pharaohs were laid to rest in the body of the earth (fig. 44). From the valley, the mound is nippled and strongly resembles the breast of Hathor herself. The dismantling of the magical machine that re-created the rays of the sun could go no further. One returns to the sacred mountain in its traditional form. The whole process suggests an abandonment of what can only be called inventive technology in favor of ancient organic traditions embedded deep in the consciousness of mankind.

Thebes itself lay across the river. It contained at least two large temples of Amon, a local god, primarily of fertility, thus of the proper flow of the Nile and the growth it brought forth. One of Amon's temples lies along the riverbank, stretching downstream as with the river's flow (fig. 45). The god's house is upstream; the court before it is defined, indeed choked, by fat, soft-looking columns imitating the forms of papyrus plants bound together with their buds closed (fig. 46). Their rounded, vegetable sponginess may be usefully contrasted with the similar papyrus columns that the nineteenth-century American architect Henry Austin used for the gateway of his Grove Street

44. Thebes, Egypt. Valley of the Tombs of the Kings.

45. Luxor, Egypt. Temple of Amon. Reconstruction drawing with "Qurnain."

Cemetery in New Haven, Connecticut. Their buds are cut sharp-edged as gears. They are entirely nineteenth-century in character and suggest machinery themselves. But Amon's temple is all vegetable growth of river plants, while a current like that of the Nile flows from the narrow darkness of his sanctuary outward to court after court, hall after hall, added over the generations. The hypostyle hall uses open papyrus columns (fig. 47), like those engaged in the wall at Saqqâra. Their smooth bells spread broadly to mask the impost blocks they support, upon which the beams of the ceiling were placed. Hence, as seen from below, the ceiling would have seemed to float like the sky.

In the temple at Luxor, the hypostyle hall was never finished, leaving the two rows of high columns standing alone. But inland, in the Temple of Amon at Karnak, which was also part of ancient Thebes, the central columns of the hypostyle hall were surrounded by multiple rows of the short, fat, closed-bud columns that were needed to set them off (fig. 48). The entire complex must have been experienced as a great swamp, like the swamps of Egypt before the all-powerful Pharaoh was able to drain the land and control the Nile's flow.* We are wholly in the hands of older gods once more. The innermost row of short columns supports clerestory windows that bring light from above into the central row. More than ever, the sky above the high central columns would have seemed to float, elevated as it was above the major source of light itself. So the current flows sluggishly out through the choked vegetation and rushes triumphantly at last

*The germ of this concept is in Wilhelm Worringer, *Egyptian Art,* London, 1928, esp. pp. 62–63.

46. Luxor. Temple of Amon. Circa 1390–1370 B.C. Forecourt of Amenhotep III.

47. Luxor. Temple of Amon, Court of Ramses II. Circa 1280–1260 B.C. North end of hypostyle hall.

through the final gates, like the cliffs of the Nile upstream, and along the Avenue of Rams before it. The force of the Nile has been released, flowing from the god. Amon gives forth the waters of fertility to the waiting land. That is why his image is often rendered ithyphallic; he fertilizes with his flow.

Once shaped, the great New Empire temple type hardly changed over the centuries, except perhaps to insist ever more richly upon the vegetable softness of its column forms. At Edfu, built in the Ptolemaic period, the open-bud capitals of the central axis are much more elaborately foliated than those at Thebes (fig. 49). Their shapes are softer and more complex. A generation ago, when art historians cared about such things, we might well have called them "baroque" in character. Certainly they are even more naturalistic than they were before. That process continued into Roman times, as on the island of Philae. There, in the kiosk of Augustus and Trajan, the papyrus capitals are the most vegetable of all, and the river imagery could hardly help but be enhanced by the fact that the buildings at Philae soon came to be inundated periodically by the Nile. So Antinoüs, Hadrian's favorite, eventually was to become a god himself by drowning in the Nile under mysterious circumstances, and his cult in late antiquity played a part in the continuity of Egyptian riverine imagery into the Christian era.

By that time, the old cult of Ra and of his sacred mountains of light had long since receded into the past; indeed, the slapstick account of the building of the pyramids written by Herodotus in the fifth century B.C. shows us that its every meaning had been forgotten long before. But during the second millennium B.C.,

48. Karnak, Egypt. Temple of Amon. Circa 1530–1280 B.C. Hypostyle hall. Reconstruction.

49. Edfu, Egypt. Temple of Horus. Interior.

the cult of the sacred mountain as such continued with unabated force throughout the Ancient East and in the Aegean.

Minoan Crete was apparently its purest sanctuary, and its deepest traditions would seem to have directed all the major rituals of religious and political life in that sea kingdom. All the Cretan palaces are oriented toward sacred mountains and adjust their courtyards to them. Knossos, the very seat of kingship, is oriented on Mount Jouctas, cone-shaped and cleft, where, in later myth, the Cretan Zeus was buried. The palace at Phaistos is directed toward Mount Ida, wide-horned, where Zeus was born. So in Crete, unlike Egypt and Mesopotamia, the sacred mountains

were there in natural form. They did not
need to be constructed by mankind. Instead, the manmade forms were laid out
to complement and receive their mass
with open courtyards from which they
dominated the view. There, in their sacred
presence, the major rituals of kingship
took place.

At Knossos, a traveler coming from
the northern shore of Crete is led along a
single-file pathway toward the north side
of a long, rectangular courtyard (fig. 50).
There, a short stair mounts directly to the
central axis of the court, with a columned
portico rising up above it on the right-
hand side. The view from this spot is directed in a strong diagonal across the court
toward the southern propylon, beyond
which a mounded hill rises, with Mount
Jouctas lifting full and silent beyond it.

Beneath the summit of that mountain
was a cave sanctuary of the goddess of the
earth, and she, as embodied in Cretan ce-
ramics (fig. 51), wears a headdress that is
both conical and horned, so reproducing

51. Crete. Female idol from Gazi with crown of doves and
horns. Terra-cotta. 13th century B.C.

50. Knossos, Crete. Central court and Mount Jouctas from northern entrance. Circa 1600–1400 B.C.

52. Knossos, Crete. Palace of Minos. Circa 1600–1400 B.C. Throne room.

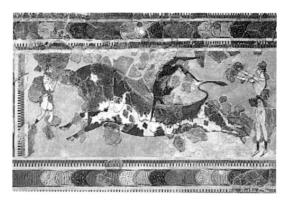

53. Knossos. *Bull Dance,* fresco. Circa 1500 B.C. Reconstruction.

her mountain's mass and profile. The roofs of the palace, certainly flat, may also have been crowned with horns, as its excavators thought, and as it is shown in frescoes and gems. The goddess would seem to be the old earth mother of Paleolithic times brought up to date, big-breasted as of old but svelte and elegant, though still the being from whom the horned animals, the food of mankind, are born. She is also the Earth-Shaker, mother of terrors.

At Knossos, the southern propylon, the most elaborate gateway to the palace, is directly on axis with the mountain, as is the range of rooms behind it. One of these contains the pillar cult of the goddess, set deep in the earth. Another is the throne room (fig. 52), where the king sat in a little throne just big enough to hold him. Through its bucket seat and high back, a deep ripple like an earthquake tremor runs, while long ripples flow as well through the frescoes on the wall behind it, and fires seem to spring up from the earth below. Knossos is, in fact, placed at a point of maximum seismic disturbance, and the king, representing his people, received that force in his own body.

If we believe Greek myth he may also have been, at least at times, bull-masked as Poseidon, Earth-Shaker, the goddess's consort, bringing on the earthquake through her power and in a sense sacrificing himself to her. So as the horned beasts of Paleolithic times ran along their cave walls deep in the womb of the earth, and as the horned dancers took up their burden for them in places shaped by men, so here the major event for which the courtyard was formed was the great bull dance, an ultimate refinement of all the rituals that had been directed to the earth since Paleolithic times. The bull charged straight. The spectators on the flat roofs of the palace could see him and the horned mountain at the same time. He brought

56. Phaistos, Crete. Mount Ida from the central court. Circa 1500 B.C.

55. Puye Pueblo. Buffalo dancer.

58. Cyprus. Mycenaean krater. 14th century B.C.

its power down into the courtyard, where human beings received it and hugged it to themselves, seizing the horns and propelled by them through the air like birds (fig. 53).

In this context, we can hardly fail to recall the court at Puye and the bull dancers whose horns conduct the power of the heavens into the plaza (fig. 55). We recall

their link with the serpent, image of rain, and in this conjunction of animal heroes, the words of Euripides in the *Bacchae,* describing the birth of Dionysos and of Tragedy itself, ring most apt of all:

> And when the weaving Fates fulfilled
>   the time
> The bull horned god was born of
>   Zeus,
> In joy he crowned his son,
> Set serpents on his head.*

So the Pueblo bull dancer and the stucco relief of the charging bull on the wall of the pavilion above the north entrance at Knossos go very well together (fig. 54). Far apart in time and place, their rituals are clearly celebrating much the same moment of human consciousness. Is it simply a matter of multiple invention of similar things, or can there have been some great diffusion of the earth religion long ago, of which, in the Old World, the rituals of Crete represented a kind of climax? In their own way, the Greeks were later to believe exactly that.

At Phaistos, there was no throne room, so that the axis of the courtyard could itself run directly toward the mountain (fig. 56). What a contrast with Jouctas Ida forms. We can understand how the Greeks associated the former with death—did it recall or suggest the conical tholos tombs of the Mycenaean lords?—and the latter with birth, as the mountain opens in a kind of exalted physical release and joy. To celebrate the axis of view to Mount Ida, the doorway in the court at Phaistos that leads toward the mountain

*From *Bacchae* by Euripides, trans. William Arrowsmith, in *The Complete Greek Tragedies,* Volume IV: Euripides, eds. David Greene and Richard Lattimore, Chicago and London, 1958.

is flanked by niches in which round columns are engaged (fig. 57). It is a rich manipulation of column and wall not to be found again until Roman times. Of course, as from much of the court at Knossos, the view of the mountain itself would have been blocked from the doorway by the mass of the buildings, but that did nothing to mitigate the potent magic of the alignment or the fact that all of it was perfectly visible from farther out in the court and from the roofs—from which, as at Taos or Puye, the essential ceremonies were in any case always best viewed.

The relationship of humanity to nature is made abundantly clear: Nature's mountains dominate, as does the goddess who surmounts them and whose body in fact they are. The manmade courtyard opposes no countersculptural presence to the natural forms but simply receives them in its hollow, just as, in their rituals, the dancers receive their horned force. So mankind is dependent and, as it saw itself, youthful. A Minoan gem shows a young athlete saluting the mother on her moun-

tain, and like the gored dancer on the Boxer vase, he gives himself up joyfully to her.

This is the pre-Greek world. But by 1400 B.C., Greeks were already ruling at Knossos and Phaistos. A famous vase found in Cyprus shows the contradictions inherent in that situation during the later second millennium B.C., the Mycenaean period. The shape of the vase has the wonderfully organic curve of Minoan work, but the figures on it are not the fluid representations of fish and octopi most common to Crete. They are hard-edged, abstracted human beings, Indo-European war chieftains riding in their chariots (fig. 58). They display themselves as lords and, as the chariot wheel drawn with a compass shows, they put their instinctive trust in the abstract, geometric works of man. Out of the conflict so clearly imaged here, the dense fabric of Greek myth was to be woven, as was the Greek relationship to the landscape, something equally eloquent, shot through, as at Mycenae itself, with so much darkness, so much light.

54. Knossos. Relief of charging bull above northern entrance. Circa 1500 B.C.

3
THE GREEK TEMPLE

THE GREEK TEMPLE WAS an image of victory. It embodied the Greek conquest of the Aegean and the intrusion of the Olympian gods into the domain of the old goddess of nature. As such, the temples supplanted the long-lost courtyards of the kings with the solidly sculptural bodies of manmade divinities, expressive of human qualities and challenging the divinity who was embodied in the landscape's shapes. The old imitation of the forms of the earth, older than written history, was given up. The temples became divine persons; their shapes brought the human presence into a new, fundamentally dramatic dialogue with the land. Indeed, out of that confrontation

87. Paestum. Second Temple of Hera with conical hill.

between nature's fact and human desire, the luminous structure of Greek Classic thought took form, and tragic drama explored the hero's fate. Architecture itself was never to be the same again. It developed a new language, strictly structured, supple, and intense, and very nearly as alive toward the end of the twentieth century A.D. as when it first came into being.

84. Paestum, Italy. Second Temple of Hera. Colonnade. Entablature. Pediment.

Surely, the myth of the king as hero, perhaps even as a Gilgamesh seeking immortality, lay behind it all, but it is clear that the Greek chieftains of the Bronze Age, the first Hellenic invaders, wanted very much to conform to the sacred patterns of the goddess's earth and its law if they could do so. Eleusis, the site of the oldest and most enduring mysteries of her ancient religion, was a sacred site for them as well, and it is marked by the same kinds of mountain forms that were sacred in Crete. On the Sacred Way from Athens, for example, the island of Salamis, dedicated to Aphrodite, a goddess of mountain and sea, lies directly ahead, deeply cleft and horned (fig. 59). At the point where the Sacred Way reaches the shore of the bay, Mount Kerata (meaning "horns") (fig. 61) comes into view on the mainland across the water. It rises directly above the caverned mound that was the site of the Mysteries (fig. 60), and seen from there, it opens like the female cleft, organic and tremulous in profile, "the gate of true dreams," the gate of horn (fig. 61).*

*See Gertrude Rachel Levy, *The Gate of Horn*, London, 1948.

Into this world resonant with the goddess's symbols, the Greeks brought their own gods and wove them into the old pattern in a lively syncretism of old and new. It has been the fashion among all too many scholars, and perhaps especially among the hard-nosed American archaeologists of the generation just past, to deprecate the Greek religious sense and condescend to the Greek gods. The nineteenth-century prejudice, nourished from Judaic and Christian sources, that monotheism represents a "higher" set of religious conceptions than polytheism, clearly played a large part in the formation of that attitude. Does it make sense? Surely not. It is difficult to imagine that the belief in a single jealous male god of uncertain temper represents a "higher" spiritual state than the belief in many gods, male and female alike, each an embodiment of some aspect of human life as it can be empirically known and experienced. Each balances and checks the other to some degree. It is true that the Greek gods most realistically promise mankind nothing, but they will, and do, aid human beings who pursue their ways with spirit. Any modern man who says he does not know them does not know his own mind, because, if he has tried to deal with the realities of things as they are, the appropriate Greek gods have been there with him, cloaking him in their power: Aphrodite in love, Apollo in clear reasoning, Dionysos in ecstatic possession, Zeus in justice, Athena in right action and divine effrontery, Ares, the big-kneed, in the loutish skills of war.

Beyond that, every religious document of the early Greeks that we possess, from their sacred sites to their literature, attests to the depth and authenticity of their religious feeling. Homer was not

59. Sacred Way from Athens to Eleusis. Shrine of Aphrodite with horns of Salamis.

61. Eleusis. Mount Kerata from the Acropolis.

writing until perhaps the eighth century B.C., but he was reflecting not only the beliefs of his own age but also those carried by oral tradition from a much older time. For English-speaking people, the incandescent translation of the *Odyssey* by Robert Fitzgerald brings the Greek gods and goddesses to life much as the Greeks must have felt them to be. So Athena leaps into the ship with Telemachos, as he goes to seek news of his father, and it is as if the spiritual voyage of Western civilization, curiously open, literal, and magnificently simpleminded, begins right here:

> Telemakhos then stepped aboard;
>   Athena
> took her position aft, and he sat by
>   her.
> The two stroke oars cast off the stern
>   hawsers
> and vaulted over the gunnels to their
>   benches.
> Grey-eyed Athena stirred them a fol-
>   lowing wind,
> soughing from the north-west on the
>   winedark sea,
> and as he felt the wind, Telemakhos
> called to all hands to break out mast
>   and sail.
> They pushed the fir mast high and
>   stepped it firm
> amidships in the box, made fast the
>   forestays,
> then hoisted up the white sail on its
>   halyards
> until the wind caught, booming in the
>   sail;
> and a flushing wave sang backward
>   from the bow
> on either side, as the ship got way
>   upon her,
> holding her steady course.

> Now they made all secure in the fast
>   black ship,
> and, setting out the winebowls all
>   a-brim,
> they made libation to the gods, the
>   undying, the ever-new,
> most of all to the grey-eyed daughter
>   of Zeus,
> And the prow sheared through the
>   night into the dawn.

60. Eleusis. Telesterion and Salamis.

And the dawn comes, alike for gods and men:

> The sun rose on the flawless brim-
>   ming sea
> into a sky all brazen—all one bright-
>   ening
> for gods immortal and for mortal
>   men
> on plowlands kind with grain.
>   And facing sunrise
> the voyagers now lay off Pylos
>   town,
> compact stronghold of Neleus. On
>   the shore
> black bulls were being offered by the
>   people
> to the blue-maned god who makes
>   the islands tremble. . . .*

*Homer, *Odyssey,* trans. Robert Fitzgerald, Garden City, New York, 1961, pp. 43, 47.

62. Pylos, Crete. Palace of Nestor. Megaron.

65. Sparta, Greece. Menelaion from the east with Taygetus and the Valley of the Eurotas.

In this landscape, Nestor's megaron at Pylos is oriented south toward the coned and horned mountain that flares so dramatically on that horizon (fig. 62). The king's fire burns in the center; his throne is set to one side, and a porch opens out to a courtyard on the south (fig. 63). The simple shape of the megaron is set within the labyrinth of the palace as a whole. Near its southeastern boundary, a small room opens toward an altar, behind which the secondary conical formation of the mountain mass lies on axis before the horns. Just to the left, the east, lies the lord's tholos tomb, restored by the excavators (fig. 64). It, too, is a cone, built up into a corbeled dome and then covered with earth, so that it exactly echoed the natural landscape cone and, it should be said, recalled the conical mass of Mount Jouctas as well, where in Greek myth, as we have noted, a Cretan Zeus was buried. Clearly, Pylos, like Knossos, has the kingly view, and its major symbol is the protective cone of the goddess, within which the king himself is laid to rest at last.

Telemachos soon traveled on to Sparta, through the wild passes of Mount Taygetus, and if the present Menelaion set on the eastern height above the sown lands was indeed the site of the megaron of Menelaus and Helen, then their palace, too, was set to take advantage of the mountain's clefts and horns: Here it is Alcman's dark Taygetus, deep-gorged and fanged, bursting with power (fig. 65).

Northeastward, on the Argive plain, lies armored Tiryns, fortified, as no Cretan palaces were. The Mycenaean lords are Indo-European intruders. They are at war with the people of the countryside and with each other. But still the megaron of the king is oriented exactly upon the hill

63. Pylos. Palace of Nestor. Throne room of the Megaron. Reconstruction drawing.

64. Pylos. Tholos tomb.

66. Tiryns. Megaron and Palamedes above Nauplion.

68. Mycenae. Tomb of "Agamemnon."

of Palamedes to the south, lying behind a mounded hill, its body notched and cleft exactly on the central axis of the megaron's view (fig. 66). The king would clearly like to lock his palace into the landscape's protective powers, but he is a military chief above all else, and he builds with enormous stones, like those employed by his Indo-European cousins, the Hittites, in their capital at Hattusas, far off in central Asia Minor. There is a romantic violence in the stones; they are far larger than they need to be, the biggest that could be lifted into place by human resource, and appreciated by the later Greeks as Cyclopean, built by giants.

So it is the lords' will and their joy to rule, and to be true kings, but they seek to govern through the power of the goddess as well, and to invoke her protection if they can. Out of that fundamental human dilemma the myths of Mycenae took shape. The king's megaron was set in the cleft of the most powerful natural embodiment of the goddess to be found in the Argolid (fig. 67). In Greece, it is matched only by Delphi. Two great horns lift up and out, suggesting spread knees, with the goddess's lap open between them. In that throne, like that of Hathor in which the Pharaoh sat, the citadel glows

golden in the sunlight, a conical mass, looking from the plain, to modern eyes, like the turret of a tank in defilade. So emplaced, it controls the main road between Corinth and the Argolid and looms above an intersecting track leading eastward toward Epidauros. Directly between it and the plain of Argos lies a broad, mounded hill; in it the greatest of the tholos tombs is buried, named by Schliemann for Agamemnon (fig. 68). A dromos built of enormous stones leads to it. Originally, that road, too, was filled with loose stones and covered over so that all the members of the House of Atreus who were buried there slept within an unblemished hill.

Inside, the hollow cone of stone is full of whispers. Acoustically, it is an echoing shell. A shuffle of feet in the dust of the floor will bring a rustling as of many little wings above, like the flutterings of Homeric, batlike souls. The declamation of the Greek language will bring on eldritch screeches, the whole hollow tomb sounding like the bronze cauldrons in Greek

67. Mycenae between the horns.

theaters, which the actors were reputed to be able to detonate into clarion sound by the pitch of their voices. It is a marvel of haunted space, a cavern crowded with the resentments of the dead, the great lintel over the doorway swinging up, lamenting like shrouded arms.

Outside, along the axis of the dromos, the slope of the southern horn of mountain can be seen. The path to the gate of the citadel continues northward beyond the tomb and then turns back southward up the contours to come to the Lion Gate with the southern hill, now perfectly conical, rising behind it (fig. 69). In this view, the triangular tympanum slab above the lintel of the gate echoes the cone of the mountain beyond it, and the column between lions that is carved in relief upon it (fig. 70) reflects the image of the goddess as she is engraved on Minoan gems. The citadel is thus dedicated to her, given over to her care. Directly behind the gate lies the grave circle, and on that line of sight, the cone of Argive Hera can be seen far down in the plain (fig. 71). Again, the kings in their golden death masks are being laid to rest under the protection of the goddess. One mask (fig. 72), named Agamemnon's by the excavators, resembles Henri IV, a wide-mustached, saddened, aging king. His megaron is higher

up, at the very summit of the citadel, looking westward toward the clefts of Artemis' strongholds on Mounts Kyllene and Artemision (fig. 73). A deep gorge plunges down directly behind the megaron, and the cone of Hera at Argos can be seen from it in the depths of the plain beyond the hill of the tomb.

Now the king is supreme, and he will be king of all the Greeks if he can. He will go so far as to sacrifice his daughter at Aulis for a fair wind to Troy. When he

69. Mycenae. Lion Gate with Mount Zara on approach.

returns from the war, puffed up with pride and bringing Priam's daughter, Cassandra, with him as his captive, his wife and her lover will kill him without pity, he and all his men as they sit at table. Homer has Agamemnon's shade tell Odysseus the story in the underworld:

70. Mycenae. Lion Gate. Circa 1300–1250 B.C.

71. Mycenae. Grave circle A with Treasury of Atreus, cone of Argos beyond.

72. Mycenae. Funeral mask of "Agamemnon" from the royal tombs, beaten gold.

73. Mycenae. View from the citadel.

In your day
you have seen men, and hundreds,
 die in war
in the bloody press, or downed in
 single combat,
but these were murders you would
 catch your breath at;
think of us fallen, all our throats
 cut, winebowl
brimming, tables laden on every
 side,
while blood ran smoking over the
 whole floor.
In my extremity I hear Kassandra,
Priam's daughter, piteously crying
as the traitor Klaitemnestra made to
 kill her
along with me. I heaved up from
 the ground
and got my hands around the blade,
 but she
eluded me, that whore. Nor would
 she close
my two eyes as my soul swam in
 the underworld
or shut my lips. There is no being
 more fell,
more bestial than a wife in such an
 action . . .

 . . .

that woman,
plotting a thing so low, defiled herself
and all her sex, all women yet to
 come,
even those few who may be vir-
 tuous.*

And Aischylos, in the fifth century, causes Cassandra, waiting in the courtyard, to cry out:

See there, see there! Keep from his
 mate the bull.
Caught in the folded web's entan-
 glement
she pinions him and with the black
 horn strikes . . .*

So the horned site suggests the bull king and, in myth's typical reversal, his murder with the horn. Like the bulls in the Vaphio cups, he is snared in a net and sacrificed to the goddess for his crimes against her. With this event, a deep suspicion of all women was sown in the Greek mind and was to mark its history. So, at the last, Agamemnon counsels Odysseus to beware: "Land your ship/in secret on your island; give no warning/ The day of faithful wives is gone forever."[†]

Disillusioned, the kings fall before the new invaders, the more primitive Dorian Greeks from the north. They are driven to the eastern shores of the Aegean. The Peloponnesos and Crete are overrun. The Dorians sweep through the islands all the way to Rhodes. They attack Athens and, traditionally, fall before her walls, driven back by her last king, who dies in the battle. So Athens stands between east and west Greece, neither quite Ionian nor Dorian but in touch with both, herself a condensation of two opposing ways of life as the dark ages come down.

Archaeology is beginning to bring rays of light into those centuries and to illuminate some continuities with the past.[‡] But on the whole the phenomenon was of

---

*Homer, *Odyssey,* p. 210.

*Aischylos, *Agamemnon,* trans. Richmond Lattimore, Chicago, 1959, pp. 1125–28.

†Homer, *The Odyssey,* p. 211.

‡So is philology. See in general: Stephen Scully, *Homer and the Sacred City,* Ithaca and London, 1990.

rupture. The shock was very great. An amphora from Attica of about 1100–1000 B.C. shows it well. All the old organic images are given up, as is the continuous curve of the vase itself. Its profiles are built upon a strict geometry, and its decoration is purely abstract. In a sense, it is now wholly Greek, as the Mycenaean vase from Cyprus was half Greek, half Minoan. Now, too, the heroes have disappeared; all the glorious pretension is gone. Symbolic imagery starts over with careful, abstract forms. By the eighth century, the geometric system has become elaborate, symphonic, monumental in scale. A big meander may dramatize the body of the vase or elongate its neck like a powerful spring.

Some of the vases are big as a man. They were funerary and in some instances, as in the Kerameikos Cemetery in Athens, they stood out above the grave in which the burned ashes of the dead were interred and, filled with oil, dripped a steady libation through a hole in their bases over the charred bones. By the eighth century, too, the heroic figures had returned, but they were now constructed of purely geometric forms, which, like the imagery of Homer in the same years, were not only repetitive and conventionalized but also showed some clear memory of the old Mycenaean days: chariot drivers in the shape of the Minoan double ax, for example. Above all else, the dead man rests upon his high, creaking funeral cart, while the women, subjugated, mourn him in battalions and the cormorants, the seabirds, skitter between the horses' legs and beneath the bier.

The whole vase stands out in space above the grave, just outside Athens' Dipylon gate, with the Acropolis rising in the middle distance. Its great temples have

74. Perachora, Greece. Temple of Hera. The sacred formation.

not yet been built upon it, though the megaron of the Erechthids that stood on its summit had surely been transformed into the Temple of Athena Polias long before. But of the new architecture that was about to be invented (it is not too strong a word), the vases were the precursors: big, architectural hollows themselves, abstract in form, looming over the graves as emblems of the paternal cult and introducing into the old landscape a new shout of human grief and defiance.

It was just then, in the eighth century, that the Greek temple as we know it began to take form. The old sacred landscape formations were still holy. Perachora, at the head of the Gulf of Corinth, directly across the water from Corinth itself, is conspicuous among them (fig. 74). From Corinth, the headland looks like a great sphinx facing down the bay. On approach from the water, it opens up into a broad-shouldered figure with a high, rocky head and a protected harbor tucked into its body down below. Right by the harbor, facing toward the head, all the successive temples on the site were placed.

The first, of the eighth century, was a little, apsidal house with a rounded back and a high, frontally gabled roof, supported on a couple of columns in front (fig. 75). A model found on the site shows the type. It is made monumental by a large fret around the enclosing wall, exactly like that on a contemporary vase. The image of the divinity was housed within, back to the wall and facing out toward the doorway. The whole building leaps up and out with the energy of that presence. There is no Minoan flat roof any longer; that, too, becomes an active element now. The temple is a sculptural embodiment of the force of the divinity whose house it is.

By the sixth century, it was succeeded at Perachora by a much larger rectangular temple set farther back and filling almost all the narrow area of flat ground between the harbor and the cliffs. The building was now surely a good deal like the old megaron of the kings, but it is as yet impossible to trace any link between them. Yet in the enthusiasm for old Crete that clearly played a part in ushering in the Daedalic style of sculpture of the late seventh century, it is certainly possible that some consciously archaeological revival took place in architecture as well, at that time.

By the late seventh century, in any case, the Greeks seem to have decided that the way to make their new temples express their divinities as they imagined them, with human characteristics distinct from those of the sacred topographical formations in relation to which they took their stand, was to surround them with a peripteral colonnade of columns. In eastern Greece, those colonnades became multiple, shaping a grove around the god's house and suggesting an Egyptian temple turned inside out.

This system, as it was developed in the Temple of Hera on Samos and that of Artemis at Ephesos, created the Ionic mode, wherein each column leaped up to a voluted capital with something resembling hydraulic force that also came to be associated, surely from a very early date, with the female form (figs. 145, 146). The Aeolic mode, as it was used on Lesbos and elsewhere, also suggested powers associated with the sea in its great capitals, eyed and octopus-armed. But in the Doric mode, which was to dominate mainland Greece and the western colonies, the colonnade was kept single and the columns were made as muscular as men. The rectangular house of the god was thus screened with vertical figures suggesting the human body, masking the fact that the building was an abstract container of space and transforming it into a sculptural presence distinct from that of the landscape's forms. The Doric temple became not a grove but a person.

75. Perachora. Apsidal temple. 8th century B.C. Model.

At Perachora, there was no room for the peripteral colonnade, but at Poseidonia in southern Italy, the Roman Paestum, for example, there was plenty, and the three Greek temples there were peripterally conceived. The columns of the earliest, that of Hera I of circa 550 B.C., should be compared to the wonderful little Daedalic bronze in Delphi (fig. 76), of perhaps eighty years before. The figure wears an Egyptian headdress, flattened across the top to turn the head into a capital, below which the supple body of a Cretan athlete has been stiffened into a column. One straight axis runs down the center, expressive of the imposition of a point load upon the figure, around which the body swells symmetrically as it takes that compression from above. This is the Doric column (fig. 77).

It is true that stone columns had been Egyptian, too, as was the stance of the bronze Kouros figure itself, but now both transformed the Egyptian model in order to dramatize a new, steadfast, muscular resistance to architectural weight. And since the column, though abstract, clearly suggests the erect human body, the human observer empathetically associates his own vertical stance and its muscular resistance to gravity with its own. So the columns of Archaic Greek temples are part of the same sculptural program, celebrating bodily force, that produced the monumental stone Kouroi of the sixth century. Each temple, like each Kouros, is different from all the others but is also so much like them that absolute differences of character can be distinguished among them, as is possible only among beings of the same species. So all Greek temples are perforce very similar: The type is never compromised, precisely so that each being can be read as distinct. Now the old imitation of

76. Daedalic Kouros. Bronze. Mid-7th century B.C.

the forms of the earth is given up. The temples are divine persons; their shapes bring the human presence into a dialogue with the land.

The site at Paestum (fig. 78) had two major sanctuaries within the city limits, that of Hera on the south, with two temples, that of Athena to the north, with one. Inland of Hera's sanctuary, the boundary hills break out into a decisive cone shape, reminiscent of the conical hill of Hera in

77. Paestum, Italy. Second Temple of Hera, from First Temple of Hera. Detail of columns.

78. Paestum. Temple precincts. 18th-century engraving.

the Argolid. Toward the cleft alongside the hill both temples of Hera are precisely oriented (figs. 83, 87).

The second is circa 450 B.C., thus a hundred years later than the other. What had the Greeks done to make it work better than the first temple for the divinity within and the worshipers without? The worshipers may be imagined as approaching the temples primarily from the sea, then along the main street of the town behind the temples and, normally proceeding only afterward to the altars on the

east, as standing at last between the temples and the conical hill. All along this route, the second temple clearly reads as a more powerful sculptural body than the first (fig. 79). It has only six columns across the front; they are bigger than those of the first temple; the whole body is more powerful, upstanding, and compact. It is thus more "Doric" than the other, whose colonnade of nine columns is widespread, as if not unaffected by influence from the Ionic mode. At the same time, the west end of the second temple has been opened into an opisthodomos, which makes it look the same as the entrance pronaos on the east (fig. 80). The word *opisthodomos* means only "the work at the rear." Its function is visual: to refuse any sense of the building as a closed box of space and to permit it always to face the observer—who will often, as here, approach the temple from the rear.

The first temple had no opisthodomos (fig. 80); on approach from the main street, it would have shown as a simple box behind the much wider peripteral colonnade, stretched to nine columns in contrast to the other's six (figs. 81, 82). This difference has two effects. The human eye can easily take in six columns all at once, without "counting." The impression is therefore of bodily unity. Nine columns

79. Paestum. Temples of Hera. Air view.

82. Paestum. Second Temple of Hera.

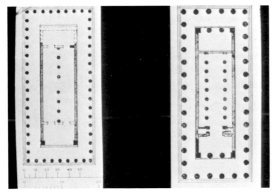

80. Paestum. First Temple of Hera. Circa 550–540 B.C. Second Temple of Hera. Circa 450 B.C. Plans.

83. Paestum. Second Temple of Hera. Interior.

begin to become a continuous colonnade, additive and harder to grasp as one body, so moving toward the Ionic grove. Moreover, with an odd number of columns, the image of the divinity cannot be placed on the central axis of the building. Its own visual access to the sacred landscape shapes and to the sun of its name day is blocked, just as the worshipers' view of it, when the doors of the temple are opened, becomes an indecisive one.

We noted that both the temples of Hera at Paestum are oriented exactly on the landscape notch. The central colonnade of the first obscures that relationship; the second temple locks into it (fig. 83).

81. Paestum. First Temple of Hera.

The divinity is thus one with the landscape but different from it. Her interior structure suits her nature; it is not adjusted to the reception of human beings within it. She is intended to be seen primarily from outside, and there once again the increased sculptural power of the second over the first is evident enough. We must further imagine a broad, high pediment stretched across the broad face of the first temple, below which the columns, with a very low center of entasis, are made to look compressed. The effect would have been more a structural than a sculptural one, because the support of the weight would have been dramatized and the two elements of load and support distinguished from each other. In the second temple, the columns are bigger and even more mus-

cular, but their center of entasis is a little higher and the pediment above them much lower and less broad than the other. Again, the effect is of unity, of one organic body, all integrally heavy and brooding and weighing grandly on the earth (fig. 84).

With the Parthenon, its contemporary, the Temple of Hera at Paestum is the most thoroughly overwhelming image of divinity in temple form that remains to us. Its body is like those of Kleobis and Biton as they are represented in the two great Kouroi dedicated at Delphi (fig. 85)—the sons of one of Hera's priestesses, who for services rendered to her were given the goddess's interpretation of the greatest blessing that mankind could receive: They were put to death in their sleep. Together,

88. Paestum. Temple of Athena. Circa 510 B.C., from the southwest.

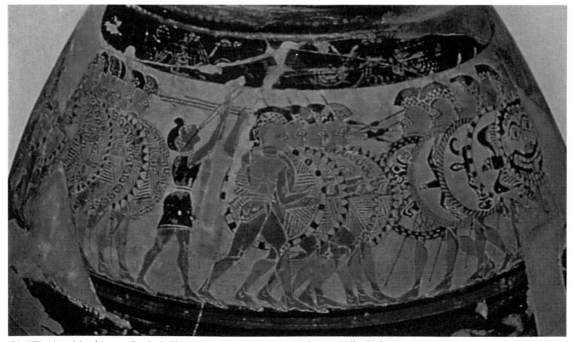

86. "Warriors Marching to Battle," Chigi vase. Circa 640–630 B.C. Rome, Villa Giulia Museum.

they had dragged their mother's cart across the muddy plain of Argos to the Heraion, and like a yoke of oxen they stand, and like oxen sacrificed to Hera they are ox-eyed, like her, and their hair is braided like that of her sacrificial ani-

85a. Taos Pueblo. North House with Sacred Mountain.

mals. All this brooding animal power, this aura of death and sacrifice, perhaps of men, is in the looming body of the temple itself no less than in the human figures. What a presence it is, its columns surrounding us at their own intervals, marching forward in their own massive tread around us as we move among them. It is not a simple building to shelter us. It is the goddess herself in majesty and terror. Contrast should be made with, for example, North House at Taos (fig. 85a), all abstracted mountain mass; it is the earth's sanctity intensified. Hera's temple is humanity terribly suffused with the divine.

In this vein, the whole body of the temple is one compact mass made up of vertical, self-sufficient, geometric units. Exactly so stood the Greek hoplites of the

85. Kleobis and Biton, marble. Circa 580 B.C.

84. Paestum. Second Temple of Hera. Colonnade. Entablature. Pediment.

Archaic period, massed shoulder to shoulder in their dense phalanx, as we see them on the Chigi vase of the later seventh century (fig. 86), advancing in step to the music of the flute. The poet Tyrtaeus should be quoted in this connection, as I have done perhaps too often over the past forty years. The Spartans imported him from Ionia to teach them how to march in step, and the lines he wrote for them are still the best auditory accompaniment to the temples' advancing masses. He entreats the hoplites to stand steady, foot to foot, to raise shield to shield, plume to plume, helm to helm, and strike blows. In Greek, it is the ferocity of the sound that moves us, its pounding of feet and clangor of arms.

Kai poda parpodi theis ep aspidos
   aspid ereisos
En de Lophon te lopho kai kyneen
   kynee
Kai sternon sterno, peplemenos andri
   mechesto

The temple is a divinity; however much it suggests the phalanx, it is not a gang of armed men (fig. 87). But like the phalanx, the temple was one of the essential Greek cultural structures through which human power was focused, aggrandized, and brought to bear on the rest of creation. Each temple is therefore different in power, as each divinity is different. This shows spectacularly well at Paestum. The two temples of Hera are much the same; the second is simply more successful at embodying the whole of Hera than is the first. But the Temple of Athena is totally different (fig. 88).

It dates from about 500 B.C., right between the other two temples in date, so that chronological developments in this

89. Paestum. Second Temple of Hera. Detail.

case have nothing to do with the issue. Athena's columns are thin; their point of maximum swelling—of entasis—is high. So they seem to thrust up rather than to be compressed or to weigh down. Unlike the two temples of Hera, which are placed on flat ground, we must approach this temple from below, which increases its lifting effect. Moreover, the pediment here never had a horizontal cornice. Hence, the eye continues upward beyond the columns' thrust. Athena does not stand heavy like Hera, Goddess of the Earth, and, at Paestum especially, of Childbirth. She rears up and raises her aegis above her city, whose embodiment she is, the expression, in particular, of its active political ambition. She has nothing to do with the conical hill to the south. She rises before the mountains inland, defying them, bringing to life what Sophocles was to call "the feelings that make the town."* How different a being from Hera she is. Contrast with Hera's second temple is telling—with the dark, brooding shadow of its horizontal cornice most of all (fig. 89). Hera is ancient and secret in the end. Athena is open, accessible to

---

*Sophocles, *Antigone,* 354, trans. E. Wyckoff, Chicago, 1959, p. 191.

mankind, and here she had a little porch of columns, which may have been Ionic, to greet humanity at the entrance side. Most of all, her columns are active, upward-leaping, as she would have men be, while those of Hera I seek the ground.

One should go further. Contrast with other divinities is equally telling. Apollo at Corinth, dated within the same decade as Athena at Paestum, stands with a positive immovability in the center of the mighty goddess shapes that haunt the landscape of the Isthmus; the upward-rolling acropolis held by Aphrodite, Hera's sphinx-mountain flaring at Perachora across the Gulf (fig. 90). In this confrontation, Apollo's columns have no entasis at all. They are purely conical in section, slanting straight-sided. In fact, none of Apollo's developed temples have any entasis whatever. Why should they, since this god neither weighs down upon the earth nor leaps up from it, but stands solid and sure as an embodiment of Hellenic dominance in the goddess's old world? He is discipline, self-knowledge, rationality, and calm light; his brightness illuminates, civilizes the wild land. His temples are the most like a phalanx of them all, each column a solidly geometric hoplite fixed in place by his own firm will and the fellowship of his kind. And if there is a contrasting darkness within the hoplite as within Apollo himself, some ambiguity in the bright, unyielding image, that is kept, literally, inside; it is not shown to the outer world.

All of that is best seen at Delphi, where Apollo most conspicuously subordinates the old goddess of the earth and assumes her prophetic powers. He kills her great snake, the python, and cries, in the Homeric hymn, "Now lie there and rot, on the earth that feeds man." Deep inside his

90. Corinth, Greece. Temple of Apollo. Circa 500 B.C.

91. Delphi, Greece. View from near sanctuary back toward Itea.

temple, a dark adyton was hidden, whence a priestess, a female, prophesied in ambiguous phrases. Outside, everything was different. The columns of the present temple were rebuilt in the fourth century B.C. after an earthquake, so that they are taller and more slender, markedly less robust than Apollo's Archaic columns were. But, like them, they have no entasis; they stand in perfect stasis, triumphant over the mountain and the void.

For the pilgrim in antiquity, the experience of the site of Delphi normally began at the port of Itea on the Gulf of Corinth (fig. 91). From there, the road winds upward through olive groves. A river, the

92. Delphi. Horns of the Phaedriades.

Pleistos, flows down through the gorge, like a giant serpent undulating along the valley floor. From the slopes below the sanctuary, the whole approach is visible, and the landscape seems markedly unstable. The heavy feet of Parnassos push down among the olives, as if the mountain mass was still in flow as well. It is, in fact, a center of earthquake tremors, as Knossos was, and when we move forward toward the shrine, the grandest and most menacing of all the earth's fighting forms rise before us. They are the horns of the Phaedriades (fig. 92), shaking up and out against the sky; the light moves across them, and they swing with it, shining and shadowed, restless with power.

The sanctuary of Apollo lies just below them (fig. 93), but the pilgrim in antiquity would in all likelihood have stopped for a moment at the Sanctuary of Athena Pronaia at Marmaria, a little lower down the slope. The major temple there was a circular one, a new kind of tholos, and entirely suggestive of the navel of the earth, which Delphi was also supposed to be. Up above it, the columns of the Temple of Apollo in his sanctuary at first show very small before two wild sets of landscape horns. The temple seems to be carried forward on an unstable slope, entirely at the mercy of the earth's force and especially menaced by the enormous horns above it.

There is little doubt that by the later Archaic period, when the sanctuary was in its heyday, a very conscious drama between the natural and the manmade had been orchestrated on the site, a drama calculated to embody the eventual victory of Apollo over the earth's cataclysmic power. To begin with, when we approach the horns more closely, the temple remains small and far above us; as we come near the entrance to the sanctuary, it is almost out of sight. The major entrance is on the east, so that we must turn our backs on the Phaedriades and move forward past a throng of treasuries and monuments, all in competition with one another—like the cities that built them—and all jockeying like a Greek crowd for points of vantage along the Way (fig. 94).

The treasuries, each like a little temple *in antis* that can face and turn and push forward, are set in the most advantageous position that each can find. The "planning," if such it should be called, derives

93. Delphi. Temple of Apollo under the horns.

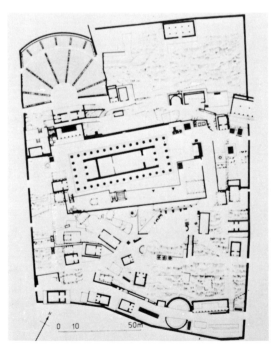

94. Delphi. Plan of sanctuary of Apollo. Restored.

96. Delphi. Portico of the Athenians, polygonal wall, and Temple of Apollo with the cliff.

97. Delphi. Temple of Apollo. Altar of Chios, left.

mainly from ritual and sculptural, not spatial, concerns. The whole takes shape only as each treasury finds its place along the Sacred Way, whose route from below to above is the determinant of the site's shape as a whole, its serpent spine. The rest is all action and aggression. The Treasury of the Athenians seizes the ideal position (fig. 95), right where the Way up the contours turns to approach the temple, so bringing the horns of the cliffs into view once more, with the winged sphinx of Naxos rising on its Ionic column in that line of sight. It is lifted high above the cavern of the Pythoness by the Ionic jet of hydraulic energy, and it echoes the mountain's profiles with its flaunted wings.

On that approach, the delicate Ionic columns of the Portico of the Athenians also come into view (fig. 96). Behind them, the fine limestone wall is like a sophisticated comment on the Cyclopean masonry of the heroic past, but now the stone surfaces are flattened, smoothed, and covered with writing—with the language that defined the Greeks to themselves. Just beyond that wall, the Way turns up between the cliff and the heavy

masonry of the temple's platform to approach close to the god at last. But just before that can occur, the high altar of Chios blocks the view, so that the temple finally bursts upon our sight all at once, providing a surprising climax after all (fig. 97).

Here, the Archaic Greek column must have stood at its most triumphant (fig. 98). These later and rather dwindled, though taller, examples themselves capture the feeling. They are bright before the dark cliffs; they challenge the horns. Their vertical fluting and straight sides stand out with special poignancy against the wild, slanting profiles of the moun-

98. Delphi. Temple of Apollo with the Phaedriades.

95. Delphi. Temple of Apollo. From Treasury of the Athenians.

100. Delphi. Temple of Apollo from above.

99. Delphi. Theater and Temple of Apollo with mountains across the valley.

tains across the valley. Like the tall, taut, proud *Charioteer* of the late Archaic period—who has been salvaged at Delphi from the wreck of his chariot and his horses and from that of the hundreds of other dedications of his time—they stand victorious, upright, humanly divine in the face of nature's awful fact and undying power.

This is the climax of the Archaic world. By the early Classic period, its simple sense of victory had been modified and tempered. Dionysos had come to share the site with Apollo for three months out of the year. The seats of his theater nestle back into the hollow of the slope (fig. 99). Their convex shape complements an especially concave outpouring of rock on the slope across the valley, and they look out over their own low stage house and even the mass of the Tem-

ple of Apollo toward the longer view southward across the land. From higher up, that effect of union with the landscape is even more striking. Highest of all, the stadium slides into the upper slope and is anchored in the cliff. Coming down from it, uplifted perhaps by a sense of brotherhood and victory, the pilgrim sees the theater open up to vastnesses even farther off, while the temple sails out effortlessly across the world (fig. 100). Most of all, its pediment and those of the treasuries now seem to echo the profiles of the mountains rather than to contrast with them. The pediments are the only parts of a Greek temple that can be seen as evocative of landscape forms—at least sometimes, and in this case strikingly so. They lock at last into the earth, transforming ancient victory into some measure of kinship with the land.

4

OLYMPIA AND THE ACROPOLIS OF ATHENS

APOLLO RECEIVES DIONYSOS INTO his site at the end of the Archaic period to suggest a new wholeness in mankind, but the Classic movement of the fifth century is dominated by two other divinities: Zeus and Athena—Zeus as the god of *Dike,* justice; Athena as the embodiment of the city that bore her name. So the major Classic sites are the Sanctuary of Zeus at Olympia and the Acropolis of Athens, which Zeus and Athena hold. The most important work done on those sites during the fifth century all dates within one long generation of men, that at Olympia beginning in the 460s, that in Athens largely completed by 432. I agree with those historians who have suggested that most of the relief sculpture at both sites may have been carried out by one great team of artists, led by Pheidias, first as a young man at Olympia, then in Athens during his middle years, and at last back in Olympia after the death of Pericles to cram his vast Olympian Zeus into the temple that had been designed more than thirty years before.

159. Athens. Parthenon from the east. See also p. *x.*

Yet the themes of the two sites are utterly different. Between them, they comprise two complementary, or perhaps even opposed, ways of looking at the world. At Olympia, the site of the most important of the great Hellenic games, traditionally founded in 776 B.C., the Greeks of the fifth century look backward to the time of the kings and the heroes, all sons of Zeus, like Herakles and Peirithous, the Lapith king. In an incomparable group of sculptures, revolutionary in form and conservative in meaning, they explore the concept of law, the character of crime, and the limits of human behavior. They contemplate the differences between men and nature, action and tradition; the Sacred Truce is the underlying theme. Of all this, the god is Zeus, to whom Hesiod ascribes the bringing of law to mankind.

On the other hand, the Acropolis of Athens celebrates the breaking of limits, the ready acquiescence of nature to human action, the victory of the polis over everything. It is the Athenian Empire, expressing a new unity of Dorian and Ionian

128. Athens, Greece. Acropolis. From the Pnyx.

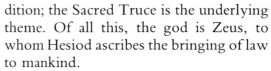

102. Olympia, Greece. Temples of Hera and Zeus, with Pelopion.

Greece, embodied in the Athena of the Parthenon, the ship of the Athenian state under way. The Zeus of Olympia is aristocratic; kings stand in his pediments. The Athena of Periclean Athens is democratic; the people of Athens crowd into her frieze.

Olympia is the quietest of all the great sacred sites (fig. 101). It is the opposite of Delphi, violently caught up in its naked horns of rock. Olympia is marked instead by a conical hill, well grown with trees, which rises above a flat, low plain defined by the crossing of two rivers—the Alpheios flowing down from high Arcadia, the Kladeos flowing into it just below the sanctuary. How can this gentle place embody the king of the gods? At Delphi, the Temple of Apollo stands out in victory before a majestic view. Here, the two temples in the wooded Altis (the word means "grove") are set quietly in what amounts to a meadow (fig. 102). The old Temple of Zeus, later rededicated to Hera, lies close under the hill; the Classic Temple of Zeus stands a little farther out on the plain.

At one time, the stadium lay directly in front of the two temples, running eastward across the front of the long platform on which the treasuries of various city-states jostled each other to watch the games. By the fourth century, with the increased professionalization of athletics, the stadium was pushed eastward all the way out of the sanctuary, which was then fenced in by a stoa, the Echo Colonnade, along that side. Even then, however, the meaning of the site remained clear. The games took place in front of the conical hill, just as they had done at Knossos in sight of Mount Jouctas (fig. 103). It is once again the kingly site, and the place where a king is buried. Pindar, in his tenth Olympian Ode, tells that the games were initiated by Herakles, who then named the

101. Olympia. From the west. Hill of Kronos, Altis, valleys of Alpheios and Kladeos rivers.

103. Olympia. Hill of Kronos and Hellenistic stadium.

conical hill, calling it the "Hill of Kronos," the dead father of Zeus. The hill is his tomb, conical like those of Nestor and Agamemnon and like Mount Jouctas itself.

Pindar further specifies that Herakles began the games at the tomb of Pelops, the eponymous hero of the Peloponnesos, at the place "where two rivers cross." And the Pelopion is, in fact, the center of the site (fig. 104). The approach to it in antiquity showed the conical hill directly ahead, unemphatically but wholly dominating the sacred enclosure. In front of it stood the altar of Zeus, built up of ash and blood. It, too, was conical, echoing the shape of the father's tomb. Directly under the hill lay the first Temple of Zeus, long, low, and rather open, with

the columns, originally of wood, set far apart. Pausanias records, apparently with some surprise, that in it Hera sat enthroned on the axis, with Zeus standing beside her. He was to get a temple all to himself only in the fifth-century campaign of building, when the old temple was rededicated to Hera alone and given a small altar of its own.

Doxiadis' fine perspective (not beautiful perhaps but very informative)* shows how the two temples related to each other as seen from the northwestern entrance to the site (fig. 105). The line of view falls directly over the Pelopion in the center, as do the sight lines from all the major entrances to the sanctuary. To the left, Hera, seen with the new temple, now looks positively low, gentle, and open, while Zeus looks big, upstanding, sculpturally solid. Brother and sister, husband and wife, male and female. In any event, the Temple of Zeus is very large, and, standing well out in space, it is able to balance the conical hill: the old dead god in nature, the living king of the gods in human form (fig. 106).

*From an early and perceptive study of the organization of Greek sanctuaries by a city planner: K. A. Doxiadis, *Raumordnung im griechischen Städtebau*, Heidelberg and Berlin, 1937.

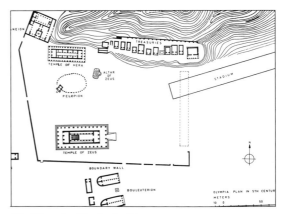

104. Olympia. Plan in the 5th century B.C.

105. Olympia. Temple of Hera, left, Pelopion, and Temple of Zeus, right. Reconstruction drawing.

That great contrast was enhanced when Pheidias finally placed his vast ivory and gold figure of the enthroned Zeus within the temple, bursting its seams (fig. 107). It was far too big for the interior, surely consciously so. One of the Seven Wonders of the World in Hellenistic times, it loomed in the darkness above a shining pool of oil, intended to lubricate it in the damp site but certainly adding to its awe as well. Such a figure of majesty: It is hard to think of its degradation when it was taken away by a Christian emperor in the late fourth century and brought like a captive king to Constantinople, where

it somehow perished. On the site at present, with the temple flattened, and especially at night when the cicadas and frogs are singing, one contemplates the terrible vulnerability of Zeus, god of human justice, in our fanatic world. But once there was a true, calm balance at his site, opening out a space for human beings by the tomb of Pelops, defined by the big temple of the son and the big hill of the father with the smaller temple of wife, sister, and daughter resting between them. It was Greek, and paternal, right enough, but the autonomy of Hera was growing, as her temple became hers alone.

107. Olympia. Temple of Zeus. Circa 462–457 B.C. Reconstruction drawing, section through cella.

The major entrance to the sanctuary during antiquity was on the southwest, at the rear of the Temple of Zeus. There again an opisthodomos made it a front view, while the pediment stood out above the conical hill and, if we credit Doxiadis' drawing, continued the line of its slope (fig. 108). As one moved toward the Pelopion, that pediment loomed ever more tumultuously overhead. In it, the Sacred Truce, the very cement of the Olympian Games and of Hellas itself, was being broken. Again, Pausanias tells the story. It is the wedding feast of Peirithous, king of the Lapiths, a northern Greek tribe. He

106. Olympia. Zeus and Hera, with Pelopion and Hill of Kronos.

has invited his good friends Kaineus and Theseus, the king of Athens, and his old cronies, the wild centaurs, half man, half horse, from the mountains nearby. They, not being Hellenes and therefore knowing neither self-discipline nor Apollo's law of moderation, get savagely drunk. They grab the boys and girls, including the bride, for carnal purposes, and a war begins that lasts a year, during which Peirithous as king and general destroys them all. The first bloody scuffle of that war is taking place in the pediment (fig. 109). The figures are all arranged within the triangle of the gable with dramatic unity of action, like a picture in a frame. Contrast should be made with such sculpturally dominated earlier pediments as that from the Temple of Artemis on Corfu, where the great gorgon in the center is at one scale and Priam and his killer in the corner at another. Each is sculpturally autonomous, but Olympia's pediment is pictorial.

In this it reminds us that, during antiquity, it was the painter Polygnotos, not any sculptor, who was regarded as the greatest artist of the early fifth century. The pediment may legitimately be regarded as having been adjusted to his example or at least as reflecting the whole trend toward pictorial values that he apparently led. Whatever the case, I believe that this pediment, coupled with Robert's conjectural reconstruction (of 1893) of Pausanias' description of Polygnotos' *Iliupersis** in the Lesche of the Cnidians at Delphi (fig. 110), was the major model for one of the most important paintings of the modern age: *Guernica,* of 1937, by Pablo Picasso (fig. 111). This picture, in-

*Carl Robert, *Die Iliupersis des polygnot, Hallisches Winckelmannsprogram,* Halle, 1893.

108. Olympia. Temple of Zeus. Reconstruction drawing.

109. Olympia. Temple of Zeus. West pediment, Battle of Lapiths and centaurs.

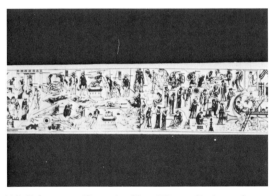

110. Polygnotos. Iliupersis. Circa 475 B.C. Conjectural reconstruction by Robert, 1893.

stigated as it was by the German bombing and strafing of the Basque town of Guernica on market day, was also set up in a place where, as Pindar wrote of Olympia, "many strangers" passed, the Spanish Pavilion at the International Exhibition of 1937 in Paris. A critic wrote at the time that *Guernica* looked like a Greek pediment

112. Olympia. Temple of Zeus. West pediment. Battle of Lapiths and centaurs. Detail.

111. Pablo Picasso. *Guernica.* 1937.

that had been hit by a locomotive, and that is, of course, exactly how the west pediment of the Temple of Zeus looks in its reconstructed fragments. But there are other resemblances beside the pyramidal organization. The human figures in both compositions are subjected to distortions that are expressive of their states of mind, at Olympia no less than in *Guernica,* where arms inflate and knees melt and throats swell to a scream. A Lapith tries to reach out to rescue a maiden, but his foot is twisted and his knees pinned down by heavy drapery (fig. 112). His knife just barely reaches a centaur, who has seized the maiden by the ankle. She falls, her right knee hidden by drapery and thus visually unsupporting, her body a long, unstable diagonal culminating in the exaggeratedly heavy mass of her arms and shoulders, falling with increasing momentum like the crown of a felled tree. Indeed, her drapery resembles oak bark, and Pindar tells us that Herakles planted the trees in the Altis "to shelter the god from the sun's fierce rays." The trees, like the maidens, are helpless and need protection. Rape and violence may be directed to sacred nature, as well.

But unlike *Guernica,* where the scene is illuminated by technology's electric light bulb, which in a sense makes the whole horror possible, Olympia has a king to enforce the law (fig. 113). Pausanias tells that the figure in the center is Peirithous himself. A good many modern scholars want him to be Apollo, another son of Zeus, claiming among other things that the Greeks would never have put a mortal man in the pediment. I see no convincing reason to agree with them. What may be more or less this same team of sculptors was to put the citizens of Athens on the Parthenon's frieze. The Classic Greeks, in fact, were capable of almost anything. Whatever the case, god or human, it is a kingly figure and a son of Zeus who rises above the strife. The struggling figures around him are now properly rearranged in the museum at Olympia, so that the king is clearly seen as ordering, not striking, and heroes who, according to Pausanias, should be Kaineus and Theseus, flank him on either side. It is all meant to be seen from below, in pictorial perspective, and in that view the quiet majesty of the central figure, ruling through light and grace, can be most fully perceived.

On the other pediment, the figures are still (fig. 114). They looked toward the stadium, standing out above the altar of Zeus, where all the oaths before the games were sworn. There was never a Hippodameion in the sanctuary, as Doxiadis and others once believed there to be. In fact, the original stadium filled that space. So above the place of the games and the

113. Olympia. Temple of Zeus. West pediment. Apollo.

Olympic oaths, an oath is being broken. Pausanias is again our guide. He tells us that it is the oath before the chariot race between the king, Oenomaus, and Pelops, a suitor for the hand of the king's daughter, Hippodameia, in which the king is killed. Sterope, the queen, is also present. Mother and daughter are still wrongly placed in the museum's present reconstruction of the group. Hippodameia, proud bone of contention, lifting her mantle to climb into the victor's chariot, should stand next to Pelops, who is young, awkward, and aggressive. Hippodameia's mother, arms locked in anxiety across her stomach, should stand next to the proud, cruel, and fated king on the other side.

The myth is savage. Oenomaus, "going," as Pindar puts it, "backward out of life without a son" will lose his crown in the end to the young man who marries his daughter. To prevent that, he already has raced thirteen suitors and killed them all. But this time Pelops has bribed Oenomaus' charioteer to cut partway through the king's chariot axle, so that in the race he is thrown and dies. Zeus stands between the rivals as they falsely swear. It is an *agalma Dios,* Pausanias tells us, an "image of Zeus" as on an altar. The image does not move to aid Oenomaus; some think his body suggests a slight turn in Pelops' direction, the victor's side. But on the other side of the pediment, the aged

116. Olympia. Temple of Zeus. East pediment. Kladeos.

seer who backs Oenomaus lifts his hand to his cheek in dismay, knowing that the king will be killed (fig. 115). As in contemporary drama, he is a Teiresias figure, telling us, the audience, what the principals in the tragedy do not yet know. The mood is tense, dark. Each figure, like a fine actor, reveals his soul by the movements of his body, and all again are quite obviously meant to be seen from below.

114. Olympia. Temple of Zeus. East pediment.

Farthest below the central figures on the pediment itself, and looking up toward them, were the figures of the Alpheios and the Kladeos, the river gods. The surviving example (fig. 116) comes coiling sluggishly out of his drapery like a water creature from its shell, turning heavily like the river current of Homer's Scamander at Troy. It is pure nature. Its face is therefore as devoid of human intelligence as Picasso's light bulb. But it watches the central figures; they are exposed to its blank look, which is as unmitigatedly uncommunicative as that of a bluefish. Before it, the human actors, seen from below, stand revealed in their cruel pride, most of all in their secret intent (fig. 117). Nature is clearly separate from mankind. It intends nothing, hence means nothing. It does not communicate; it simply is. Therefore, it neither condemns nor forgives. Above all, it does not consent. Eventually, the rivers were to flood the site.

So, on his pediments, Zeus explores for us the character of human intention and its crimes, which makes law necessary for mankind. But his own character is deeper than that; it has to be penetrated step by step before we can stand in the shadow of him enthroned. This is the way the sculptures in the metopes work. They embody the labors of Herakles, after which, so Pindar tells us, he founded the games, and they are placed not in the outer metopes of the peripteral colonnade but in the six metopes above the opisthodomos and the six above the pronaos (fig. 118). In them Herakles is shown, like the kingly figure on the west pediment, carrying out his labors with and through grace, giving off light like the figures on contemporary red-figure vase painting against their dark ground (fig. 126). Unlike the hulking Herakles of the Archaic

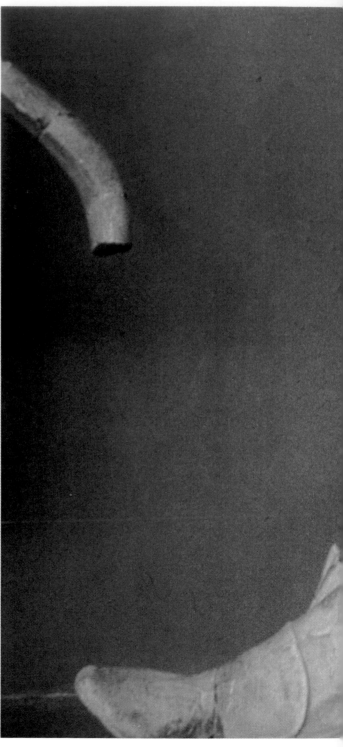

115. Olympia. Temple of Zeus. East pediment. "Old Seer."

117. Olympia. Temple of Zeus. East pediment. Central group: Zeus, Oenomaus, Hippodameia.

isthodomos and thus is meant to be seen first from the major entrance to the sanctuary at the rear of the temple. Moving from left to right, the first scene is that of the Nemean lion (fig. 119). Here Herakles is only a boy. He has already killed the lion but is exhausted from the struggle. Athena stands behind him to comfort him; here at the very beginning of his labors he seems already discouraged. One line of care across his brow marks his otherwise unlined, boyish face. The long, hard trials of his life all lie before him, and the first has shocked him almost more than he can bear. Well might he fear, because in the next metope he is alone, tangled up with the Lernaean Hydra in the ultimate snake dream. Nothing could be worse, but he comes through, and in the next metope, wherein he brings the Stymphalian birds to Athena, the boy has become a man (fig. 120). His face is lean and bearded; the line is deeper across his brow. He has matured through his labors, but in the next metope, where he must exert all his physical force to curb the Cretan bull, he is brutalized by them; his head is thick and round, his face distorted (fig. 121). He is alone again with his mortality and with what his labors have made him. But later, in the metope of the apples of the Hesperides, Athena is with him again, working alongside him like an equal partner, though her aid in holding up the world is shown as primarily symbolic, spiritual

period as depicted in the old black-figure style, the new Herakles is no longer a mindless, slightly comic, often drunken smasher and basher. Now he understands the nature of his heroic responsibilities and accepts his burdens with a dignity equal to that of his patron, Athena, who stands with him in some of the metopes.

The sequence of labors is also important. It starts over the entrance to the op-

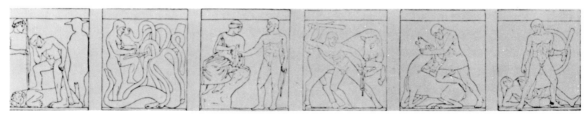

118. Olympia. Temple of Zeus. Metopes. Labors of Herakles. Reconstruction drawing.

rather than humanly physical like his own. In the very last metope, which stood to the far right as one finally entered the temple through the pronaos on the east, Herakles has become old and, perhaps it is not too much to say, anachronistically, saintly (fig. 122). He is sweeping out the Augean stables, the dirtiest job of all. He is disgusted, but he does his duty to the last.

Athena directs him to it, and a word more should be said about her character throughout. She, like Herakles, grows and develops from metope to metope. It might better be said that she grows as he grows, as he is able to imagine her at any stage of his life. In the first metope, when he is a boy, she looks like a boy, too (fig. 123). Her hair is up, her face lean-profiled. She is what he as a boy is able to project: a friend in the palaestra. In the metope of the Stymphalian birds, when he has become a man, she has become a woman (fig. 124). She meets him as an equal, sitting on an irregular outcropping of rock like a girl in the park. As she receives his

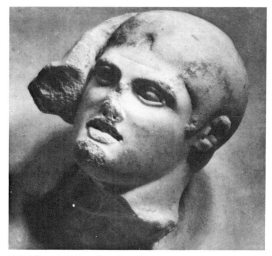

119. Olympia. Temple of Zeus. Metopes. Herakles and the Nemean lion. Detail, head of Herakles.

gift, her face is soft, full, and rounded; her hair has filled out into a thick, maidenly bob. It is as if the sculptor is saying that men make their gods—or that at least they make Athena, who is the sum of their ambition, their identification of themselves.

So this head of Athena may be the noblest surviving Classic head of all (fig. 125).

120. Olympia. Temple of Zeus. Metopes. Herakles presenting Athena with the birds from Lake Stymphalus. Detail, head of Herakles.

121. Olympia. Temple of Zeus. Metopes. Capture of the Cretan bull. Detail, head of Herakles.

122. Olympia. Temple of Zeus. Metopes. Cleansing of the Augean stables. Detail, head of Herakles.

It is broad and powerful, gentle and tender, physically as solid as that of a great athlete, proud in flesh and spirit, a bright image of what humankind, male and female, might hope to be. And thereafter, as we have seen, Athena is Herakles' equal partner, as they together support the world (fig. 126).

At the very last, though, Athena becomes the only thing that the old man has left to him: his devotion to his duty, his kingly will to do Zeus' work in the world (fig. 127). Only in this last metope of the Augean stables is Athena armed, the cheek pieces of her helmet up, harsh duty embodied, all that remains to Herakles: the courage, hard-earned, to face the end of things.

It was the armed Athena who held the Acropolis of Athens. There Pheidias' Athena Parthenos, the Maiden unspoiled, stepped forward in ivory and gold, the

123. Olympia. Temple of Zeus. Metopes. Herakles and the Nemean lion. Detail, head of Athena.

124. Olympia. Temple of Zeus. Metopes. Herakles presenting Athena with the birds from Lake Stymphalus. Detail, Athena.

125. Olympia. Temple of Zeus. Metopes. Herakles presenting Athena with the birds from Lake Stymphalus. Detail, head of Athena.

cheek pieces of her helmet raised once more, her shield beside her with the coiling snake of the Erechthids within it and Victory in her hand. As she loomed forward in her broad cella, the whole bulk of the temple expanded, too, blazing white on the Acropolis height, filling the sky.

The first fact of the Acropolis is that it was a fortress, a steep plug of rock rising in the Attic plain within a magnificent circle of land and water, Athena's olive groves and Poseidon's sea, all defined by a ring of mountains and islands and in those smogless days even by the mountains of the Peloponnesos across the Saronic Gulf (figs. 128, 129). The only easy slope up the Acropolis height is at the western end. Mounting there and looking down the long west–east axis of the summit, one sees the cleft, coned, and horned masses of Mount Hymettos closing the view (fig. 130). When the light is right across those slopes—today, in the brutal

pollution, an occurrence all too rare—Athens indeed seems "violet-crowned," as Pindar said she was (fig. 130). As a Theban, Pindar resented the hubris of Athens with all his heart, but his invocation of her splendor is one of the finest utterances of antiquity. He calls her "renowned, and violet-crowned, and sung by

126. Olympia. Temple of Zeus. Metopes. Atlas brings Herakles the apples of the Hesperides.

127. Olympia. Temple of Zeus. Metopes. Herakles cleansing the Augean stables. Head of Athena.

129. Athens. Acropolis. Destruction of the Parthenon in 1687. Print by Fanelli.

poets, shield of Hellas, beloved Athens, god-filled city state."

    O tai liparai
    Kai iostephanoi
    Kai aoidimoi
    Hellados ereisma
    Kleinai Athanai
    Daimonion ptoliethron

The last line rolls like earthquake and thunder, making us feel the physical presence of the gods in the ground as no other language has ever quite been able to do.

In the Archaic period, there were always two major temples of Athena on the Acropolis, along with one great altar dedicated to her and various sanctuaries of other divinities, including an altar of Zeus at the highest point (fig. 131). As one came up through the old western propylon, climbing at a diagonal with the Mycenaean defensive bastion looming over one's unshielded right shoulder, the Archaic Temple of Athena Polias was seen on the right, lying directly along the axis of the summit and oriented exactly upon the horns of Hymettos, with the cones of the Sanctuary of Aphrodite at Kaisariani also in view (fig. 132). If the stone bases still in situ in the ruins of the temple were, in fact, the bases for Mycenaean wooden columns *in antis,* then the megaron of the Mycenaean kings stood here as well, with the same orientation and the same sacred

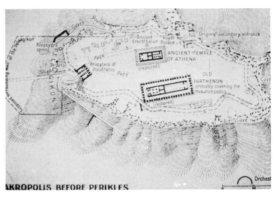

131. Athens. Acropolis. Before 448 B.C. Plan.

132. Athens. Acropolis. Temple of Athena Polias with possible Palace of Erechtheus and Horns of Hymettos.

130. Mount Hymettos from the Acropolis.

133. Athens. Kore wearing peplos. Circa 540–530 B.C.

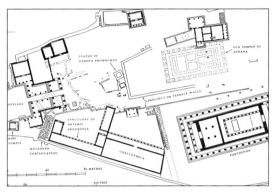

134. Athens. Acropolis. After 432 B.C. Plan.

mountain view, which in this instance was much like that from the megaron at Tiryns. It seems clear enough that the temple succeeded the megaron here, apparently with that wonderful historical continuity that was the Athenians' special pride.

The altar of Athena lay directly ahead, between the temple and the horns; but to the right, set just on the precipitous southern edge of the height, there was always another Temple of Athena, one constantly rebuilt. This was the Parthenon, where

Athena was not the ancient sacred wooden image that was dressed by maidens on her feast day in the other temple but, like Pheidias' vision later, the most up-to-date image of what the city of Athens in any given generation could imagine herself to be.

Around both temples, Athena's handmaidens, the Korai, stood, some wearing the Dorian peplos (fig. 133) and some, especially during the splendid, eastward-looking Peisistratid era of the later sixth century, the chiton and hymation of Ionia. How well these two types evoked the situation of Athens standing between western and eastern Greece, and they embodied the character of that Archaic Aphrodite-Athena as well. Many of Sappho's lines might well have been written about them. Of the touching Peplos Kore: "This is the grave of Timas, who died before she was married. In memory of her, her friends took hard iron and cut locks from their hair."

In 480 B.C., the Persians took the Acropolis and burned both temples, the Parthenon under construction as usual. Those of the Korai and the other sculptures that were not taken back to Persepolis were broken and thrown down, and similar fates may well have been suffered by the priestesses of Athena themselves, if the purported Athenian order of battle of 479 B.C. is authentic. In it, the priestesses and others are ordered to remain on the Acropolis rather than to withdraw to Troizen or to join the fleet at Salamis. After the war, the Greek states agreed to leave all the shrines destroyed by the Persians in ruins as a fitting memorial to impiety, but a generation later Pericles unilaterally set the treaty aside, and his new campaign of building was begun. But the old Temple of Athena Polias was, in fact, left in ruin. Perhaps no more of it was visible above ground than can be seen today, probably much less. So the center of the Acropolis, in front of the Altar of Athena, was now open (fig. 134).

The present Parthenon was built, a vast, broad temple set in part on newly filled ground that broadened the Acropolis on the south and wherein the broken Korai, defiled, were used as fill. Eventually, a new, complex Temple of Athena Polias, the Erechtheum, was constructed just at the northern edge of the burned temple, but, if indeed it was ever completed as intended, this temple was not finished until late in the century. The Parthenon and the new entrance to the Acropolis, the Propylaia, were both finished in 432, just before the Peloponnesian War so ruinously began. The Propylaia was aimed directly up the center of the Acropolis, so that the human worshiper now moved directly along the axis of the height, with the horns of Hymettos before his eyes and the two temples on either side defining a space and a perspective for him.

The most important building of all in this new scheme of things was of course the Parthenon itself. It may perhaps be regarded as the first developed Greek temple to be designed from the inside out. Its cella was made especially broad in order

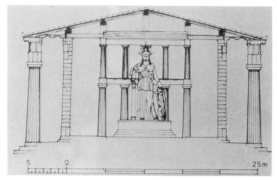

135. Athens. Parthenon. 447–432 B.C. Ictinos and Callicrates. Section.

136. Athens. Parthenon. Interior looking east.

137. Athens. Parthenon. View from the Propylaia.

to give Pheidias' statue plenty of room, and was finished on three sides with an interior colonnade in order to frame Athena grandly (fig. 135). As the temple broadened inside, it stretched to an eight-

140. Athens. Acropolis, from the Areopagus.

column width on the outside (fig. 136). Eight columns across the front rather than six had been characteristic of the Archaic Ionic temples of eastern Greece, especially on Samos and at Ephesos. At the same time, in all likelihood influenced by the hypostyle halls of Egypt, the Ionic temples also used one or more rows of columns behind the outer colonnade. Therefore, they were, as I have mentioned, more grove than body, unlike Doric temples with their six-columned fronts and single peripteral row. The Parthenon also employs a second row of columns across front and back. The pronaos almost disappears, as does the opisthodomos. Only enough projection of wall is left to refuse a boxlike corner. Within, however, a true closed chamber appeared, a treasure house with four columns, probably Ionic, holding up the roof, as in an ancient megaron.

Most of all, through its conspicuous use of Ionic features, the Parthenon may be regarded as asserting the hegemony of the Athenian Empire in the eastern Aegean. But it is in every other way a Doric temple. Unlike the wide-spreading Ionic examples, it is pulled tautly together as one active, unified body, rising at the summit of its hill (fig. 137). The upward rush of its columns, unified by a low, comparatively light pediment, should remind one of the similar quality in the Temple of Athena at Paestum, where there was also a second set of columns, possibly Ionic, at the entrance side. Athena

138. Athens, Acropolis. From Hill of Philopappos.

139. Athens. Agora. Sacred Way and reconstructed Stoa of Attalos.

is clearly complex. Her city is both eastern and western Greek, Ionian and Dorian at the same time. The lift of the Parthenon's columns may also be regarded as, in part, an Ionic feature. Ionic columns rush up like water jets. Indeed, a paddle stroke in the water will make a fine Ionic capital and shaft—volutes, flutes, and all.

But it is the whole body of the Parthenon that is stretching and rising, pushing to the very limit our visual and conceptual capacity to take it in. The eight columns demand much more than six do to be counted as units in a series, but the Parthenon will not permit that. The columns lean up and in together, tightening the corners. Yet so broad is the facade that we somehow constantly feel that we are

looking at it in pure elevation, even though one long side may also be visible to us at the same time. So the body is always swinging out off the corner column as if to turn toward us, perhaps even to envelop us within two vast opening planes.

This effect is especially marked because of the way we are normally made to see the temple: up the slope of the Acropolis height, for example, where we cannot read any diminishing perspective on the north side because the lower part of the farther columns is masked, or from the Hill of Philopappos across the way on the southwest (fig. 138). There, the angled slant of wall below the temple, built, we remember, precisely as a setting for this building, makes it difficult to fix on a horizontal ground line, so that not only does the western facade seem to turn toward us but the whole body of the temple also appears to be dipping to the southwest, like a ship in the sea—indeed, like the great shining, blazing white Athenian ship of state itself, turning in victory to salute the ships in the war harbors at Phaleron and Piraeus down below.

The Parthenon does literally blaze. For the first time, a Greek temple was not stuccoed white over darker stone but was built of white marble all through: Pentelic marble shot with iron pyrites, which sometimes modify the clearer white with a deeper fiery glow. Therefore, as the contemporary Temple of Hera at Paestum, for example, stands heavily locked into the plain, as solid and permanent as the mother who shelters us (fig. 87), so the Parthenon rises, turning on its height, the embodiment of a collective will impossible for us to fix or dominate with our individual minds, asserting the victory of the city of Athens over everything.

On her feast day, that triumphant being was approached along the old Sacred Way from Eleusis, through the Kerameikos Cemetery, from which the shining white body can be seen standing out against the sky. The Panathenaic Way then passed through the Dipylon gate—the procession itself began there—and moved on through the workaday world of the agora (fig. 139). The present Stoa of Attalos, built only in the second century A.D. and reconstructed by the American excavators of the agora, now directs our eyes toward the Acropolis, upon the far side of which, in this view, the Parthenon has largely disappeared. The Way then angles westward and passes by the Areopagus, the Hill of Ares (fig. 140). Here, in myth, the Amazons had raised their altars to the god of war, and from here, in fact, the Persians launched their assault on the northwestern face of the hill. In this view, the vastness of the Propylaia is apparent, with the big marble box that contained a picture gallery sticking out awkwardly into space. The importance of painting in the Classic period could hardly be more underscored.

To the right, the exquisite small Temple of Athena as Victory (hence Victory is wingless here: *apteros*) sounds the clarion note of the Acropolis, looking toward Salamis, proclaiming Victory. To approach the Propylaia, the Way takes a circuitous route up the contours, emerging well past the gate, where a corner of the Parthenon just comes into view. From here, however, the Temple of Victory most attracts the eye, pulling us along the path that passes beneath it (fig. 141). A calculated drama of natural and manmade is established. The natural rock is exposed below, seething in wild masses. Upon it rests the broad, blunt masonry of the Mycenaean

141. Athens. Acropolis. Temple of Athena Nike. From the Sacred Way. Mnesicles.

142. Athens. Acropolis. Propylaia from below the Temple of Athena Nike. Circa 437–432 B.C. Mnesicles.

143. Athens. Temple of Athena Nike.

bastion, while at the top the intricately crafted, articulate body of the temple stands, a final manmade achievement in total contrast to the natural rock below. The temple is oriented east, and there was no room on the bastion for an opistho-

144. Athens. Propylaia.

domos. So the side wall ends are just slightly advanced as pilasters to keep our eyes inside the mass on the west and to suggest that it is, in intention at least, facing toward us.

This was clearly the point from which the architect, Mnesicles, intended that the viewer should get his first and most important close view of the Propylaia (fig. 142). Nothing could be more conscious, in a sense more modern, than the way the viewer is jockeyed into position here. The key to that is the placement of the door to the picture gallery up above. It is set markedly off center in its wall so that it can be seen, perfectly framed by columns, precisely from the critical point of first viewing below the bastion.

But the Propylaia is still high above our heads. How do we get up there? By the Roman period, there was a good broad stair filling the space between the Propylaia's wings. What did Mnesicles intend? American archaeologists have proposed a system of ramps, for which there is really no evidence whatever. It is the result of a modern Romanticism, which would deny the Classic Greeks the straight axial approach of a stair, though that is what I think Mnesicles himself intended. On the other hand, the Greeks have recently suggested the presence of an enormous ramp of super-highway scale that seems to extend halfway down the hill. This seems gratuitous as well. One still prefers Mnesicles' stair. As one mounted it from below the bastion, the Temple of Victory began to stand out against Pericles' new harbor at Piraeus, far below (fig. 143).

Finally, from the height of the Propylaia, the overscaled Ionic volutes of the temple marked the view toward Salamis, which lies directly on axis to the west (fig. 144). Since Pausanias specifically cites the

145. Athens. Propylaia. View to Acropolis with Ionic column.

146. Athens. Propylaia. Ionic column, detail.

relevance of the sea view from this point, some archaeologists have been moved to suggest that the rest of the Acropolis top was surrounded by a wall so high that the sea could not have been seen from it: the ultimate absurdity of all, as the most cursory tour of the summit of the Acropolis can show.

The Propylaia itself is a wholly amazing building. We know that Mnesicles intended it to be symmetrical. It would thus have been enormous, but the sanctuary of Brauronian Artemis refused to give up ground for its southern wing. So Mnesicles made it look symmetrical from below by a little optical trickery on that side. The building is in every way environmental and viewer-oriented. Everything about it is intended to lead the spectator in a direction, to shape his views, and to change his attitudes. First, the Doric colonnade receives him with a more widely spaced central intercolumnation (fig. 142). Within, the Ionic columns leap up (figs. 145, 146), taller and more slender than the Doric, changing the scale and seeming to push the roof upward with their famous

148. Athens. Acropolis. Old Temple of Athena Polias with Erechtheum, left, and Parthenon, right.

149. Athens. Parthenon. West front. Reconstruction drawing from propylon.

hydraulic jet, so actively expanding the space.

The doors to the Acropolis height may often have been closed. After the bright light outside we are therefore in deep shadow. Then the doors are flung open, and the utter blazing white and blue of the Acropolis height bursts upon us, and the Parthenon stands hugely to the right, seen in an angle view from between the Propylaia's final range of Doric columns (fig. 147). "Nothing left but these closely knit and violent elements," Le Corbusier wrote of this view, "sounding clear and tragic like brazen trumpets."* It is a fair description. Almost directly ahead, just slightly to the left of the central axis, the colossal figure of Athena Promachos, Athena of the Vanguard, would have stood, the gleam of her spear point visible from far out to sea. Beyond it, as we approach the crest, the altar of Athena would have come into view directly before us,

with the horns of Hymettos rising behind it on that bearing. To our left the long wall of the Erechtheum defines the space and enforces that perspective, as does the marching bulk of the Parthenon on the other side (fig. 148). As at Olympia, we are in a room, now a vast one, defined in part by nature, in part by manmade forms. The axis of the Acropolis, which, as Le Corbusier also wrote, "runs from the sea to the mountain," is now also running right through our own bodies, from the place of victory behind us on the sea to the old sacred mountain of the goddess and the kings before us.

It was at that moment, too, that we first stood at the gate to the Parthenon's own enclosure, and from that point the whole mass of the temple literally explodes upon our senses, filling our eyes, consuming the world (fig. 149). It is precisely then, and as we approach the stairs

150. Athens. Parthenon. Pheidias. West pediment, De Laborde head.

*Le Corbusier, *Towards a New Architecture,* trans. Frederick Etchells, London, 1931, p. 206.

147. Athens. View through Propylaia to Parthenon.

that lift it even more imposingly above us, that all the temple's major sculptural groups are seen together, or were all seen until one of history's consummate idiots, the Venetian Admiral Morosini, smashed the pedimental sculptures to fragments in 1687, attempting to lower them to the ground. There, Athena, her face electric with victory (fig. 150), strove with Poseidon for the Attic land, and the river gods consented to her triumph, their bodies swept by it as by a wind (fig. 151). They are literally shaped by it, unlike the river gods at Olympia, whose rhythm is wholly internal, their own (fig. 116).

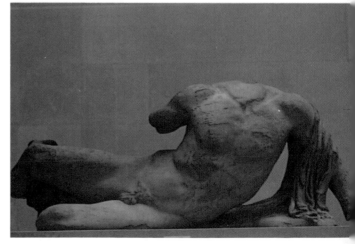

151. Athens. Parthenon. Pheidias. West pediment. Kephissos.

152. Athens. Parthenon. Southwest corner with metope of Lapith and centaur.

153. Athens. Parthenon. Pheidias. South metope, Lapith and centaur.

154. Athens. Parthenon. West front. Detail, with pediment, metopes, and frieze.

This is the hubris of Athens, certainly. She presumes to conquer nature at last. Similarly, just as Aischylos in the *Oresteia* claims for Athens the power to change all the old laws and to reconcile the old antagonisms, especially those between mankind and the goddesses of the earth, so in the metopes of the Parthenon the archetypal antagonists of Greek and Persian, Greek and Amazon, and—especially since it is these that best remain to us—centaurs and Lapiths, still fight as of old, but are each shown to be dependent upon the other (figs. 152, 153). Each pair would fall to the ground if the structural links between them were to be loosed, and the slayer can never free himself of the slain. In the end, there must be harmony. As in the *Oresteia,* it is Athena's will.

Finally, the continuous frieze is seen (fig. 154), this, too, an Ionic feature, but set back above the entrance to the treasure chamber like the Doric frieze of triglyphs and metopes at Olympia. Here, though, it runs all around the temple, starting at the observer's right, not his left, and moves from that point back toward the central space of the Acropolis once more,

155. Athens. Erechtheum, west side.

while on the southern face of the temple, out of sight from here, it rushes straight eastward toward the entrance side.

So led back toward the center of the Acropolis, we are made to face the Erechtheum, which had otherwise been marching up the hill and leading our eyes toward the Parthenon from the moment we had seen it on our approach from the Propylaia (fig. 155). Now it can be perceived as another of those astounding innovations in which the Acropolis is so rich and which, in fact, all its major buildings are. It is the very record of the struggle between Poseidon and Athena, true *architecture parlante* in every way.

157. Athens. Acropolis. Erechtheum. Porch of the Caryatids, view of the Propylaia and Salamis.

156. Athens. Acropolis. Caryatids of the Erechtheum with Hymettus from old Temple of Athena Polias. Altar of Athena ahead.

It is conceivable, as Wilhelm Dörpfeld believed, that it was originally intended to be a symmetrical building, and arguments can be made for that, especially, as I will mention in a later chapter, from certain analogies with the sanctuary of Athena at Lindos on Rhodes. But whatever the case, the Erechtheum was finally left as we now see it, and its message is clear. Poseidon strikes the rock, and the high Ionic columns of the north porch leap up. But Athena's olive tree sprouts in the sun southwest of them and is backed and framed by a unique wall, originally of columns and metal grilles, finally of columns

158. Athens. View westward from the height of the Acropolis.

other side, the caryatids populate the view toward the sacred mountain: all its cones and horns are dark behind them (fig. 156). The great altar of Zeus is set close to the Parthenon's northeast corner. We are led to it and past it to enter the temple itself, and as we turn back westward on the approach, the contours of the Erechtheum can be seen sinking into those of Parnes behind it, picking up the slope where Xerxes leapt from his throne as he saw his fleet destroyed.

Finally, the Parthenon stands alone against the seaward view (fig. 159). The gulf and Salamis lie far below it. Seen in straight elevation from the east, the temple's springy mass defines a strong arc, as

engaged in the surface of the wall, as columns had not been, except at Akragas, since the days of Phaistos.* Athena wins, and her maidens come splendidly forward across the Acropolis height (fig. 156). They swing out in majestic procession to the very edge of the old destroyed temple lying below them, and there they pause, like the dead Korai brought to life once more.

Victorious, they stand out above the view toward Salamis, in which the mass of the Propylaia has now sunk down below the line of sight (figs. 157, 158). We see *over* its pediment. (What price a wall high enough to mask the sea?) On the

*At the gigantic Temple of Zeus at Akragas, another unique structure, engaged columns were used even earlier in the fifth century B.C.

161. Athens. Parthenon. East pediment. Horse of the moon setting.

160. Athens. Parthenon. East pediment. Horse of the sun rising.

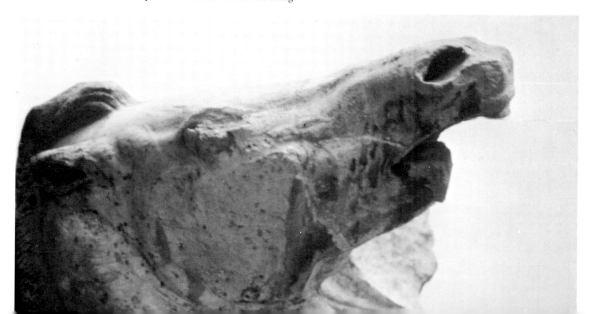

if responding to the whole bowl of sky in which it stands. In the pediment, that arc was emphasized. The wild horses of the sun sprang up on the south (fig. 160), even as the exhausted horses of the moon slipped downward on the north (fig. 161). On the southern slope, Ares opened his body like a mountain meadow to the sun (fig. 162), and the mountainous seated mothers from Eleusis (fig. 163) raised their arms toward the central group, blown out in Morosini's bombardment, where Athena once leapt forth from the forehead of Zeus. Northward, the mountain mothers of Hymettos reclined, their forms, like that of Ares, echoing the mountain's own

163. Athens. Parthenon. East pediment. Demeter and Persephone.

164. Athens. Parthenon. Pheidias. East pediment. Aphrodite and Dione, detail.

162. Athens. Parthenon. East pediment. Ares.

profiles and invoking its masses. Aphrodite and Dione lay in each other's arms, like the pointed mounds of Kaisariani before them resting in the mountain's body, and they are literally swept by drapery like a rush of waters, like headlands on which the sea foam crashes and subsides (fig. 164). Now the gods and the earth are all one in human form, all victorious, consenting, complete.

Below them, in the frieze, the gods sat again with mankind, as the maidens brought the Dorian peplos to the old Athena on her feast day. They sat with drapery across their laps like the clouds that drift across the middle heights of Olympus itself. Below them, the doors of the temple would have swung open and the Parthenos would have been seen at last (fig. 135), framed in her broad cella with a Victory in her hand. But at the same time the whole body of the temple itself is rising and lifting in a broad and obvious upward curve across the summit of the

165. Athens. Parthenon. North flank.

hill (fig. 165), carrying us back westward with its peripteral colonnades—its *ptera,* its wings—lifting us high in space like a vast ship of the air, with the fleet in its harbors and Salamis before us (fig. 166). We are victorious, each one of us who rides that ship westward into the night (fig. 167), westward through the darkness like Telemachos with Athena, as this her greatest ship cleaves through the long night into the dawn.

166. Athens. Parthenon. Detail of Pteron with view toward Piraeus.

167. Athens, Greece. Parthenon. Sunrise.

5
HELLENISTIC AND ROMAN: THE IDEAL WORLD OF INTERIOR SPACE

UNTIL THE MIDDLE of the fifth century B.C., each Doric temple was physically different from all other temples in ways that were expressive of the character of the divinity it embodied. We have seen all that clearly enough at Paestum, Corinth, Delphi, and Olympia. It was especially true of the Parthenon itself, which was the climax of the series in terms of the complexity and power of the being it shaped. All the more curious is the fact that by about 430 B.C., just after the Parthenon was completed, that special individuality and sculptural force drained out of the temples almost overnight. They stiffened up, took on a kind of canonical correctness and uniformity, and became all at once more like simple

205a. Constantinople. View from the Bosphorus with Hagia Sophia at center.

buildings than unique sculptural presences. Soon, indeed, the Greeks apparently began to forget why the temples had been built as they were, and, from about 430, began to invent a series of literary myths to explain their forms. Many of these found their way into the writings of Vitruvius, who probably offers a fair idea of how temples were thought of and their parts named by the first century B.C.

The temples that were built during the middle years of the fifth century along the ridge between the Acropolis and the sea at Akragas, on the southern coast of Sicily, are excellent examples of the very early stages of that development (fig. 168). Perhaps it is significant that we have no idea whatever who the divinities inhabiting the temples called "of Hera" and "of Concord" actually were. Nor do the temples themselves reveal it; they are stiff, linear, and dried out, though still exquisite, like good American Greek Revival work, for example. But the old awe is measurably gone. That loss of sacral aura was soon to be encouraged by the sudden rise of philosophical thought of a kind that apparently made it difficult to believe with the old conviction in the actual physical presence of a god in a building. Surely, the abstraction of Platonic thinking was also to play a considerable part in deprecating the very physicality of the older temples.

177. Lindos, Rhodes. 4th century to 1st century B.C.. View of town and acropolis.

168. Akragas. Temple of "Concord."

But the temples at Akragas were built long before that. Perhaps production in series played some part in the desiccation of their character. Gangs of Carthaginian prisoners worked on them, and they are laid out like simple landscape elements along their ridge, more like picturesque spatial markers than demanding individual beings. The general effect is already remarkably Hellenistic in ways that prefigure the environmental layouts at Lindos and elsewhere. Sicily was not Greece, after all. It was bigger in scale, more barbarous in its associations. Its cities were larger and richer than those of Greece. In a landscape less sacred, they clearly set out to define themselves and to shape an environment. This was especially true of Akragas, largest of all in ground covered and with a grid plan from the very beginning. So the ridge of temples was arranged to give scale to the town.

At the same time, some curiously original temples appeared all at once in the same years, as if some fundamental conceptual restriction also had been cast off, as it had been at Athens itself. Again, this too had already been the case at Akragas when, earlier in the century, the Temple of the Olympian Zeus at the lower end of the ridge markedly broke with the scale of earlier temples which, though of all conceivable sizes up to a point, had never become so colossal or "abnormal" as to suggest a Titanic rather than an Olympian presence. But the temple of Zeus at Akragas does exactly that (figs. 169a, 169b), blowing up the scale to an enormous degree and employing the figures of Atlantean giants to support the wide span of lintel between the columns, which were themselves engaged in a solid masonry

169a, b. Akragas. Temple of Olympian Zeus. Restored model and Atlantean figure with the town.

wall. The temple thus became, literally, gigantic, monstrous in view of the Olympian peripteral type that had been the norm. It is likely, therefore, that many of the myths about columns as the figures of captives and so on that Vitruvius was to repeat so avidly later began to be shaped right here, where the figures of barbarian prisoners were made to assist the columns in their task. It is just possible, of course, that the temple of Zeus was reviving a much older, early Archaic tradition; if so, it was one that had previously failed to shape the Archaic and Classical Doric temple to any degree. And all of Vitruvius' literary myths describing the use of human figures, representing captives as columns, are late themselves and refer to events that are of post-Archaic date.*

The Temple of Apollo at Bassae, of the later fifth century, shows another kind of invention. This unique temple was built by Ictinos after the death of Pericles and the return of Pheidias to Olympia. The marvelously complete study of it by Frederick Cooper (now in preparation) shows among other things that it had a pediment so shallow that no sculpture could possibly have been set in it. It is as if Ictinos, the designer of the Parthenon but probably always under Pheidias' thumb, had made up his mind that no sculptor was going to be allowed to dominate his very own temple in this remote place.

Beyond that, the site of Bassae, in high Arcadia, may well have been regarded by the Athenians of the later fifth century as an especially primitive and violent one (fig. 170). It might not be too much to suppose that they enjoyed its wildness from a new, liberated, proto-Romantic

*Cf. George Hersey, *The Lost Meaning of Classical Architecture. Speculations on Ornament from Vitruvius to Venturi,* Cambridge, Mass., 1988.

170. Bassae. Temple of Apollo. From Mount Kôtilon.

point of view. At the same time, Ictinos certainly invoked traditional qualities in his building. His columns, for example, are wholly without entasis, as had always been the norm in Apollo's temples. They stand in a rigid phalanx at the edge of a deep gorge beyond which the cone of Mount Lykaion rises, sacred to Apollo of the Wolves. Mount Ithome, associated with human sacrifice, looms like a flat-topped Mesoamerican temple base far southward down in the plain, and the long body of Apollo's temple carries our eyes toward it. The temple also has, uniquely, a side door in the east wall of its adyton. Many years ago, I speculated that the door might have been opened there so that a small statue of the god at the far corner of the adyton could have had a view of Lykaion between the peripteral columns. Frederick Cooper happened to be in my class at the time. So he went off and slept with his head in the appropriate position

171. The sun rising on the summit of Mount Lykaion as seen through the east door from the presumed position of the statue of Apollo. Photo by Frederick Cooper.

on the eve of Apollo's feast day and was awakened by the sun rising exactly on the summit of Lykaion as seen between the columns (fig. 171). Among the many nice things my students have done over the years, this was perhaps the most moving to me.

Ictinos was not finished with innovation. He also led a line of engaged Ionic columns down the two long walls of the cella and placed the first Corinthian column directly on axis ahead, just about where the image of the god would have stood were it not for the special demands of the site (fig. 172). The Corinthian is the most treelike of Greek columns and could thus most appropriately stand for Apollo; the tree that sheltered his birth was sacred on Delos, and he had a bronze tree in his sanctuary at Delphi. Ictinos then let a sculptor loose on a continuous, thus Ionic, frieze running around the interior of the cella. The Parthenon is surely being recalled and profoundly modified in this association of Ionic columns and Ionic frieze. The sculptures of the Parthenon metopes were also modified, with a view toward lateral movement and augmented violence, in some of its figures, others of which strongly suggest those on the west pediment of the Temple of Zeus at Olympia. The effect is somehow consciously archaizing, primitivizing: It is tumultuous and wild, like the landscape outside. Indeed, it seems to be bringing the landscape inside the temple, where so many of the other complexities of Apollo's character, suggesting unexpected links with nature, are also being explored. Outside, he is still the immovable Archaic hoplite in the light; inside, he gathers the old earth, its forests and mountains, into his own darkness.

Bassae is one of a kind, but its concern

172. Bassae. Temple of Apollo. Restored perspective of cella.

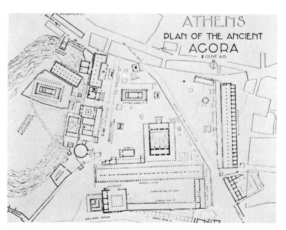

173. Athens. Agora. Plan in 2nd century A.D.

for interior space is not uncharacteristic of the more general movement of Greek architecture from the later fifth century onward. That movement was away from the sculptural embodiment of divinity in the temple, which clearly had been the obsessive concern of the Archaic period, toward the development of architectural form as an environing element, able to shape the spaces of everyday, inside and out.

174. Miletos. Plan.

175. Priene. 4th century B.C. Reconstruction drawing.

176. Priene. The Temple of Athena as originally seen from altar in agora.

By the later fifth century, therefore, the Agora of Athens rivals its Acropolis (fig. 173). The Temple of Hephaistos and Athena, which is built above it, is so placed that it must be approached on the axis of its east front. The eastern porch was much deepened over the rest of the *ptera* to accommodate that approach, and regular rows of trees were planted along the temple's sides and back. It is the first example we yet know in Greece of *landscaping* rather than of the landscape worship encountered so far. The difference is enormous. This was not the first time that the Greeks acknowledged the landscape, as one or two truly blind archaeologists have affirmed. It marks instead the beginning of the *end* of the old awe of landscape. Now human beings, not only gods, shape it, as part of an environment they create for themselves.

Elsewhere around the Agora, the stoa type, an invention of the Archaic period, was used more and more to define the space, culminating in the Stoa of Attalos of the second century A.D. The best examples, however, of the shaping of the environment by architecture were the new grid plans with which the name of Hippodamos of Miletos was associated. The Greeks had employed the grid from a very early date, especially in colonial sites like Akragas, but Hippodamos is supposed to have been the first to shape the town as a whole, balancing the residential grid with large public spaces in the center of the city.

In the plan for Miletos (fig. 174), more or less credited to him, the Agorai have become regular in form, shaped by space-defining colonnades. It is the same in the grid-planned towns that were built in many locations from the fourth century onward. Priene in Asia Minor remains one of the best examples (fig. 175). Its grid spectacularly runs down the sloping contours, as it does in San Francisco and apparently had also done in the town that Hippodamos designed for Pericles above the new war harbor of Piraeus. At Priene, a savage rock rises above the grid; it is the acropolis of the town. Doxiadis showed long ago how the Temple of Athena, now a taut, thin, elegant but rather lifeless Ionic being, was calculated to be seen from the town altar in the agora as standing out in striking contrast to the dark Acropolis rock (fig. 176). The columns of the temple are high and close together; those of the stoas are lower and far apart, but they are all comparatively thin cylinders compared with earlier examples. Everything is losing sculptural body, while the stoas especially are gaining spatial control.

The effect at Priene is much like what Western civilization has come to know as neo-Classic; the contrast between rock and temple is theatrically dramatized. We again sense attitudes that can be described as at once Classicizing and Romantic, like those that shaped early modern architecture in the Romantic-Classicism of the late eighteenth century. The sanctuary of Athena at Lindos on the island of Rhodes exhibits similar qualities. Thirty years ago, the site still looked like Classical Greece: a tiny, white town, a harbor for Telemachos and Athena, and a brown acropolis rock rising above the line of the dark blue sea into the light blue sky (fig. 177). Now the beach may well be

178. Lindos. Acropolis. Model.

crammed in summer with shoals of topless English, peculiarly shaped and burned a lobsterish color, a daunting spectacle. But the rock above is surely still as it was, with its thin, white amphiprostyle temple pushed forward to the very seaward edge of the summit, from which the strange circle of the hidden harbor called "the eye of the sea" is visible far below. The effect of contrast is again consciously dramatized, but most of all, it is the environmental axis that controls the site. Here the plan of Lindos should be seen in relation to those of Delphi and the Acropolis of Athens (figs. 94, 134).

Delphi was, as previously noted, all sculpturally dominated. The temple was oriented as it ritually had to be, and the individual treasuries jostled anarchically for position along the Way that led up the contours toward it. Each building, the temple included, acts on its own, and each one individually seizes the attention of the human observer as he takes the ritual way between them. At Athens, on the other hand, the axis of human movement was led straight up the center of the site, while the Erechtheum on one side and the Parthenon on the other set up a space for the human observer and directed his gaze toward the altar of Athena and the mountain's horns. The temples themselves were

180. Lindos. Conical promontory, with "Tomb of Cleobolos."

thus becoming in part environmental, space-defining elements. At the same time, the Parthenon is still a dominant sculptural being, the most powerful of them all.

Lindos may be regarded as the Athenian Acropolis with the Parthenon lopped off. Its elaborate Propylaia can be seen as a direct elaboration of that of Mnesicles. A stairway runs up the center; the wings of the colonnades open out to enclose the space at the sides, and a second big Propylon opens behind it (fig. 178). The southern colonnade is extended as if to take up some of the perspective containment that the absent Parthenon had achieved, and the Temple of Athena looks a bit the way Dörpfeld thought the Erechtheum was intended to have been completed, minus, of course, the Porch of the Maidens. We are led straight up the stairs in the center (another after-the-fact indication that Mnesicles may have intended stairs in his Propylaia), and the top steps are cut to keep us from straying off the axis (fig. 179). Here we are reminded of Knossos (fig. 50) as well as Athens, and from here our eyes are led by colonnade and temple to a conical headland that rises beyond the acropolis on the east. It is thus still Athens, but with the great Athena gone forever.

179. Lindos. Axis of view from Propylaia.

The slender columns that surround us on the height show how Greek art as a whole had changed since Archaic times. Then, it had all been sculpturally dominated: the temple itself, its aggressive figural decoration, freestanding sculpture, and black- and early red-figure vases with their sculpturally carved and active figures. Now, it has become much more pictorial. So the brushstroke colonnades at Lindos (fig. 180), as well as the man-shaped headland (a conical tomb) that they frame on the west, demand comparison with Roman landscape paintings of the kind that probably derived from Greek landscapes of as early as the fourth century B.C. (fig. 181).

Solid forms dissolve in light. Most of all, the shapes of the earth, its sacred mountains, are now painted, thus controlled, by men. The old awe is being transformed into a Theocritean idyll; the gods are still there more or less, but now in a literary, nostalgic, rather melancholy guise. Again, this does not represent the *first* time that human beings responded to nature, as some archaeologists still seem to think, but the beginning of the last phase of that response, a pictorial one. When painting shakes itself free of sculpture and discovers its capacity to create environments through illusion and to people them as it wishes, it cannot help but change the way human beings feel about their relation to the natural world. They are psychologically in charge of it as never before.

From the very beginning, and deeply conservative as they were, the Romans were determined to control and to shape their rituals so that men might feel protected from nature as much as might be, and could even conceive of enclosing the space of nature and shaping them-

181. Pompeii, Italy. Sacred landscape. Wall painting. 1st century A.D.

182. Praeneste, Italy. Sanctuary of Fortuna Primigenia. Circa 80 B.C. View from a distance.

selves. So Roman architecture both pursues its own ancient objectives and adapts those developed by post-Classic Greece. The most characteristic and culturally dominant of all Roman sacred sites was that of Fortuna Primigenia at Praeneste south of Rome. The colonnades recall Lindos, but the whole structure of the site is vastly different from that of any in Greece.

There, the landscape is characteristically formed into bowls of plain ringed by mountains, with the temples standing out three-dimensionally in the space so formed (fig. 128). In Italy, the mountains run down the center of the peninsula in a spine. Individual peaks rarely stand out among them, and are even more rarely identified as sacred. It is the slopes that count. Down along them and through them runs the water that fertilizes the incomparable Italian agriculture of the lower hillsides and the coastal plain. So it is the seaward slopes of the mountains that are holy, and there the major sacred sites are to be found (fig. 182).

Praeneste was always the most important of them all. Its theme was the fertile earth. Its goddess was at once the first-born and the nurse of Jupiter. Her waters are led down through the manmade structure and released to the fields below. It is the Temple of the Moon at Teotihuacán, now actually articulated for the passage of the mountain springs through its own interior cracks. So, unlike that temple, Praeneste is part of the slope, built into it (fig. 183). It is a sacred mountain itself and surely recalls the ziggurats of Mesopotamia, of which the Romans in all likelihood knew no more than they did of Teotihuacán. It is, however, all part of that pervasive pre-Greek, non-Greek world of magical imitation, reflecting ancient conceptions probably worldwide.

There is no central ramp at Praeneste. The side ramps emphasize the sheerness of the mountain wall—and it is, indeed, all very high and steep, looming dizzily over the coastal plain. Only high up do the ramps join and the stair turn to march straight up the mountainside. The whole structure opens out laterally around that movement, its Hellenistic colonnades

spreading like veils of rain before the deep, vaulted caverns where the pools of mountain water lie (fig. 184). At the summit, there is no opening to the upper slopes. The experience is concluded, indeed closed, by a manmade hemicycle crowned with columns, above which, in the center, rose a thin circular tholos like a high head. It is the goddess opening out her arms to enclose us in her sacred space—much as if the site of Perachora (fig. 74) were manmade.

Indeed, for the Romans, the word *templum* meant a space, not a building, so that Frank E. Brown, the greatest Roman archaeologist that any of us now living are likely to know, began his lapidary work on Roman architecture by writing, "The architecture of the Romans was, from first to last, an art of shaping space around ritual."[*] More than that: If the Greek temple is like the Greek phalanx, which won its battles by marching in step as a solid body and smashing the enemy, Praeneste is like the Roman legion itself, wherein the legionnaires were trained to fight in open order, like the columns here, and so could open out and envelop the enemy, enclos-

[*]Frank E. Brown, *Roman Architecture,* New York, 1961, p. 9.

183. Praeneste. Sanctuary of Fortuna Primigenia, with Renaissance palace.

184. Praeneste. Sanctuary of Fortuna Primigenia. Model.

ing him within a ring of iron. It is fitting that when we arrive high up in the hemicycle at Praeneste and look back toward the Tyrrhenian Sea, we are indeed the commanders of the vista, as the whole great structure opens its intervals around us and extends its wings like the legion deploying to enclose the world (fig. 185).

It is the Roman view; it envelops the entire visible landscape. Exactly so was the Roman Empire to enclose the Mediterranean basin, and exactly so did Roman architecture eventually come to enclose space entirely, to create perfectly controlled interiors, set off from the messy inconsistencies of the natural order. Therefore, the Pantheon was a planetarium and Hagia Sophia a perfect embodiment of Neoplatonic wisdom in its condensation of the ideal shapes of circle and square. All that was the foundation of medieval architecture in Western Europe, where the major preoccupation remained the creation of transcendent interior space. Similarly, when Western Europe began to look back out to nature again during the Renaissance, Praeneste became the dominant model for the great new gardens, of which the first was Bramante's Court of the Belvedere in the Vatican, where the architect brought the old pagan sacred mountain right into the papal enclosure to balance the dome of the basilica that he was building at the other end of the court.

185. Praeneste. Sanctuary of Fortuna Primigenia. View from hemicycle toward the sea.

186. Timgad, North Africa. Air view of city.

187. Timgad. Triumphal Arch. A.D. 165.

188. Epidauros. Theater. View northward.

189. Aspendos. Theater. Restoration.

All that is for later consideration. The important point here is that Rome changes the Greek relationship to nature by enclosing it within a hollow shell. This is the empire itself. It is also any given colonial city within it that was founded on the legionary model. A city like Timgad in North Africa (fig. 186) differs from Miletos in the fact that it has a fixed edge that encloses it in a square. Through it the *cardo* and the *decumanus* run, crossing in front of the forum where once the commander's headquarters were to be found. The Roman stamp is laid on the world.

Everywhere is Rome. Above the main road out of town, the Roman triumphal arch rises (fig. 187). It is a great signboard, telling us that in the face of nature, this is Rome. Greek columns and Roman arches are attached to it precisely as signs, informing us that the point of these is more than structural; they are the images of civilization and authority. Like the relief carvings of columns and arches that the conquistadors were to affix to the walls of their first churches in Yucatán, these forms are now instruments of cultural indoctrination and intimidation, framing the road to Rome, claiming the world for Rome. Along that road, the round-headed Roman arches swing in aqueducts and bridges, consuming space, conquering distance. Down below, the carefully drained paving of the roads tames the earth for marching feet and leads us all to the high walls and the gates of Rome. There, too, the rusticated surfaces and the broad letters of the inscriptions that the gates bear are signs that enforce belief in the city and its authority.

So Rome's instinct is to enclose, to keep nature out, to trust in the manmade environment as a total construction, and, finally, to tell us about all those things

190. Rome, Italy. Basilica Julia. 30–13 B.C. Interior.
Reconstruction.

rhetorically. In the Greek theater, as at
Epidauros (fig. 188), the seats nestle into
the arms of the hill, and the spectators look
out over the low stage house toward nature, which frames and is itself the major
theatrical backdrop for the human action
taking place below. In the Roman theater,
as at Aspendos (fig. 189), the stage house
is raised to the height of the seats and
closes the view not with the natural landscape but with the elaborately baroque,
manmade optical devices of the Roman
scenae frons. So the Greek stoa, open along
one side, can be seen as one of the pro-
totypes for the Roman basilica (fig. 190),
where it is faced by a second stoa, the ends
closed, the whole roofed, and light intro-

duced into the nave (the ship) so formed
through clerestory windows cut just
under the roof. The basilica was the
Roman court of law; the statue of the emperor stood in it, normally with its back
to one of the short walls. Human law gave
a reasonable shape and direction to the
world.

The old Forum Romanum itself grew
up over the centuries and eventually
turned out to be a much more disorderly
conglomeration of buildings than the Romans normally cared to deal with. It was
in fact a good deal like Delphi, with the
temples, basilicas, and other civic buildings crowding in at all angles along the
Sacred Way that ran through the marshy
valley below the Palatine Hill from the
Capitoline on one side, with the Arch of
Septimius Severus below it, through the
Arch of Titus on the other. So the Romans
built a new series of fora under the em-
perors, culminating in the Forum of Trajan with its elaborate market above it on
the slope of the Quirinal Hill (fig. 191).

All the imperial fora have the same
shape, most developed in Trajan's. It is
based on the enclosure of a vast area with
small care for what the environing walls
will look like on the outside. The city will
be adjusted to them as may be. It is the
great interior courtyard that counts, and
this, on a large scale, is almost identical in
shape with the most developed of the temples of the earth goddess that were built
on Malta during the third and second millennia B.C. (fig. 192). Could the Romans
have been familiar with those enclosures?
Perhaps they were; some Roman tombs
have been found among them. But the
change of scale is so vast that the mind
boggles at the conceptual leap that would
have been demanded of the Roman architect if the derivation had been delib-

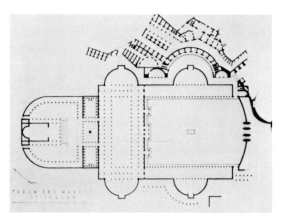

191. Rome, Italy. Forum and Market of Trajan.
A.D. 112. Plan.

192. Malta. Megalithic temples on island of Gozo. Neolithic. Air view of model, in Valetta.

erate. In any event, there are the hips, the shoulders, the head of the goddess perfectly recognizable in both.

Like Trajan's Forum, there is every likelihood that the Maltese temples, built into the earth with literally no exteriors, were also open to the sky. In one of them, the larger of the two on the Maltese island of Gozo, which was traditionally regarded as Calypso's island (where Odysseus could have had immortality if he chose), a megalithic pier stood in the head, the seat of wisdom and, perhaps, desire. So the Column of Trajan rises one hundred feet up between the Greek and Latin libraries in the head of his forum, which is the ultimate Roman achievement in terms of the handling of urban crowds. They are led and directed en masse but always remain in the body of the mother. The side colonnades and hemicycles suggest excitement and variety, but they are comfortably enclosed at the sides and lead sooner or later to the figure of the emperor, the father, standing with his back to the far wall of his temple and lecturing his visitors on proper Roman behavior.

Above Trajan's Forum, the market serves the citizens' other needs. It is of brick and concrete construction, Rome's greatest technical achievement in terms of

193. Rome. Trajan's Market. Interior of basilica.

mass structures and gangs of workmen, not all of them necessarily skilled. Two walls of brick are built up as high as is convenient for the mason (fig. 193). Concrete is then poured in between them. When it has set, the mason caps the wall and starts on up again, standing on a scaffold as required. If he has a door or a window, he will cap it with—sometimes—a wooden lintel and then build a relieving arch of brick or hollow tile above it, so that the first rush of the new pour of concrete will be directed away from it and a kind of canopy will protect it until the whole mass has time to harden into monolithic immobility. Finally, a centering of wood in the shape of a long barrel may be built up to span between the walls, as in the hemicycle in Trajan's market, and vaults of concrete, perhaps laced with brick or tile, will be poured across it. If clerestory light is desired, the long axis of the vault may be intersected by cross vaults as in the basilica in the market, so that the whole vaulting system, however heavy in fact, will look visually light, like a windblown canopy lifted up from below.

It is exactly the opposite of the point loading of Greek columns, laid up dry in drum on drum and supporting the direct weight of the lintel above them. The Greek system itself suggests the intractability of the column spacing, the sculptural dominance of the solids, while the Roman is all space, the enclosure of high air by weightless canopies. When Greek columns were applied to walls so formed and under such cross vaults, as they were in Roman baths and in New York's great Pennsylvania Station (fig. 194), which was modeled upon them,

195. Tivoli, Italy. Hadrian's Villa. Air view.

their visual effect was that of holding the upward swell of vaults down, not of supporting them. The generosity of Roman public space in comparison with the squalor that has overtaken our own during the later twentieth century was underscored by the destruction of Pennsylvania Station's high vaults in favor of low tunnels, like the burrows of rats through which we proletarians now sniff our way while the homeless, refuse of our barbarous tribe, lie huddled against the walls.

There is no doubt that Roman architecture has been severely misunderstood and underestimated during the modern period, in part because the Roman Empire has always had a bad popular press. Even the Beaux-Arts architects who, as in Pennsylvania Station, so effectively adapted Roman architecture for contemporary uses, generally wrote about it in an apologetic way, as if it had been concerned only with engineering problems. Frank Brown in particular showed that this view was far from the truth, and a whole generation of modern architects followed him to Hadrian's Villa in the early 1950s. (Le Corbusier, so he tells us, had already visited there in 1910.)

194. New York, N.Y. Pennsylvania Station. McKim, Mead and White. Interior during demolition, 1965.

196. Tivoli. Hadrian's Villa. Maritime theater.

197. Tivoli. Hadrian's Villa. Canopus.

The Villa is pure poetry (fig. 195); it is the place where the Roman instinct for enclosure most intersects nature. There the Emperor Hadrian went to "plant his pumpkins," as Trajan apparently called his intersecting compound vaults. There, as ruler of the world, Hadrian meditated on all its religions, especially those that were involved with the worship of the earth. Spread across the surface of the flat land below the sanctuary of Hercules Victor on the slope of the Apennines at Tivoli, the Villa sent its Roman axes out into space at eccentric angles, as if feeling out and exploring the avenues of movement suggested by the ground. In the center, around which all the axes wheeled, a perfect circle was placed, an island set behind a moat within an enclosing wall (fig. 196). Here, the individual, the emperor, could meditate in peace, surrounded by a melody of columns fanning out from his central presence in the secret place. Libraries rose around it. Outside, a long wall with a colonnade along both sides led the emperor to walk out along the axis of movement that led toward Rome, until at last, in Brown's telling phrase, "he could just barely not see the city."

It is the ultimate suburban refuge. Its baths were labyrinths, later beloved by the architects of Baroque Rome; their vaults were canopies lifted by the wind. Led most conspicuously across the site were the waters of the Serapeion, supposedly based upon the Temple of Serapis in the Delta of the Nile, but in reality a profoundly original meditation upon the ancient theme that has cropped up so often in these studies: of water drawn out of the earth by mankind. Here, it runs through a cavern that opens like a band shell to let it issue forth in a long basin, flanked by capricious colonnades and copies of the

caryatids of the Erechtheum (fig. 197). This sheet of water, reflecting the sky, leads the eye beyond all the domes and columned enclosures of the Villa's Roman order to focus at last on the Italian hills, round and mounded, suggestive of Etruscan tombs (fig. 198).

Hadrian was, in fact, an Etruscologist. He learned the language, and his greatest building, the Pantheon in Rome (fig. 199), is in one sense a domed Etruscan tomb raised to majestic scale and looming over the city as a whole. But it is Greek as well. Hadrian had it set so that the dome cannot be seen from the columned precinct before it, in front of the entrance door. There, everything is Greek. A Greek temple front

198. Cerveteri, Italy. Etruscan tombs. View from top of Tumulus II to west.

199. Rome, Italy. Pantheon. A.D. 118–125.

rises before us with one of the greatest of Latin inscriptions marching across its frieze and telling us, laconically, that Agrippa had made it. Agrippa, Augustus' son-in-law, had dedicated a small temple on the site, and Hadrian piously invoked the Augustan age in assigning the great new temple to him. We pass under the lofty Corinthian columns, lifting the high and mighty pediment at Roman scale, another signboard far above our heads. Up to this point there is no inkling of a dome. It is only when the vast bronze doors are opened that the new world of Roman space opens before us (fig. 200). The tomb has become the whole known world—indeed, the empire of Rome. This is the most telling of all the Imperial Roman images of the world as they controlled it: a central open space like the Mediterranean, enclosed by a thick wall like the provinces of Rome around the sea, and with the Mediterranean sun in the center, lighting up all the planets in turn as it picks them out in the niches around the walls during its passage through the day. The empire has become a cosmic order.

Of all that world, shaped by human will, the human figure occupies the center. We are reminded of the famous passage in Vitruvius, reminiscent in all likelihood of Pythagorean or even Platonic ideas, which states in effect that the human body is favored by being so proportioned that it can fit into the perfect shapes of square and circle, which are by implication those that reveal the basic order of the universe. The image this passage suggests resulted in numerous depictions of it during the Middle Ages and the Renaissance, of which the best known is Leonardo's (fig. 201). In the Pantheon, the circle, indeed the sphere, is present, the square only by projection. But it is the ideal world, ca-

200. Rome. *Interior of Pantheon.* Painting by Giovanni Pannini.

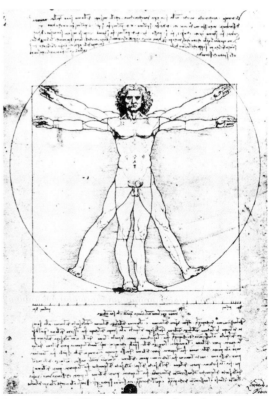

201. Leonardo da Vinci, *Man of Perfect Proportions,* pen and ink. Circa 1510.

pable of configuration only inside, whence the accidents of nature, and indeed of all matter, can be banished in favor of pure idea. It is true that the hollow volume of the Pantheon is defined by broadly solid Classical shapes, strong columns and entablatures, deep, heavy coffering and all, everything picked out clearly by the shaft of sunlight penetrating from above. When we step into that shaft, however, all matter disappears. We are blinded: Everything beyond the glow is dark. We are in the darkness of cosmic space. Planetarium in more than the simple representations of the planets, and far transcending in the end any image of terrestrial empire, the Pantheon releases mankind at last to the void, the universe, eternity.

That was what the Romans wanted, no less than that, a creation more perfect than the world we normally can know. So they became Christian and shaped domed spaces so mysterious that, though enclosed, we cannot know the edges or the limits of it all. In San Vitale in Ravenna, our experience seems to transcend matter. We are hypnotized by a light no longer natural but, in the word of the Early Christian philosophers, "heavenly." A comparison with the Pantheon shows how this effect is brought about.

The Pantheon has only one plane of enclosure, although its thick boundary walls are in fact cut with cavernous niches, screened by columns. In San Vitale, the supporting piers are brought well inboard from the enclosing walls, which are made as thin as possible and cut with windows (fig. 202). The screens of columns curve back out toward the exterior walls so that, with the dazzle of light from the windows behind them, we cannot tell where the planes of enclosure actually are. No oculus illuminates the walls from above. Everything dilates around us, magical and de-

202. Ravenna, Italy. San Vitale. A.D. 526–547. Interior, looking toward sanctuary.

203. Ravenna. San Vitale. Exterior.

materialized. We are in heaven or some other transcendent sphere. Moreover, this magical interior is all that counts, so far as the building as a whole is concerned. The exterior is a simple brick shell to contain this space (fig. 203). The Greek portico is gone. The Greek columns, with their suggestion of sculptural presences, have disappeared. The building has lost all trace of sculptural body. The fabric itself is holy no longer. It is only a device to create an ideal environment. The conceptual journey away from the old gods that began directly after the building of the Parthenon is now complete. Antiquity is over.

But the Early Christian communities also wanted another kind of church. Especially in Rome and, apparently, Western Europe in general, they desired not a vertical, domed space but a long, horizontal one. The Roman basilica, condensed, one guesses, with the shape of fora such as Trajan's, were ready at hand to serve as models. The sense of an enclosing body is not absent in the apsidal head and the transept arms. The nave and aisles of basilicas like Old St. Peter's or Santa Maria Maggiore lead toward the head and are lighted from above by clerestory windows (fig. 204). The long axes of the old fora and basilicas alike are now clarified and enforced. The enclosing walls are as thin as they can be made. Again, it is only the space that counts, and there, as in a court of law, the sacrifice of the mass is celebrated with perfect clarity, rationally exposed to the focused view of the congregation as a whole, just as the statue of the emperor had been in his time.

So there were two kinds of spaces: one horizontal and rationalized, one vertical and mysterious; the former flat-roofed, the latter domed. They can be considered as two archetypes of human experience, irreconcilable opposites, so much so that human beings quite naturally wanted them both, and they condensed them in Hagia Sophia, at Constantinople, the new center of the world. Constantinople was indeed almost the exact geographical center of the Late, Christian, Roman Empire, and its capital. There Justinian built Hagia Sophia so that it rose into the sky like some strange extraterrestrial vessel, floating above the Bosphorus, a Roman heaven on earth, carried out with a completeness and at a scale unattained before (fig. 205a).

The long axis of Hagia Sophia is that of a basilica, with the main altar backed into the apse at the far end (fig. 205). But between entrance and altar something un-

imaginable intervenes. The vertical dimension lifts out of sight. Four great piers, set on a square plan but carefully hidden by colonnaded screens of wall, support four vast Roman round-headed arches, so suggesting another square at their apexes high in the space above. Between them, however, curved sections of vault, called pendentives, are built, transforming the square on the ground into the circle in the sky. All of this was made possible and sustained over the centuries by elaborate buttressing outside, none of it visible from within, which was thus allowed to come across as irrational, magical.

Upon the circle, the dome is set, but the solidity of its bedding is made mysterious to us by the insertions of a ring of windows at the critical level. The dome floats, "suspended on a golden chain from heaven," the Russian ambassadors of the Middle Ages were to affirm. That was hundreds of years later, but they returned home to make Russia Byzantine, probably forever. Mosaics complete the illusion. The solid Classical details of the Pantheon have disappeared. The capitals of the columns, like the walls, dissolve in shimmers of surface light. No support is visible anywhere. It is all irrational, immaterial. Every surface is a dazzle. It is heaven, all of it apparently moving in orbits beyond those normally grasp-

204. Rome, Italy. Santa Maria Maggiore. Interior. Reconstruction.

205. Constantinople. Hagia Sophia. A.D. 532–537. Interior.

able by our sensory equipment, lifting us into its transcendent sphere. It is the Platonic perfection of circle and square, convincing us that it is more essential, more true, than the appearances of the natural world can possibly be, and all dedicated to Sophia, Goddess of Wisdom, who is, after all, the Athena of the Parthenon as well.

It is, of course, necessary to point out the epochal differences between the two buildings: Parthenon all body in nature (fig. 128), Hagia Sophia all shell containing a dream. But how alike they also are, especially as each is a unique condensation of opposites: the Parthenon of the Doric and Ionic modes, Hagia Sophia of the basilica and the dome. It is no wonder that they remain uniquely powerful in terms of human experience, glowing as they do at the very edge of our capacity to perceive them.

Still, it was Hagia Sophia that set the course of European architecture for a thousand years, one that in a sense dominates it to the present time. To control nature, or to keep it out, was to become Europe's obsession far beyond Christianity, so that in the middle of the twentieth century, the leaders of East and West could for a time speak of the conquest of nature in much the same way. Hence, the preoccupation with interior space that has dominated European architecture and has largely superseded, in symbolic terms, its relationship to nature, should be regarded in larger historical perspective as not necessarily the only normal way of things. It was a Roman construction, and it was to be explored to the very edge of experience during the Western Middle Ages, shaping a very special, and very strange, relationship between humanity and the natural world.

6

THE GOTHIC CATHEDRAL: STRUCTURE

I N WESTERN EUROPE, at first, the transcendence of nature of the kind created at Hagia Sophia (fig. 205a) was not imagined, or at least not realized. Romanesque architecture, as for example at St. Etienne de Nevers (fig. 206), indeed came to embody a concern for solid matter, which also has normally characterized Western European architecture in one way or another. The fabric of the Romanesque building itself, with its great elephant-footed compound piers, solid, massive walls, and small windows, was still eminently sculptural, as Hagia Sophia had refused to be, but it also defined a wholly environing enclosure, and the walls often were painted in ways that

228. Laon, France. Cathedral. Begun late 1150s. Nave wall.

seem calculated to deny their mass. Moreover, the culmination of any Romanesque building was finally to be a Gothic choir, as it is at Vézelay (fig. 207). This was so because what the Romanesque came to want, eventually, was that very blaze of light that would dematerialize all the masses of the building, illusionistically, magically, into an image of heaven on earth.

237a. Chartres, France. Cathedral. Nave wall. Begun 1194.

Out of that impulse, Gothic architecture came into being. We are sometimes misled—surely, we are all seduced—by the wonderfully solid Romanesque forms. Nonetheless, their architects were all struggling to bring light into them. Here, Otto von Simson has touched on the basic point, which is that the choir is the image or symbol of heaven, and the crossing is its facade, its gate.* Hence, the effect of Gothic light is to transcend the statics of the building masses, the realities of this world. Therefore, the fundamental reason for being of Gothic architecture, as of any architecture, is not technical, or structural, or even functional in a restricted physical sense. It is symbolic; its builders want it to mean something.

All works of art have to do with meaning. We can never, in fact, experience form without deriving meaning from it. All forms have their physical and associational meanings built into them, and all

*Otto von Simson, *The Gothic Cathedral: Origins of Gothic Architecture and the Medieval Concept of Order,* New York, 1956.

those meanings, but especially those involved with association, will change as cultures change. As our cultural codes are modified, we literally "see" differently, since our associational faculties also affect our physical ones. It therefore follows that we cannot describe works of art in ways that are, in the misleading terminology of a few generations ago, purely "objective." All experience of art, all writing about art, is deeply involved with the viewer's cultural stance and with his or her own capacity to conceptualize the physical and associational experience that he or she personally has of works of art.

Having said that, though, I would still like to try to do something in these two chapters which is on the face of it equally fallacious. I would like to write primarily about the structure of Gothic cathedrals in this chapter and about the symbolic experience of them in the next. Of course, this chapter, too, has to do with experience, since the structural instinct in mankind is itself engrossingly physical and symbolic all at once. Ideally, everything should be discussed together in one complex unity, as it is in the end experienced, but there are some good reasons for taking this approach.

To begin with, it is perfectly reasonable to discuss Gothic architecture at some length from a technical point of view. In one way, everything that happened from St. Denis in the 1130s on through the middle of the thirteenth century had to do with an excited, highly technical conversation between architects. It is true that their clients, their critics, their workmen all participated in that wonderful hubbub: so French, the first in that incomparable tradition of French "movements" through which the close analysis of art in an obsessively technical way came to change society itself, even for those who did not

206. Nevers, France. St. Etienne. 1063–1097. Interior, choir.

participate in it. The history of Impressionism comes to mind: The experience of the urban and suburban world changed with it. Without any question, something of the sort was happening even more intensely during the twelfth and thirteenth centuries.

The conversation clearly had a good deal to do with how the new churches were going to be constructed in order to let in as much light as possible. Some of the issues that arose can be seen in the four-story elevation of the interior of the Cathedral of Laon, which was begun in the late 1150s (fig. 228). The wall is actually very thick in section but is handled visually in such a way that it seems to dematerialize and to dissolve into moving colonnettes, gathered together in skeletal bunches. Right away, we are beyond simple structure to a complex illusionism that is intended to create the impression that the wall is magically dissolving in light. Or, at Chartres (fig. 237), we see a three-story elevation in which the tribune, which is the vaulted vessel at the second level, is eliminated, and only the triforium passageway in the thickness of the wall now remains between the nave arcades and the clerestory windows. The wall is now being supported in part by the flying buttresses of the exterior, which, like the massive buttresses of Hagia Sophia, are not visible from the inside. It, too, is a world of illusion, shaped by and for the heavenly light of the enormous stained-glass windows.

These effects were all made possible by complex structural manipulations, and it was almost exclusively in terms of that structure that Gothic architecture was studied by many generations of French critics. The method was initiated by the greatest of them all, Viollet-le-Duc, who projected his own nineteenth-century materialist, structural positivism upon Gothic architecture itself. His incomparable *Dictionnaire raisonné de l'architecture française* traces the growth of Gothic forms out of what he sees as structural demands and possibilities.* But there is more than that in the *Dictionnaire,* most of all a wonderful structural imagination, through

which Viollet-le-Duc thinks himself, feels himself empathetically, into the forces that are moving through the building. He imputes such feelings to Gothic architects, in all likelihood not incorrectly.

The article that first triggered my own enthusiasm for this topic, and perhaps for this admittedly limited method, is in that empathetic tradition. It is by Jean Bony, who is, I think, the finest critic and historian of Gothic architecture now living, and is entitled, "La Technique normande du mur épais à l'époque romane."* It seemed to me at the time that this concept could be applied to Gothic architecture, and it was the first work I did as a graduate student under the late Professor Sumner Crosby, the excavator of St. Denis. Since then, it has been explored as a Gothic phenomenon by the late Robert Branner and others.†

On the other hand, even if we are determined to concentrate on the structure of the wall, we find that we cannot really begin our study of Gothic architecture with it. Even to get at the structure, we have to begin with the human intention, the program out of which Gothic architecture was born. That program was first conceived and embodied by Abbot Suger at St. Denis. In 1134, Suger began to add a big new narthex, only a bay and a half deep, to his old Carolingian Abbey of St. Denis, where the kings of France were buried (figs. 208, 209). The high, comparatively shallow narthex was like a great banner, an enormous signboard hung in front of the old church, and Suger clearly believed that this was the most important

---

*Eugène Emmanuel Viollet-le-Duc, *Dictionnaire raisonné de l'architecture française du XIᵉ au XVIᵉ Siècle,* Paris, 1873–1875.

*Jean Bony, "La Technique normande du mur épais à l'époque romane," *Bulletin monumental,* 98, 1939, 153–188.

†Robert Branner, *Gothic Architecture,* New York, 1961. A fine general account: Whitney Stoddard, *Art and Architecture in Medieval France,* Wesleyan, 1966.

207. Vézelay, France. La Madeleine. 1120–1136. Interior, nave and choir.

208. St. Denis, France. Abbey Church. Abbot Suger. West facade. 1137–1140.

209. St. Denis. Abbey Church. Model with Suger's westwork.

210. France. Circa A.D. 1100. Map.

the level of the roadway has risen since that time. During the nineteenth century, too, one tower collapsed following a disastrous attempt at reconstruction with stone that was too heavy.

We ask ourselves, in any event, what Suger was trying to do. The first fact of importance is that Suger was in many ways the first man of consequence in the kingdom after the king himself, whose close personal friend he was. Later, he was regent of France while the king was on crusade. As Abbot of St. Denis, he was the custodian of the tombs of the kings of France, who controlled at that time only a comparatively small area around Paris (fig. 210). Over their heads, just a short way down the Seine, loomed the great kingdom of England and Normandy and, northward, with its boundary hardly beyond Picardy, the Holy Roman Empire flooded across the Rhine. Paris was very

addition to make, the place to start. He did not begin at the choir. His first instinct was to build a new facade. It was crowned by two towers, but, most important of all, it set the first rose window high in its central bay. The proportions were somewhat more vertical than at present because

211. Caen, France. St. Etienne. Begun circa 1065. West facade.

much on the frontier of a tiny kingdom, around which, especially to the south, powerful feudal areas owed only nominal allegiance to the king.

Hostile Normandy was hardly more than just outside the walls of Paris, and the first image Suger's facade suggests is that of Norman architecture. It is clear that Suger had looked in Normandy at the great facade of St. Etienne at Caen (fig. 211), which was finished shortly after the conquest of England. It has a military stance: masculine, proud, and upstanding, with high, pointed spires that gesture boldly to the heavens. It is organized in three bays with three entrances, the larger one in the center. The windows are quite small.

Suger adopted its *parti* but then opened the whole thing up, first by expanding the size of the entrances, which now for the first time can be called Royal Portals. He made them fill the spaces between the buttresses, while windows of comparatively large size rise above them. The harmony of half circles that is set up by doorways and windows alike culminates in the circle of the rose. Here, in the first Gothic facade, the first rose window appeared. It opens at the highest level, a pure circle, set in a square bay and filled with stained glass.

The new facade now reminds us not only of St. Etienne but also of the major image of imperial majesty that the Western world knew at the time: the Arch of Constantine in Rome (fig. 212). Suger had been to Rome, and his Royal Portals open the space between the piers in a way that recalls that arch. Up above, the Hadrianic tondi that are built into the facade of the arch are circular, and they may well have suggested the circle of the rose to Suger. It is interesting, though, that the tondi are archetypally antique in the sense that they are solid sculptural reliefs, while the rose is supremely medieval in the sense that it is transcendent, dematerializing into light.

On the other hand, it is likely that Suger also had still another source in mind, iconographically an even more crit-

212. Rome, Italy. Arch of Constantine. A.D. 312–315.

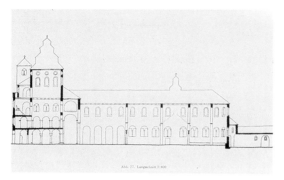

213. Corvey, Germany. Abbey Church. Section.

214. Laach, Germany. Abbey Church of Maria Laach. Circa 1156. West facade and narthex.

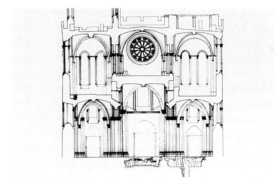

215. St. Denis. Abbey Church. Abbot Suger. Section of narthex looking west, showing chapel of the king.

ical one: the imposing basilicas of the Holy Roman Emperor along the Rhine. From the time of Charlemagne, many of the most important churches of the Rhineland had been built with two apses, one for God and the other for the emperor. The emperor's throne was placed in a raised gallery in the western apse, looking down the long axis of the nave toward the altar lower down on the east (fig. 213). The western apse, with its aggressive towers, was in effect the emperor's castle, and, as at Maria Laach (fig. 214), it sometimes had round windows in it. It may be felt that Suger took over the whole conception, so claiming the succession from Charlemagne for his own king. He transformed the scattered round windows into a single monumental rose, opening to the western light. Everything in the facade builds up to that transcendent wheel, to the circle of light spinning up above.

Suger's circular rose lighted the chapel of the king. That chapel was a simple square (fig. 215), not much larger than the rose itself, which thus opened its entire outer wall to the afternoon sun. Its inner wall was, in turn, open to the interior of the narthex, and its light filtered down into the nave below it. In the thirteenth century, the king's rose would have been in view from almost everywhere in the church, most especially from the altar,

where the priest, turning to bless the congregation, could have seen the king looming high above him in the western light (fig. 216).

To make all this structurally possible, at least in Suger's mind, to open up a whole wall and fill it with glass, the ribbed vault was employed. In section, we can see that the rib itself is springing from a point far down in the walls, well below the springing of the vault (fig. 217). It is embedded in the piers. It thus becomes clear that with the new technique of the ribbed vault, in which the rib was built first, an unprecedented flexibility in vault shape becomes possible. The rib could be started from almost any elevation on the supporting piers and might take an asymmetrical route across the bay. It could be

216. St. Denis. P.N. Guerin. *Philippe II le Hardi apporte à S. Denis les Antiques de St. Louis.* Oil on canvas in Sacristy. Circa 1808–1811. Before installation of organ masked Suger's rose window.

buried deep in the haunches of the supporting masonry on both sides, so giving an enormous sense of security to the builders. Suger's writings* communicate his own feeling of excitement about the rib's nearly miraculous powers, and he used it to further his major aim: to let in the light. Each bay, defined by the crossing of the ribs, with the deep web built up between them to accommodate the windows, becomes a marvelously light-filled architectural unit. We feel that its function is to model light and to direct it with the profile of the rib itself. The whole is a trap for light. That is the essential way in which

*Abbot Suger on the Abbey-Church of St.-Denis and its Art Treasures, ed., trans., and annotated by Erwin Panofsky, Princeton, 1946; second edition by Gerda Panofsky-Soergel, 1979.

Suger's use of the ribbed vault differs from the way it had been used before. At Morienval, for example, only its flexibility had been exploited. Every bay in the choir there has a different and irregular shape, of which the vaulting is made possible by the rib. Suger exhibited its flexibility, too, but fixed on its capacity to create regular, airy volumes of space.

Having finished his narthex, Suger went on to build a new choir and to make at least a beginning toward the rebuilding of the rest of the church (fig. 218). That, as we have noted, was to take place eventually, and on an even grander scale than Suger envisaged. His choir, however, was as revolutionary as his narthex. One of the major glories of Romanesque architecture had been its radiating chapels, which projected as magnificent half-cylinders well outward from the ambulatory of the choir. The windows in their splendidly solid walls are very small, which means that little light penetrates from them, through the ambulatory, to the altar in the center of the choir. What Suger did was to increase the size of the windows and to bring the radiating chapels in, indeed to diminish their projection to almost nothing. They begin to merge with the ambulatory, and the rib is now used to increase that effect of flowing unity. It draws the volumes of the chapels into the volume of the ambulatory and produces a dynamic canopy, springing from the tiniest columns Suger thought he could get away with, between whose slender shafts the ambulatory opens onto the choir in the center. The light thus penetrates almost without interruption from the chapels to the high altar, and the whole becomes that crown of light at the head

217. St. Denis. Abbey Church. Abbot Suger. West facade, rose window.

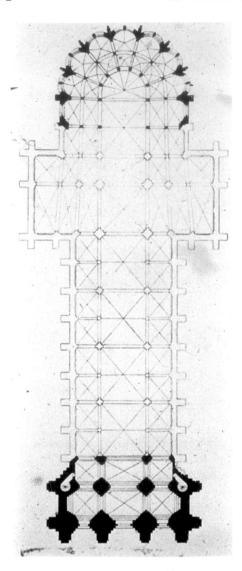

218. St. Denis. Abbey Church. Abbot Suger. Plan. Reconstruction. 1137–1144.

220. St. Denis. Abbey Church. Abbot Suger. Plan of choir.

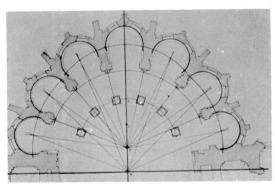

219. St. Denis. Abbey Church. Abbot Suger. Plan of crypt.

of the church that Suger desired, the crown of "heavenly windows."

Another of St. Denis' important characteristics is that the choir is higher than the nave. It is a half level up; the crypt, a half level down. Burials of different periods took place in both crypt and nave, but the crypt was increasingly reserved, as time went on, as a sanctuary for the saint's relics that were gathered there. The choir rose above everything but was of course supported by the crypt. Suger's plan for crypt and choir alike is an affair of intersecting circles, about which more must be said in the next chapter (figs. 219, 220). Down below, in the crypt, the piers are massive in section and separate the spatial circles, while up above, in the choir, the whole dematerializes, the columns becoming very thin, as we have seen, and the windows much larger. Differentiation between the circles breaks down. They intersect each other in light. The mass of the exterior wall seems to be pushed out and aside by the ribs. Hence, we go from dominant mass in the crypt to dominant space—and light—in the choir. At the same time, the thin columns of the ambulatory are brought in slightly toward the center of the church in relation to the massive cylinders below (fig. 221). It is as if Suger was trying to set up a diagonal

221. St. Denis. Abbey Church. Abbot Suger. Ambulatory and crypt.

222. St. Denis. Abbey Church. Abbot Suger. Ambulatory vaults.

angle of support for diagonal thrusts imagined as coming from the vaults high above. Part of that thrust is certainly passing through, and the whole mass of the walls is being carried by, a column so thin as to seem almost supranatural itself.

Suger's column was even thinner than the one we see today (fig. 221), which was encased in cast stone in the nineteenth century. Despite their experience with cast iron, the architects of the nineteenth century, a materialist-realist age, simply could not believe in this column. It is an example of Suger's complete success. He had clearly wanted a column as miraculous as his rib, and he caused a dancing play of almost pure line to burst out above it in the ribs it supported (fig. 222). We are brought into an architecture in which mass is totally dissolved in favor of cylinders and tubes that seem so taut and tense that we can imagine them ringing as an iron column will ring when we strike it. The whole system seems to push the piers of the outer wall outward, so splitting the

223. Sens, France. Six-part vaults with *colonnette-en-délit*. 1140s and later.

walls between them to allow the light of the windows to appear. And when we go outside to see what has happened, we find that the grand geometric solids of the radiating chapels of Romanesque architecture have disappeared and Suger's wall is, indeed, made to look thin and torn apart (fig. 246). The windows push their way through it, and where he could not have windows because of the profile of the vault above, Suger split the wall again with the molding that recalls the rib inside and makes us feel the whole thin membrane as stretching in space for light. The great clerestory windows above are of the thirteenth-century rebuilding. It is obvious that they culminate a development that Suger initiated down below.

The effects that Suger wanted were thus immediately achieved. That is ap-parent if we compare the view down the nave of St. Etienne at Nevers with that of Vézelay (figs. 206, 207). In one, we are looking into darkness; in the other, to light. The compound piers of the nave of Vézelay contrast with the crown of light at the head of the church, and we have seen how Suger totally abandoned them in his ambulatory. Because of the later rebuilding, we do not know how Suger built the upper works of his choir. A reconstruction by Crosby suggests a six-part vault, in which each discrete vault unit spans two bays but is split and stiffened by a central rib between the bays, so breaking up the web of the vault into six parts. We can see such a vault at Sens, begun after St. Denis (fig. 223). Its web was heightened at a later date in order to make room for larger clerestory windows, but the fundamental principles of the six-part vault were at work there from the beginning, as they had been in other churches, such as St. Etienne at Caen, even earlier. Therefore, the vaulting of a nave in six-part vaults predates Suger. In general, it tends to involve an alternation in the piers of the arcade, since at every other pier five colonnettes are being gathered together, at every alternate pier only three. Hence, big piers, perhaps rather Romanesque in character, may alternate with smaller supports.

There is some indication that, at first, such alternation was regarded as desirable both structurally and visually, suggesting a stable, traditional structure under the new ribbed vault and larger windows. There is certainly evidence of timidity about the vault itself. A simple four-part span and a big bay seem to have been worrying; two smaller bays spanned as one with a central stiffener was, in any event, the almost universal choice.

With that system, the character of the smaller responds becomes of considerable importance. At Sens, they are *colonnettes-en-délit,* among the first of a line that was to have a spectacular, if quite short, architectural history. The bearing wall itself is, of course, made of blocks of Ile-de-France limestone, which was laid up as it was cut from its bed in the quarry, the grain running horizontally and with mortar between the blocks. For those two reasons, the builders felt that it might be possible for the wall to compact under compression, to settle. And as they began to put those big vaults up, with the semi-miraculous ribs that they felt were somehow concentrating the weight and directing the thrust, they began to fear that the wall might indeed settle and let the whole thing down. So, at first, where they had an intermediate support, and later everywhere, they employed the *colonnette-en-délit,* which looks to our eyes like a slender tube of iron. In fact, it was cut horizontally from the bed of the quarry as a cylinder but then turned vertically against its grain, against the bed; that is, "*en délit.*" Therefore, in the twelfth-century view, it could not compress. Moreover, it was cut in short sections that were set dry, without mortar, and joined with masonry rings, called annulets. Again: no settling, at least in theory.

It is a fact that the system will not compress under weight, although it can break, and such colonnettes may well crack and buckle and come away from the wall, as they seem to have done in parts of Noyon, Meaux, and Reims. That fact, however, involves another rather wonderful property, which is that if too much compression is put on a *colonnette-en-délit,* it will normally exfoliate, like the wall of a quarry when it weathers; and the French word for exfoliate is *déliter.* What

224. Noyon, France. Nôtre Dame. Choir, circa 1150–1185.

a magnificently expressive term it is, one of an unparalleled semantic density resembling that of its own material character: the *colonnette-en-délit,* hero of the mid-century, which signals its own distress *en délitant.*

Beyond all else, the *colonnette-en-délit* is a visual element. We see it beginning to approach its optical best in the choir of Noyon, which was begun in the 1140s (fig. 224). It has a four-story elevation with arcades, the vaulted vessel of the tribune, a triforium, and finally the clerestory windows. There is no true passageway in the thickness of the wall at triforium level but simply a blind colonnade applied to the wall. The wall itself, however, is very thick in section at that point; perhaps a true triforium was orig inally intended. An earlier, more structurally positivistic generation might have concluded that structural timidity caused the idea to be abandoned. We cannot be sure of that, but it is obvious that, whether they had a triforium passage or not, the builders liked having the triforium colonnade break up the wall between the bundles of *colonnettes-en-délit* that are supporting, or which the builders hoped would support, the ribs of the vaults above. Here, they do look, in fact, like sheaves of nineteenth-century cylindrical iron columns, and we can see how all the ribs are being brought down upon them, an effect that was obviously desired visually as well as conceptually. Nor are the colonnettes, theoretically incompressible, bound into the wall behind them, which might compress. They shape a separate structural and visual system, so that there are two systems in operation. One is the very thick section of the wall itself; the other is the cylindrical "iron" skeleton of the *colonnettes-en-délit* running up the wall's interior face.

Another important thing to be noted in the elevation of Noyon's choir is that the springing of the vaults, as at Sens, is at the very bottom of the clerestory windows. Again, the builders were exploiting the flexibility of the rib to start the vault as low down as they could on the face of the wall so that its pressures could be brought more rapidly down to the vertical. To that end, they also loaded the haunches of the vaults with masses of masonry which were intended to weigh down on the thick wall below them and so help bring the pressures vertically down toward the ground. It was already traditional to spring the ribs from that point. The first time we find it in a nave or choir is early in the century at St. Etienne at Caen, of which we have already noted the importance of the facade. Here, too, Normandy figured as a model and a spur. At St. Etienne, the six-part ribbed vaults were added to a nave that was originally spanned, in the earlier Norman manner, only by a wooden truss and ceiling. When

the vaults were added, they were made to spring from well down the wall alongside the clerestory windows, whereas the truss had rested, of course, on the top of the wall.

The passageway in the thickness of the wall is also significant at Caen. It, too, is Norman. At St. Etienne there are arcades, a tribune, and clerestory windows that are joined by a passageway in the thickness of the wall. The desire for such a passageway may indeed have motivated the building of an unusually thick wall, and we can see that the wall is indeed enormously massive in section, a fact that must eventually have encouraged the builders to "insert" the vaults. Then, in England, the clerestory windows and the wall passageway came to separate, so forming, as at Tewkesbury, a four-story elevation, consisting of arcades, tribune, triforium passageway—opened out to the nave through an arcade—and clerestory windows.[*] That is exactly the elevation of the choir of Noyon (fig. 224), except that here the triforium is reduced to the visual device of the blind colonnade; but, as is visible in the piers at tribune level, the thick wall is there, passageway or no.

The importance of the thick wall at Noyon can be seen in section (fig. 225). It apparently acts with the loading of the haunches of the vaults to stabilize their diagonal thrust. Down below, the columns of the arcade are as close to Suger's slender cylinders as the builders apparently felt they could go. They are as thin as possible, and in the hemicycle of the choir, they are all single columns; there are no piers. They, too, are monoliths, supporting enormous weights, and some of them, in fact, were replaced in the six-

*Jean Bony, "Tewkesbury et Pershore. Deux élévations à quatre étages de la fin du XIᵉ siècle," *Bulletin monumental,* 96, 1931: 281–290.

225. Noyon. Nôtre Dame. Section of choir.

teenth century. Above them, at tribune level, the wall is very thick; it deeply overhangs the columns supporting it. The great mass, so offset, must have been empathetically felt by the builders—since there is no positive way, even today, to calculate in any sure formula just what is going on—to be pushing down upon the wall below it, even as the loaded haunches of the vault above are pushing down on it. It is as if the whole wall was being made dynamic in order to support the vaults, indeed to dramatize compression and settling, while the separate, taut skeleton of the *colonnettes-en-délit* was regarded as working in its own very different way to do the same thing. It is unlikely that any nineteenth-century rationalist ever would have arrived at the combination of two such wildly divergent, even contradictory, systems. But how intricately wonderful they are, and how they seem to let us see into their builders' minds.

The nave at Noyon (fig. 226), built later than the choir, has a true four-story elevation, with a triorium passageway behind a colonnade at the third level. The arcades show a pronounced alternation of heavy, almost Romanesque piers and single columns. Noyon is, however, a very unusual church, especially in the transepts (fig. 227). They are rounded, like some of those along the Rhine. Moreover, their interior elevations are dematerialized into a skeleton web of passageways and colonnades that are at least made to look like *colonnettes-en-délit*. They, much more than the choir itself, create the crown of light, here before the altar, which is the glory of the church. But their method remains an eccentric one except in its objective, which is to dissolve the wall into bundles of colonnettes.

That is exactly what the architect of Laon achieved. Noyon was clearly very important to him, and it is interesting that when my late colleague Charles Seymour, Jr., set out to write his doctoral dissertation for Henri Focillon, it was to Laon that he turned, only to discover that the topic had already been claimed by Hanna Adenauer, whose father was to become chancellor of West Germany. Seymour then turned to Noyon, about which he wrote a monograph that is still a model of excellence.* He realized, however, that the first sequence of Gothic experiments really culminated at Laon.

The nave of Noyon still employs Romanesque piers; Laon wholly eliminates them (fig. 228). It retains the six-part vault, but the alternation has been almost entirely abandoned at arcade level. Above the capitals of the round columns, the *colonnette-en-délit* completely takes over. There is a clear break at that point. The

*Charles Seymour, Jr., *Notre-Dame of Noyon in the Twelfth Century. A Study in the Early Development of Gothic Architecture*, New Haven, 1939; *see also* H. Adenauer, *Die Kathedrale von Laon*, Düsseldorf, 1934.

226. Noyon. Nôtre Dame. Nave.

227. Noyon. Cathedral. South transept.

228. Laon, France. Cathedral. Begun late 1150s. Nave wall.

capitals visually support the colonnettes. But around the shafts of those columns that are the closest to the crossing, above which are extremely high towers, the colonnettes continue down to the pavement wherever five of them occur. Above the alternate piers, the three colonnettes stop at the capital. As we move westward along the nave, the whole bundle of five colonnettes is also made to rest on the capitals of the nave columns. Now the architect was insisting that he would have only pure columns, like Suger's, with no residual memory whatever of the Romanesque compound pier, not even a thicket of colonnettes.

All this exaggerates the thick wall section (fig. 229). The wall at tribune level is very deep, the columns below all comparatively slender. The tribune is assisting the wall in bringing the thrust of the central main vaults down within the section of the side aisles. There is also a triforium passageway. It is apparent that no flying buttresses were needed in this system, and none were imagined. Much later, some were added for purely visual effect. The thick wall and its associated *colonnettes-en-délit* (none of which, at Laon, have ever buckled or broken) create their own internal security, so long, it would seem, as they can be assisted by the vaults of the tribune, thus requiring a four-story elevation.

One does not like to call the nave of Laon a "solution," as if art were made up of problems rather than possibilities. Nevertheless, the system at Laon completely destroyed the old Romanesque wall system, of which St. Etienne at Nevers once again can be cited as an excellent example (fig. 230). It is a solid wall with few and sharply cut openings, all very clear, static, and stony. If one loves material and its expression in architecture beyond everything else (as the nineteenth century sometimes thought it did), one really cannot love this early Gothic architecture (fig. 228); it transcends material. The wall of Laon is not like stone: It is like pipes of iron.

Indeed, Laon resembles those nineteenth-century skeletal structures that were in fact built of iron. In that regard, its plan is interesting, as well (fig. 231). Its original conformation recalls that of Noyon, except that there were no radiating chapels in the choir, but it was rebuilt

in the thirteenth century as a simple shed. The choir was extended to a flat east end, almost like that of a Cistercian church, and there is a big rose in it as well. The interior became one large skeletal volume, suggesting that of the Crystal Palace of 1851. In nineteenth-century structures of that type, the influence of the *colonnette-en-délit,* with its annulets, is highly apparent. Whenever Viollet-le-Duc was able to do so, he used iron in similar shapes, evoking those of the *colonnette-en-délit.*

At Laon, we already tend to feel that if the twelfth-century builders had possessed iron at industrial scale, they would have used it. That particular sensibility for the thin, linear member had a special effect on English architecture. We can see how at Salisbury and elsewhere in England colonnettes of a different color are made to

229. Laon. Cathedral. Section.

230. Nevers, France. St. Etienne. Nave.

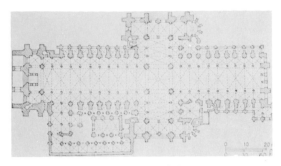

231. Laon. Cathedral. Plan as extended to east.

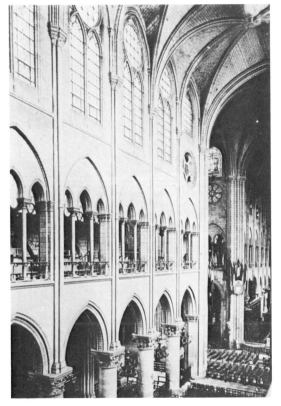

232. Paris. Nôtre Dame. Begun 1163. Nave, north side, circa 1178–1200.

stand at an exaggerated distance from the shaft of their columns: They are already celebrating that gift for building in thin, linear elements of metal that was so brilliantly developed in England during the nineteenth century. Even at Laon, when the colonnette is brought down into the arcade, it is kept clear of the column (fig. 228). It already stands free, as intransigent as an intrusive cylinder of iron.

We think, in our modern way, Well, this must be the "solution." This must be the new way, the logical way, in which these things had to be done in order to accomplish everything their architects seemed to want to do: to let in the light most of all. It might be tempting to think so, but instantly the architect of Nôtre Dame of Paris decided to show that it was not the only way. Under no circumstances would he employ those bundles of colonnettes, least of all those revolting *colonnettes-en-délit,* refusing categorically to gather bundles of tubes together to make a wall that looks so thick, hectic, and cluttered. So he made his colonnettes very thin, hardly cylindrical in profile, and he bonded them into the wall, which he treated as an unbroken plane, a very thin, stretched membrane (fig. 232). All is now one mural system, at least visually. To that end, only three colonnettes are brought down everywhere, even when there should be five, as we note when we look up at the vaults. The architect simply would not employ them all. But we can imagine him worrying about that. It is obviously a visual effect he wanted: a wall that looks utterly thin, taut, and integral. But he did not want it to fall down. So he applied all those colonnettes he refused to show in the main elevation to the thick intermediate piers of his double side aisles. He hoped that this would do the trick, but in any event he was determined to keep his nave wall flat, and, in fact, it is built in a "thin wall" technique. It does not thicken at tribune level as the walls of Noyon and Laon do. How then does it support the vaults? The architect was thinking about that problem, too; out of it the flying buttress came into being.

First comes the thinness of the wall, which means that there is no triforium passageway. What to do, then, with the wall at that level between tribune and clerestory? If we can believe the reconstruction by Viollet-le-Duc, the first decision at Paris was to use what amounted to small rose windows at that point. But this decision, if actually made, was fairly illogical in view of the fact that those windows opened only under the roofs over the tribune vaults; they gave no light. Perhaps they were wanted for other reasons, better explored in the following chapter. Whatever the case, the solution was not integral, as that of the thick-wall triforium passageway had been. It was in no sense a structural solution. Which, then, came next: a desire for larger clerestory windows to admit more light and to fill up the awkward area or a determination to stabilize the thin wall structurally? It would appear that the structural instinct carried the day, since the clerestory windows were not enlarged until the 1220s, long after the flying buttresses were added. They may even have been suggested by the big clerestory windows at Chartres, for example.

Perhaps we can try to think ourselves a bit into that structural decision by looking at the wall in section (fig. 233). Doing so, especially after having looked at thick-wall sections, we cannot help but sense a diagonal line of potential fracture running down through the tribune just above the arcade. The nave vault can almost be felt to push and the wall to crack through right there. The whole thing simply looks too high and thin. The architect must have felt something of the sort, because a glance at the section with the flying buttress added shows him leaping up to push the big vault back with the flying buttresses, trying to get as high as he possibly can to take the

233. Paris. Nôtre Dame. Section of nave.

intolerable strain off that point of fracture down below.

As a matter of fact, the section of Bourges, which represents one direct reaction to Paris (Chartres is the other), shows how the architect there used that upward leap to create two elevations: a higher one on the nave side and another one in the side aisle. Both rise into the level once occupied by the tribune, because, with the flying buttress, its vault was no longer necessary to help take up the thrust of the high vaults. So Bourges is like the section of Paris opened up vertically as well as laterally, and its plan, as well, is a lot like that of Paris. It, too, is moving toward the unity we saw in another way at Laon and which Gothic architecture in general had seemed to desire from the beginning.

In Paris, however, there is a transept, a crossing in plan and interior elevation and expressed in exterior massing, though it does not project in plan beyond the sides of the nave and the choir. Later, other chapels were built between the buttresses, thus widening the interior in effect. But what we can see about the plan and massing of Paris which should be stressed now is that it is like Laon in being a long shed: a thin, stretched body with a lot of glass. It really seems to be the culmination of Suger's original idea.

Like his St. Denis, as it stood when Paris was begun in the 1160s, the west facade of Paris is a high screen, with a massive pair of towers. Behind it, the church is lower, with an elongated, stretched mass (fig. 234). The flying buttresses further dematerialize its body. Indeed, they shred it. Many of the flying buttresses we see today have been reconstructed, but their form seems to be close to that of the originals: thin, taut, as minimal in section as one can get. The view of the apse especially, where the buttresses are very late, shows how new, how magical, the effect of the flying buttress could become. Now there is absolute thinness and tautness. All the massiveness of previous architecture is completely masked by the skeleton profiles the buttresses create.

234. Paris. Nôtre Dame. View from the south.

Again we, poor creatures, think, Well, yes, that is what Suger was after; all of it is as dematerialized as one could wish inside and out, and it is concealed behind the incomparable frontispiece of its facade with its perfect, mighty rose, the ultimate circle in the square. Perfect, but the architect of Chartres obviously did not think so (fig. 235). The body of his building is like that of a crouching animal, solid and organic in appearance; it is not a shed behind a screen of towers. Its towers are integral with the mass and somehow grow out of it. The facades of the transepts are widened to cover at least one bay of choir and nave alike, in order to diminish any sense of a stretched shell. The whole is a solid physical presence rather than the thin hollow that Paris is. Further, if we look at the flying buttresses of Chartres—and Chartres is the first major church where flying buttresses were planned from the beginning—we note that they are almost Romanesque in scale and section compared with the thin buttresses of Paris (fig. 232). They line up close together in what is in effect a solid wall engulfing the western towers and pulling them into the mass. Behind the outer buttresses, the "flying" arches spin heavily in toward the nave with great, almost Romanesque, round arches (fig. 236). They are monumental, archaic even. Everything is the reverse of Paris, and indeed of almost everything Gothic architecture seemed to have been moving toward since Suger's time. Chartres' forms are not thinner, or more skeletonized, or more dematerialized than earlier Gothic forms. They are thicker, heavier, and more massive.

Inside, too, the same effect holds. The thin membrane of wall is gone, and we are in the presence of massive piers that march down the nave and rise together as

235. Chartres, France. Cathedral. Circa 1140–1220. View from the south.

236. Chartres. Cathedral. Flying buttresses.

potent physical bodies toward the shadows of the vault (figs. 237a, b). The tribune is gone. The flying buttress has made it structurally unnecessary. Now the piers, massive as they are, rise up through its space. For the very first time in Gothic architecture, we are in the presence of a vertical lift that starts from the floor and, uninterrupted by pier capitals, rises to the springing of the vaults. Nothing, however heavy, appears to press down. The great bases rest ponderously on the pavement. Still, our eyes read everything up. Above the nave arcades, the triforium passageway destroys the wall between the bundles of massive colonnettes, and above it the clerestory windows open into a new and vast expanse. They and the arcade divide the elevation almost equally between them. We see the difference. In Paris, it really is wonderful how stretched the wall is. But everything at Chartres is rounded, massive, three-dimensional, sculptural, not planar, certainly not dematerialized in any sense at all. It is a miraculous blending of opposites, a point to which we must return.

Here, though, we should notice in that connection how sorely the architect at Bourges was torn in two ways. He wanted the great piers of Chartres, but he also wanted the stretched wall of Paris, and he used the same thin, linear molding above his triforium that the architect at Paris had used above his tribune. So he made his utterly unique church, which had no progeny in France. Its descendants were to be found in the south, in Spain, and in the New World. But the French instinct, as we shall see, tended to move not toward Bourges but toward Chartres. It is the first monumental manifestation of French classicism, which would like to bring the whole of things into one vast order encompassing everything.

The adoption of the four-part vault at Chartres is important in that regard. It is a simpler system. Everything becomes clear. There are the big piers with their colonnettes, the ribs, the vaults, and the windows; there remain only solids and colored glass (figs. 237a, b). Now the desire to bring light in is totally expressed by the vaults and piers; they become simply frames for the great windows, which are enormous. The ribs spring from halfway up their sides, as in Paris, but now each window is an opening for which the curtain of the vaults has been drawn grandly aside. The old alternation is gone. The architect has gotten rid of it, but, devil of strength and subtlety that he is, he makes each pier alternate inside its engaged columns. One has flat planes; the next is a cylinder. So there is a hidden alternation, a syncopation, within the columns' mighty tread. Moreover, with the alternation, the pier remains a column, a shaft surrounded by colonnettes, not an integral Romanesque compound mass. Yet the very breath of the Romanesque is there; it has returned, or arrived.

If we compare the whole with Laon (fig. 238), for example, we see how everything that had to do with metal, everything that looked modern in nineteenth-century terms, is gone at Chartres. We are back in a primitive sculptural world of great masses that are as physical as those of any Greek temple, and more so than some. The colonnettes have become sculpturally massive themselves and are bonded into the piers, which, in turn, are bonded into the wall system all the way to the windows, and, as we have noted, there is no clear interruption of capital level; the whole pier-wall system rises up as a continuous force. At the beginning of the thirteenth century, it seems to have been felt at once that this was the system

that did everything just right. First of all, it presented the glass in the simplest and clearest way yet devised: as the "heavenly light" that was the primary meaning of Gothic architecture as a whole. Yet, as I have already suggested, it also did something else, which might seem to be utterly contradictory but which must have answered some persistent need: It brought Romanesque architecture back. Or, since there had never been any Romanesque architecture to speak of in the Ile-de-France, we might say that it produced, paradoxically enough, the first great school of Romanesque architecture that the royal region had known.

237b. Chartres. Cathedral. Nave wall. Begun 1194.

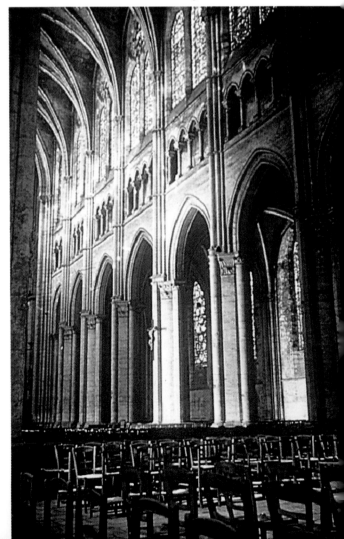

All this suggests, of course, the artificiality of our stylistic designations. We should not be imprisoned within them—as the architect of Chartres was not. He was a man who broke fashionable models. For example, if there was one thing that young architects from the 1140s onward must have agreed on as they carried on their night-long arguments, it must have been that everything had to be light—just what modern architects of the International Style all agreed on forty years ago—and that, most of all, Suger's slender columns were sacrosanct. They were the most modern element of all (like Le Cor-busier's *pilotis*), the very touchstone of being up-to-date. The architect of Chartres threw them out, at least visually, and went back to what looks like a Romanesque compound pier. His intellectual courage must have been enormous. It is true that his piers are *cantonnés,* columns surrounded by four oriented shafts, but they are in fact as visually sculptural as the truly compound piers of Vézelay (fig. 207). At Vézelay, too, there are simple four-part vaults, and the architect of Chartres brought those back as well, but with glass wholly filling their arches.

238. Laon, France. Cathedral. Wall detail from south aisle.

Moreover, at Chartres we find a plan that looks strikingly Romanesque (fig. 274), especially in the choir, where we discover that the radiating chapels, which architects had been in the process of eliminating ever since Suger's time, have come back with a vengeance. They project like Romanesque chapels. This occurred in part because Chartres is built over a very sacred crypt, that of *La Vierge sous Terre,* and some of the plan of that ancient crypt ordained the plan of the Gothic church above it. Chartres is therefore a condensation of a surprisingly diverse number of elements, including twelfth-century, "modern" art, and Romanesque, "old-fashioned" art. Moreover, as we can see in section, it is a condensation of thick-wall and thin-wall structural techniques. It has a triforium passageway in the thickness of the wall with an overhanging mass above the arcades, but the tribune is gone. The flying buttress, which grew out of the thin-wall technique, has made its elimination possible.

The "condensations" are especially interesting; it is possible that all the most memorable architectural monuments have always embodied something of the sort. We have described them in the Parthenon and Hagia Sophia and should recall Freud's critical use of the term.* It is perhaps not at all curious that Freud's categories are much like those of scholastic philosophy itself. Erwin Panofsky, in his *Gothic Architecture and Scholasticism,*† describes the first principle of scholasticism as *concordantia* (which is Freud's "condensation"), whereby opposites are reconciled to make a new unity, and he suggests that this is what is happening in Gothic

architecture. But it is happening, I think, in a deeper way than Panofsky describes. It is deeply structural, for example, especially as the thick-wall and thin-wall techniques are brought together.

Moreover, Freud also notes a principle of "displacement," in which elements are seen out of their normal context, therefore playing a part in a very new unity of meaning. Good enough: I think we can say that what happens at Chartres is, in fact, an enormous displacement, because, during the twelfth century, as at Laon, however slender and vertical the colonnettes were up above, they all weighed down on the capitals of the nave (fig. 238). The capitals *supported* them; it was still a kind of Classical (here I mean "Antique") system. The capitals are not far above our heads, and the weight was read as pressing

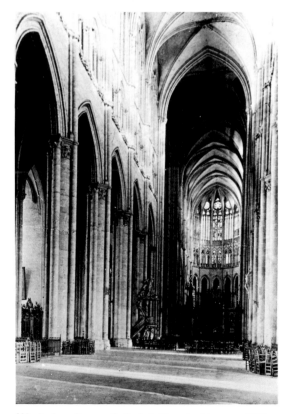

239. Amiens, France. Cathedral. Nave looking east. 1220–1233.

*Sigmund Freud, *The Interpretation of Dreams,* ed. and trans. James Strachey, New York, 1955.

†Erwin Panofsky, *Gothic Architecture and Scholasticism,* New York, 1976.

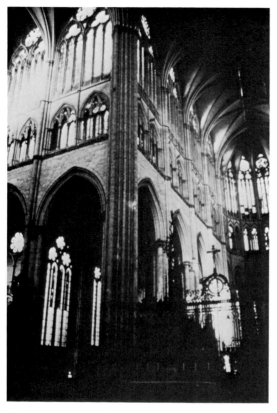

240. Amiens. Cathedral. Crossing.

241. Reims, France. Cathedral. Begun 1211. Nave, looking east.

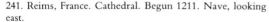

down upon them, as in Classical architecture. But at Chartres, as we have seen, the piers burst up through their capitals, so that we never read any part of the wall as pressing down; we read the piers as lifting up like trees. We feel the whole not as *built* but as growing, and while the Romantic view that Gothic architecture grew out of the trees of the forest is false in terms of development, it is true in terms of feeling when we come to the fully developed Gothic we begin to see at Chartres. We read it dynamically up, never compressively down. This is massive displacement, critically stretching and reorienting our empathetic faculty.

The solution (if I may employ that positivistic term once again) of Chartres is embraced at Amiens (fig. 239). There, however, the arcades are heightened enormously, so that they seem to leap up even more forcefully, and the clerestory and the triforium are much smaller in comparison. They are being lifted high up into the trees. Amiens was begun at the west and the building process moved toward the choir. When it reached the crossing, the outer wall of the triforium began to be glazed (fig. 240). This eliminated the last dark band in the Gothic wall. Now all is skeleton structure penetrated by light. Moreover, the colonnettes and mullions of the clerestory are brought down to incorporate the triforium into it, so forming one articulated panel. It is now Rayonnant architecture, in which Gothic architecture is, in a sense, complete. It is all trunks and branches and twigs against the light; the wall is completely dematerialized into "heavenly windows" everywhere.

At Amiens, as we have noted, this first occurs in the crossing and the choir. So one great diagonal line of sight is developed there, running up the high nave from the portals to the choir, and the eye is led out uninterruptedly to light and space as it could not have been before the triforium was glazed. Crossing and choir are now all one crown. On the exterior of the choir of Amiens, the whole mass dissolves into pure vertical buttresses with glass between them. Once again we say, Yes, this is the way it has to be done, the right and logical way.

But another architect had already chosen to do something entirely different. At Reims (fig. 241), which was begun a decade earlier than Amiens, though of course well after Chartres, the architect seems to have decided, for example, that he would not permit a continuity of visual movement from floor to vault and would also lower the apparent height of the nave. He also introduced an exaggeratedly strong horizontal element at capital level, so that

we feel the tall piers moving along horizontally like classical columns rather than leaping upward like the trees of a forest.

Reims differs from Amiens in many other complex ways. For example, Amiens was begun at the west and moved toward the east where, if we take a technologically deterministic position, we might say that it is more technologically advanced: hence the glazing of the triforium in the crossing and choir. Reims, however, progressed in the opposite direction; it started at the choir and was built toward the facade. The triforium of its choir is not glazed. It has its band of darkness. There is none of the release eastward that is found at Amiens. But if we stand in the choir of each church and look toward the west, we find that the effects are reversed. Indeed, Amiens makes no sense

242. Amiens. Cathedral. Nave looking west.

243. Reims. Cathedral. Nave looking west.

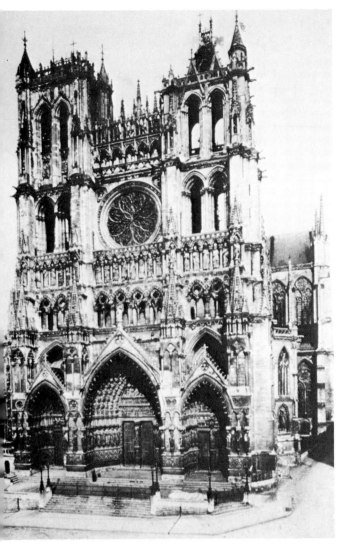

244. Amiens. Cathedral. West facade. Begun 1220.

245. Reims. Cathedral. West facade, begun 1230s. Also figs. 276, 278.

at all. The rose window looks very small and is pushed way out of contention, lost high up in the vault of the gigantic nave, while right down in front of us is the darkness of the masonry of the triforium and the tympani of the west wall (fig. 242). But at Reims, in the moderate height of the nave, the rose is enormous, filling a large part of the space (fig. 243). Below it, at triforium level, the wall is also glazed and, most of all, the tympani of the Royal Portals, until now always solid, are glass,

as well. The whole west wall is flooded with afternoon light. At St. Denis, Suger had brought that light into the chapel of the king, high above his old nave. Now, at Reims, it irradiates the entire church.

We ask whether Reims and Amiens simply became more progressive as their building programs developed. Can what happened be understood purely in terms of good old nineteenth-century technological determinism? Or were there different, much more complicated intentions at work? Surely, the builders of Reims actively wanted to do something that those of Amiens were not willing to do, and vice versa. That is, the builders of Amiens wanted height in every way, and they wanted the upward leap from the entrance that they had learned from Chartres. So, on the facade (fig. 244), we can see how the rose gets all mixed up with the towers. Height is the determinant, and because of that, the rose is too high. The towers cannot shake free of it. At Reims, however, the height of the nave, with the great rose, is brought down and so lets the towers lift up freely (fig. 245). The lower levels of the facade are emphasized by this contrast and then glazed. The statue-columns are just above our heads; they are low and close to us (figs. 276, 278). Those at Amiens are set very high above us. They start our eyes on the upward lifting diagonal we noted before. At Reims, that is avoided; our center of attention is kept quite low, although, above, again as if for contrast, the towers open up. We see the flying buttresses through their skeleton structure, and this provides, as it happens, an utterly integrated expression on the exterior for everything that had technologically occurred in Gothic architecture up to that time.

But I think that the major reason for the special character of Reims is the very special event that took place at ground level there. This was the coronation of the kings of France, of which the most important one took place in 1429, when Joan led her dauphin in through the central portal and modern France was born. At that moment, Suger's intentions were wholly fulfilled. A king of France came forward in the western light just when he was most needed. Suger had set the stage for that event at St. Denis three hundred years before. It was achieved at Reims.

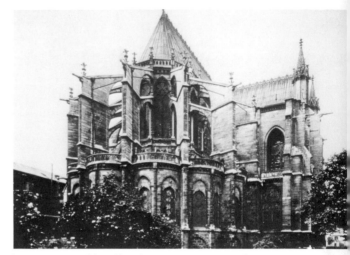

246. St. Denis. Abbey Church. Apse as reconstructed in 13th century.

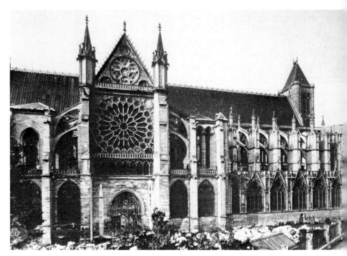

247. St. Denis. Abbey Church. 13th-century building, north side.

Then, of course, in the middle of the thirteenth century, some great architect, whose name we do not know, finished Suger's church for him, as Suger had known that someone, someday, would do. A shell of light enveloped Suger's building, enhancing what Suger had intended in every way. It swells out around the old Carolingian nave and laps against Suger's towers and balloons up above his choir (figs. 246, 247). The rose of his fa-

248. St. Denis. Abbey Church. Transept, 13th century.

cade (fig. 208), lighting his king's chapel, is now wholly visible on the interior (fig. 216) and finds three grand descendants in the high gable of the new nave and in the transepts, as well (fig. 247). They and the glazed triforia and the vast clerestory windows do in fact transform the choir into a blinding crown of light (fig. 245). As we move down the Rayonnant nave, between piers that now show a complete integration of column and colonnette into one dynamic body, we see that triforium and clerestory, too, have been firmly welded into one thin panel, wholly glazed. As as we approach the crossing, we see how gently this architect angled his much wider facade, his gate to heaven, back down into Suger's much narrower choir. Of that, only the ambulatory now remains, but the new triforium and clerestory windows rise above it to pure glory, under which the kings of France sleep, in their light and that of the roses (figs. 248, 249).

249. St. Denis. Abbey Church. Tomb of Philippe II le Hardi.

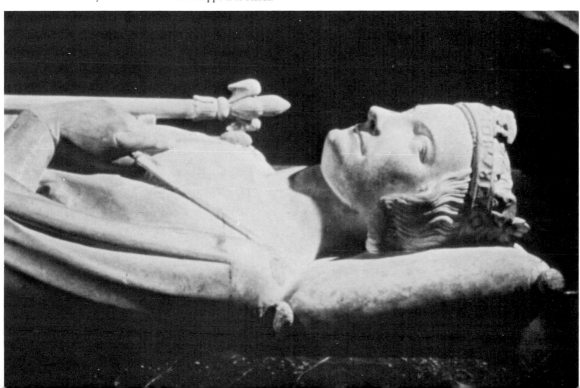

7
THE GOTHIC CATHEDRAL: EXPERIENCE

STRUCTURAL INVENTION, indeed structural daring, plays a larger part in Gothic architecture than it does in any of the other monumental architectures of the world, but Gothic architecture was not built for its structure. It was built for its symbolic content, for what it was intended to mean. Here von Simson is surely right, and his book *The Gothic Cathedral* remains the most important study of Gothic symbolism yet written, fundamentally correct in all major ways. However, it provides no single concrete analysis of the way the symbols and meanings of Gothic architecture are made visually manifest to human beings. There is no attempt to deal with Gothic architecture physically or to describe the experience of approaching, entering, and moving through a Gothic church.

276. Reims. Cathedral. West facade, with equestrian statue of Joan of Arc.

Nor is there any consideration of the way that experience varies from building to building and develops over time. Such an analysis should be undertaken, dealing with exactly the same buildings that were discussed in the previous chapter, and in the same sequence. If it accomplishes nothing else, it will help us realize how various the experience of works of art can be, how inexhaustible those works of art are in terms of meaning, and how they can be studied in any number of different ways. They never embody one truth—a fact that human beings seem afraid to acknowledge—but multiple truths, always exceeding the intentions of their makers in depth, ambiguity, and variety, and changing over time as those who perceive them change. This is true even in Gothic architecture, where von Simson is probably right in claiming a strong singleness of intention for its builders. They regarded themselves as building the image of a divine order, which would be made wholly manifest to the worshiper who finally stood in the crossing and faced the altar.

That order was embodied in the circle and the square, within whose perfect shapes, according to Vitruvius, the human body exactly fit (fig. 201). We have noted that this idea is ultimately Platonic, per-

268a. Paris. Nôtre Dame. Transept crossing and choir as reconstructed by Viollet-le-Duc.

haps Pythagorean before that. Later, during the Renaissance, the image of the human body squared and circled was to become Neoplatonism's essential emblem, but it was alive throughout the Middle Ages, as well. The power of the idea lies in its insistence on the miraculous proportioning and godlike centrality of mankind. It brings the human figure into accord with the shapes from which, in this view, everything that relates to beauty, and to the order of all things as they are and ought to be, is inescapably derived. The essential character of those shapes—and Leonardo's drawing is very expressive from that point of view—is that they are, in a Platonic sense, immaterial. The circle and the square are as thin and linear as can be. They are totally without mass. The human being is the sculpturally active object at their center. The shapes themselves are not involved with matter, and the closer they come to pure drawing, to pure *disegno,* as the Italian Renaissance was to call it, the closer they approach pure Idea and therefore, in the Platonic view, pure beauty. Anything that involves them in gross matter will always compromise them a little. Their perfection resides in their immateriality. That, of course, was what Hagia Sophia itself achieved at the beginning of the Middle Ages. It created the illusion of transcending matter with a circular dome magically floating above a square. It is an image of the perfect universe, heaven itself (fig. 205).

It is obvious that, if we start at the beginning of Gothic architecture with Suger's new facade for St. Denis (fig. 250), the circle and the square are the shapes he used. They are the crux of the design: the circle of the rose window set in its square bay between the towers. There seems to be no way of telling whether the influence of Abélard, the pioneer Platonist, played

250. St. Denis. Abbey Church. Abbot Suger. West facade. Reconstruction.

a part in this. Abélard had, of course, been teaching Plato at St. Denis right into the 1130s. We know that he praised the Platonic order and harmony of the spheres. We also know that he was thrown out of St. Denis because he proved that Dionysius the Areopagite could not be identified with the Gallic St. Denis. We do not know to what extent his influence endured at St. Denis, but we do have the archetypal Platonic image set squarely before our eyes in Suger's facade. We have seen how the king himself was intended to take up his position in that shape, in the light, in a chapel just big enough for him to stand in its center in glory (figs. 215, 216). So the king was displayed as the man of perfect proportions in the circle and the square, thus in touch with the cosmic order of the universe. Indeed, a whole universe of light

251. St. Denis. Abbey Church. Abbot Suger. West facade, center door, tympanum.

253. St. Denis. Abbey Church. Abbot Suger. West facade, rose window.

252. Moissac, France. St. Pierre. Circa 1120–1125. South portal, *Vision of St. John,* tympanum.

was being drawn in and transformed by the Western window. Exactly as in Leonardo's later drawing, all solids dematerialized around the person of the king.

Down below, in the Royal Portals, the first Royal Portals of all, we find that the central door does not have a pointed arch, which used to be regarded as de rigueur for Gothic buildings (fig. 251). Instead, it has as pure a round-headed arch as any

Roman building ever possessed. In the center of the half circle of its tympanum is the first of the great new images of the Gothic Christ. He is right in the middle, and he projects forward from the plane as he does not do in Romanesque sculpture. He holds his arms straight out, and he occupies the center of a great circle, the order of the cosmos centered on him. That circle is especially striking if we compare this tympanum at St. Denis with the consummate, southern Romanesque tympanum at Moissac (fig. 252), which is almost contemporary with it. Moissac, though Romanesque, has a pointed arch, probably because that best accords with the flamelike exaltation that is the meaning there. But emotionality is not what Suger was after. He wanted something rational, clear, calm, complete: the arch of the circle with the image of Christ displayed in the center.

Another significant fact is that the side portals at St. Denis, as if to mark off the specialness of the central portal, are slightly pointed (figs. 208, 250). Hence, the circular rhythms are concentrated in the middle of the facade, and a very conscious play of curves is developed through the middle to culminate in the full circle of the rose (fig. 253). The circular rose itself is made up of circles that are spinning out at the ends of radii within the greater circle itself. We cannot help but think of cosmic harmonies and the music of the spheres. Sumner Crosby, the major excavator of St. Denis, for a time was prepared to consider the possibility that these shapes were intended to demonstrate the epicycle in Ptolemy's system of the motion of a planet.* To von Simson, they suggested the dogmatic diagrams of twelfth-century manuscripts. Whatever the case, the rose culminates the movement of our eyes up the facade with circles spinning at the ends of radii.

Exactly so did Suger culminate the movement through his facade toward the image of heaven in his choir, because its radiating chapels are also an affair of intersecting circles, and its plan as a whole closely resembles the tracery of the rose (fig. 219, 220). The two seem to be invoking the same scheme of order. Moreover, the plan of the nave and transepts of St. Denis, reconstructed by Crosby as Suger intended to build them (fig. 218), shows what amounts to an ambulatory across the east face of the transept, on the side toward the choir, which was clearly intended to serve as the climax of movement down the nave.

It is the facade of the choir, the gate of heaven. It would have been lighted primarily by whatever windows were opened in the north and south walls of the transepts. We do not know what Suger intended there. Later, of course, there were to be the mighty rose windows of the thirteenth century, filling both transept walls (fig. 248). Whatever the case, Suger's transepts would have been shallow, so that when the worshiper arrived at the crossing and saw the whole facade of the choir, which was the culmination

*Sumner McK. Crosby, "Crypt and Choir Plans at Saint-Denis," *Gesta*, 5, January 1966, 4–8.

254. St. Denis. Abbey Church. Choir. Stained glass windows.

256. St. Denis. Abbey Church. Choir. Childhood of Christ window. Annunciation. Detail, Abbot Suger.

255. St. Denis. Abbey Church. Choir. Medallion of the Trinity.

of the experience, whatever was in the end walls of the transepts would have been well within his arc of vision. And as his eyes lifted to the choir's height, those end walls would have played a considerable part in the experience. That point must be stressed because it was to become extremely important in later buildings, where it was to be associated with the circles of rose windows.

Suger's plan of his choir, as we have noted, shows circles rotating at the end of radii from the center. And those circles progressively dematerialize from lower to higher. That is to say, in the crypt, which we remember is only half a level down from the nave, the walls are very thick in order to support the choir, so that the circles are separated by masonry. Then as we rise up to the choir—how like Suger that sounds, rising "in an anagogical manner"* from a lower to a higher sphere—we find that the circles spin free as the walls disappear from between them. The actual structural mass is being thinned out and light is taking over.

Down below is the heavy mass of the piers in the crypt (fig. 221). In the ambulatory above them, and set slightly inboard from them as if conceived in terms of a diagonal thrust from the main vaults, stand Suger's slender column shafts. We remember that they were originally even thinner because in the nineteenth century they were pasted over with a skin of cast stone. Once again, as we penetrate the ambulatory, it is the circle that consumes the mass. We are among the "heavenly windows" that were, for Suger, the objective of the whole enterprise (figs. 254, 255, 256). The original stained glass, much of which we are fortunate still to possess, is organized in circular forms, in congeries

of circles. Suger also used mosaic in various places: There, too, the basic shapes are circular.

The heavenly light of the stained glass, which transforms this mundane world into the magical harmony of the cosmos, is thus enhanced by mosaic, by which similar effects had been achieved in the East. Suger, one feels, indeed approached God not only through the Virgin but also through the great spinning circles themselves, and through the light and color they carry. He showed himself in one of the stained glass windows praying to Christ and the Virgin and prostrated right along the edge of one of those circles, in which he himself is bound up, rising "from a lower to a higher sphere" as on a vast wheel of light (fig. 256). Finally, one of the most important of the circular medallions in the windows is the great image of the Trinity, where the Son, crucified, holds out His arms in the center of the circle like a Christianized version of the man of perfect proportions, thus Himself the emblem of the order of the universe, as He was on the west facade as well (fig. 255).

Suger was ahead of his time; he broke the pattern and started something new, so that it took a few years for architectural events to begin to catch up with him. It is interesting, for example, to see what happens to the facades of the churches that were built closest in time to St. Denis. None of their builders seem quite to have understood what Suger was doing. On the other hand, they did not have his program; they did not possess the chapel of the king. We must remember, too, that up to this point, the idea of lighting into the nave through the facade had hardly arisen. So even much later, as at Sens, there is only a tiny rose high up in the center. At Senlis, in that wonderful, still-Gothic town north of

*Panofsky, op. cit., p. 65.

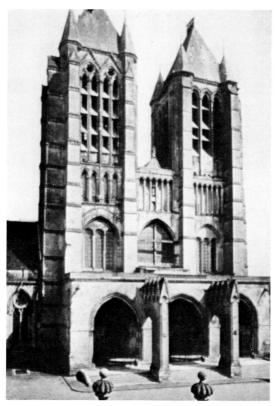

257. Noyon, France. Nôtre Dame. Facade, completed circa 1235.

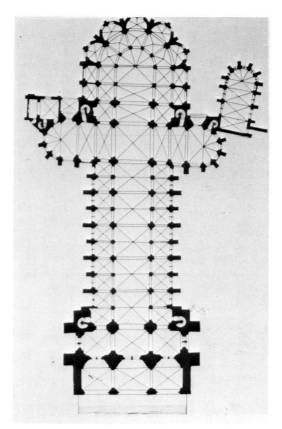

258. Noyon. Cathedral. Plan.

Paris, not so far from St. Denis and close in time to it, there are three. They have lost Suger's point and have become a decorative band. Below them, all the arches are pointed. Circular imagery clearly plays no significant part in the facade.

At Noyon, slightly later, the rose is in fact given up in favor of a pointed arch (fig. 257). It would seem that the more the builders worked with the ribbed vault and tried to calculate its diagonal thrust, the more the desire grew in them to bring that thrust down toward the vertical as rapidly as possible. That led them toward the pointed arch, which then began to challenge the circle and to exist in a kind of tension with it—most of all, to *lift*. At Noyon, where there is no rose, the towers dominate the articulation of the facade and burst free above it. Another thing about

Noyon is that the choir is in a way much more Romanesque than Suger's. The radiating chapels project; they are quite solid when compared with Suger's thin, stretched arcs, which hardly project at all. At Noyon (fig. 258), there is a whole panoply of radiating chapels which seem to be far outside the main volume of the ambulatory and are massively geometric: They are everything that Suger was trying to get away from. The same is true of Noyon's rounded transepts, so reminiscent of the Rhineland.

But on the inside those strange transepts at Noyon offer the totally dematerialized experience we noted in the previous chapter, with several passageways in the thickness of a wall that seems to break apart into screens of colonnettes (fig. 227).

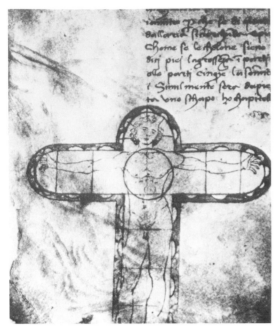

259. Francesco di Giorgio Martini. Ground plan of a church corresponding to the proportions of the human figure.

Now the climactic experience in front of the choir is created by the light that pours in through the transepts on both sides. Once more, as at St. Denis, when we arrive before the altar, something happens in the transepts, and here it is something very original. It does not seem to be anything imagined by Suger or to be developed later. It is special to Noyon.

Another image that comes through in Noyon, and in which Platonism plays a part as well, is that of a giant in the building, or of the building as a body. Such had been a very Classical idea, and it was certainly a Christian one. In the fifteenth century, for example, a drawing by Francesco di Giorgio shows us a man (whose stance suggests that of crucifixion) standing in the plan of a church (fig. 259). His body is the nave; his head, slightly slanted, is the choir, and the transepts just barely contain his outstretched arms. We notice that they are rounded transepts, like those

of Noyon, probably because a rounded transept feels stretched, here by the extension of the arms, as a rectangular, hard-cornered transept would not. The choir is also canted at Noyon, like the head of Francesco di Giorgio's figure itself.

It is difficult to say whether, throughout the Middle Ages, there was in fact any continuing idea of the body of Christ shaping or inhabiting the Christian church. In our generation, we have been much too quick to dismiss the possibility that a building can actually be thought of as a figural body. It is part of the effect upon us of the abstraction and iconoclasm of the International Style. But the plan of Laon, too, has a bodily character. Indeed, the choir abandons Noyon's radiating chapels and is more like Francesco di Giorgio's round-headed example. The whole suggests a shrouded figure lifting its arms. At least it does if we start looking at things that way.

Whether all this is so, in fact, it is clear that there are many diverse and perhaps contradictory images built into Gothic cathedrals: Neoplatonic dematerialization, the image of the human body, and sometimes architecture's other, most environmental image, that of the city as a whole. It seems apparent that the exterior massing of most cathedrals was indeed intended to evoke that ultimate image, taking shape in a crowd of towers, rising from every conceivable point to construct the City of God, a New Jerusalem, a heaven on earth. Very few churches were able to bring that vision wholly into being. Laon comes close to it with a couple of transept towers and two on the west. Tournai, in Belgium, which is part Romanesque and part Gothic, has the most complete extant group of towers around the transepts, with the lower crossing tower in the center and four higher towers around it. It was intended to be seen rising on its height above the earthly city, indeed directly above the marketplace of the town like another city in the sky. Such was also intended at Laon (fig. 260), lifting as it does high on the ridge at the eastern edge of its town, rising high above the wide plain that stretches away to the north.

One also feels that the towers of Laon are calling to the landscape as if there were some ancient cult of the earth still being celebrated on the summit of the hill. The famous oxen of Laon reinforce that feeling (fig. 261). Their horned heads peer out across the landscape from the aediculae of the towers. The clearly literary myth that was made up later to explain why they are there has them represent the oxen that dragged the stone for the building's construction. It does not ring very true. There may well be a pagan memory here, out of which the old horns emerge to flourish in the sky.

But the church is as intensely related to the town as it is to the landscape. The main street runs along the spine of the ridge. As we approach the church along it, perhaps on an early-winter morning in a chilling fog, the impression is of some

dark monster looming out of the mist (fig. 262). The square before it is very small, but the street leads straight to it, so that it opens before us until its dark bulk fills our eyes. As the light grows, one thinks of the oxen up there in the mist, and when the sun finally begins to slide across the facade, the whole troop stands out overhead, a barbaric presence, the horned animal gods in the sky (fig. 263).

It is also interesting that Laon employs little pavilions, aediculae, to house these figures. John Summerson, in one of his characteristically elegant, beautifully conceived and written essays,* put forth the idea that the aedicula was the very basis of Gothic architecture, but this cannot be correct. The aediculae were late—here in

*John Summerson, "Heavenly Mansions: An Interpretation of Gothic," in *Heavenly Mansions and Other Essays on Architecture,* New York, 1963.

260. Laon, France. Cathedral. Air view.

261. Laon. Cathedral. West tower. Detail with oxen.

262. Laon. Cathedral. View of cathedral from town.

263. Laon. Cathedral. Facade.

entrances and a deeply sunken rose (fig. 263). Now the rose comes into its own; it is a huge circle set in a gigantic frame that seems to push the sides of the facade apart and to eat up the whole center. It fills our eyes and our minds as we come out of the narrow street and approach it, while, up above, the great towers shake free and the colonnaded passageways, like those within, weave through the wall and bind the masses together. The action of the *colonnettes-en-délit* inside is thus imaged and reflected on the exterior as well. For all its brutal vitality, Laon's facade is developing toward the integration of interior and exterior, and it demonstrates the progressive encroachment of interior structures and spaces upon Suger's symbolic facade screen. But the two great form-types are Suger's still: the rose and the towers.

As we move under them and enter the building, their promise is totally fulfilled. The first thing we see, far down on the eastern wall of the choir, is another monumental rose window (fig. 264). It is, of course, part of the thirteenth-century reconstruction of the apse, which was originally half-round: a hemicycle that did not project very far beyond the crossing. As rebuilt, it was made to echo the rose of the facade. The next thing that seizes our attention as we move along the nave toward the choir is the light that is streaming down from the tower over the crossing. So, as we move to the crossing—where, originally, with the shallow apse, one was right in front of the altar—our eyes are led upward toward the light in the tower. For the first time, too, there are rose windows in the transepts, but here at Laon they are comparatively solid and dark. The transepts are also so elongated and narrow that the roses are farther away from us in the crossing than they are in

the towers of Laon as late as the thirteenth century. Therefore, they did not initiate Gothic architecture; nor were they essential to it. They do not appear in all the important Gothic buildings, but they were surely something that Gothic architecture sometimes, and increasingly, exploited— here at Laon for the first time. They, too, act to shred and skeletonize the mass. They open up the edges from which, in Laon's towers, the beasts peer.

Indeed, Laon creates the impression that animal power is moving throughout its entire body. Its facade is an inchoate, protean form with enormous cavernous

265. Paris, France. Nôtre Dame. View of cathedral from town.

many churches, and they give little sense of dematerializing the mass. That effect, at least, is not as strong as the basic one of the rise of the crossing tower, and when we finally experience the roses of the choir and the transepts all together, the major climax of that drama before the gate of heaven is still the transcendent light falling from the lantern.

All of that would appear to have been perceived, commented upon, and changed by the architect of Nôtre Dame of Paris. In 1163, when work was begun, a new street was cut through the solid mass of houses in front of the cathedral right up to its parvis, which was much smaller than it has been made at present. Its urbanistic setting, especially the approach to it, was thus made to resemble Laon's (figs. 262, 265). Some enduring Classical principle of axial approach may well have been at work in both places, but it is the conscious relationship to Laon that seems most striking in Paris.

The facade, for example, takes Laon's and cleans it up, clarifies it, indeed Classicizes it, making it reasonable, legible, and quite flat, where Laon's is physical, animal, and very deep. Paris is the most

Classical of all the great cathedrals in its facade (fig. 369). It is the most planar, the most *drawn*. It seems no accident that it is set on its island just across the narrow arm of the river from the university. In the sense that reason and human logic are the basis of Gothic architecture and of Platonism, too, it might be said that in some ways these impulses culminate in Paris. It is true that the upper levels of the facade are set back in plane above the row of kings of France who stand above the Royal Portals. Some illusion of greater height and distance is being developed. Otherwise, the wall is stretched and thinned exactly as it is inside. In that sense, it is very much like Suger's facade for St. Denis (fig. 250).

Behind it, as at St. Denis, the building is lower and wholly masked by the facade, and the towers project well past the buttresses of the nave behind them. The facade is a false front, a great signboard that—if I may employ terms made famous by Robert Venturi*—decorates what is basically a large shed stretched out behind it. That signboard has remained, of course, a fundamental insignia of Paris and of France as a whole. We are moved by photographs taken of it at the time of the Liberation of 1944, when de Gaulle walked from the Etoile down the Champs Elysées and on past the Louvre to Nôtre Dame and through its Royal Portals and down the nave to the crossing to hear the "Te Deum" sung. He was, of course, conforming to an urban structure, a ceremonial route that culminates at this facade.

*Robert Venturi, Denise Scott Brown, and Steven Izenour, *Learning from Las Vegas: The Forgotten Symbolism of Architectural Form*, Cambridge, Massachusetts, 1977.

264. Laon. Cathedral. Nave.

266. Paris. Nôtre Dame. Nave.

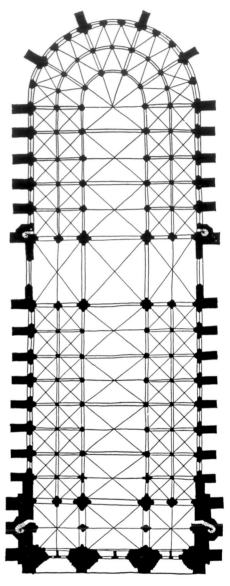

267. Paris. Nôtre Dame. Plan.

It is the most like Suger's of them all; but now an enormous circle is centered in the big square of the facade as a whole. And that, with its towers, is made up of two intersecting squares which also can be rendered as intersecting circles. It is a Classical order of what Le Corbusier was to call *tracés regulateurs,* based on the two primary shapes. In the center is the greatest of all rose windows made up to that time, in a setting of almost Renaissance Classicism that suggests more than ever that supremely Renaissance image of the heroic human being who stands in the center of the circle and the square. We recall how similar the medallion of the Trinity at St. Denis is, and we can be permitted to remind ourselves of Masaccio's later, and greatest, treatment of that theme. At Nôtre Dame, the rose is indeed used as the background for a sculptural group, here of the Virgin and Child flanked by angels. But as we pass under the rose and go through into the nave, into which the rose itself, as at Laon, now opens, we feel the high vault moving on beyond it, as it does in Masaccio's fresco, and it leads our eyes toward the choir (fig. 266).

The capitals of the nave arcades are not very high above our heads; the columns recall Suger's, despite being much thicker, and they clearly support the wall above them. There is no leap of the eye from the pavement to the vaults. There is compression on the column capitals, and our eyes are led by them on a horizontal plane toward the facade of the choir. That facade is handled in a manner that is exactly the opposite of that employed either on the west facade or on the western face of the transept, the side facing the choir. Instead of a thin wall divided horizontally, we see at first only the eastern piers of the crossing. They are bundles of rounded colonnettes, suggesting plant growth. They rise all the way up without any impediment and are so set that we see them in perspective as standing inside the plane of the nave wall. And the nave was in fact made three feet wider than the choir; I think to show them off (fig. 267). Therefore, as we are led toward the crossing, it is the great vertical burst of its eastern piers that holds our attention.

These things are impossible to photograph properly in a Gothic church. Unlike Classical architecture, nothing in this drama of forms and spaces is in any way within the camera's range. But when, in fact, we stand at the crossing, we are looking directly at those rounded eastern piers (figs. 232, 268b). Everything about them lifts. Those on the west side of the crossing, which stand beside us as we view those of the east, are their opposites in essential ways. They are not rounded bunches of colonnettes but are cut in flat, hard planes that retain the thin mural quality of the nave wall (fig. 268a). The general critical reaction to this change has been simply to attribute it to a change of architects. But that is hardly the important point, which is that the architects involved were dramatically contrasting the western and the eastern piers. The facade of heaven is thus set off as different, most of all as richer, more reflective of nature, and more

268b. Paris. Nôtre Dame. Transept crossing and choir as reconstructed by Viollet-le-Duc.

elevating than the more mundane world of the nave. Its piers force us to see them as rising, indeed as rushing up like living growth. So our eyes go up, and as they do so, the great rose windows that now fill the whole of the north and south walls of the shallow transepts come into our arc of vision (fig. 268a). They swing in and begin to spin, filling the edges of our sight, lifting and dematerializing the vaults above them in, I think, the greatest climax ever achieved in the history of architecture, and the one, to repeat, least possible to photograph.

It can and must be experienced on the spot, if we permit the building to lead us, in terms of what it means, straight down the nave to stand at last in the crossing at heaven's gate. There, empathetically, we feel it all rise up beyond matter around us.

Our flesh is not denied, but transcended. We are in the center of an expanding universe. Then, in truth at the edge of vision, but well inside its limits, the great roses lift and spring in a harmony like that of the spheres. It makes one wonder whether that was not the real reason why Viollet-le-Duc so stubbornly insisted on rebuilding the little circles at the third level. He did so, after all, only around the crossing, where this climactic drama is taking place. Perhaps he felt that cosmic spinning, so that when he decided to demonstrate how he thought the wall had originally been built before the flying buttresses were introduced, this is where he chose to do so, in order to enhance the effect.

Another significant fact about this climax in the crossing at Paris is that it, along with the facade, fulfills what Suger seems to have wanted to accomplish at St. Denis. It develops and perfects that experience. It is already a school of Paris, intellectual and idealistically immaterial. Hence the thirteenth-century work at St. Denis seems, in turn, to grow out of that at Paris. There is a similar broad and shallow transept, with a rose that fills its entire end wall (fig. 248). The tracery of the rose is very like that of the transept rose of Paris, extremely thin and linear. It, too, seems to spin as it floods its light down upon the tombs of the kings of France. We tend to feel that this was precisely the image of cosmic glory that Suger was after in his crossing and choir. Considering that, Paris seems a logical outcome of what Suger had begun, achieving as it does a largely dematerialized environment in which all solids are stretched to the flattest of surfaces and the thinnest of lines.

Outside, as we have already noted, the flying buttresses eventually complete that effect, wholly destroying the solidity of the mass. Again, however, the architect

269. Chartres. Cathedral from the wheat fields.

of Chartres did not want any of that at all. Earlier, I contrasted the signboard quality of the west facade of Paris and the shedlike character of the building behind it with the compact, crouching, integrated body of Chartres (figs. 234, 235). There the transepts are widened in order to screen at least one bay of choir and nave alike, so that the whole mass seems shorter and more compactly muscular. The towers are drawn into the rest of it, so that it is all one body rising. Those towers are one of the miracles of that principle of "condensation" I mentioned before. They are opposites joined. The whole facade is unique in Gothic architecture, just as the Parthenon was unique in Greek (figs. 271a, b, c).

The tower on the south was begun after the one on the north, both of them in the 1130s and 1140s, just at the time when Suger was working. The south tower stands today as it was built originally. The upper part of the other, above the level of the facade, was rebuilt in the late Gothic period, and we do not know what the top of it was like before. But as it comes out now, it is a wonderful complement to the south tower. It rises vertically to the point where the other's continuous cone begins to diminish and then leaps to its own spire, so that the two act dynamically in relation to each other. They shift position as they are seen from afar and engage in a stately dance against their background of sky. They are rising out of the wheat (fig. 269); and this is entirely appropriate, because the cathedral itself is a product of the great wheat fields that stretch away beyond the southern borders of the Ile-de-France. Indeed, from a distance the towers resemble an American grain elevator and, beyond that, the magnificent state capitol of Nebraska, which beautifully exploits just such a setting. Driving across Nebraska's rolling wheat fields, we see the unmistakable shapes of grain elevators everywhere on the horizon. All at once, one of them is seen shining gold on top; it is the state capitol with its dome, growing out of the place to become its emblem.

So with Chartres: It lifts as if singing out of the wheat, within which the poppies, the blood of Adonis, grow (fig. 269). A Classical connection is indeed felt; we are dealing with a temple, above which two towers move like living bodies, the cone and the spire. When we enter the town and approach the building, it begins to pivot toward us, turning on the cone, rising to the spire (fig. 270). This is analogous to what the Parthenon seems to do from a similar perspective angle. Chartres, too, is in its own way "our own dear Kore who is among us"*: always growing and breathing, and as difficult as the Parthenon to take in. Its spires are the lances of France, outdoing the Norman towers in their continuous rush up out of the

*Plato, *Laws,* 796.

270. Chartres. Cathedral. Exterior from the town.

ground, out of the wheat that was the strength of France, as the olive was of Athens and the corn of the pueblos.

Greater than Normandy, Chartres rises out of a richer earth, out of the very bread of mankind, and it rises integrally with its towers. At St. Etienne, the towers balance like military dandies on the edge of the parapet (fig. 211). At Chartres, they are intrinsic to the whole body, though built at different times (fig. 271a). It is all a matter of putting accidents together, of reacting to circumstances beyond sterile models of perfection. This is the greatest event in art, when it grows beyond concepts of perfection to an unaccountable richness of life, embracing those complexities and contradictions, as a great modern architect called them, which shape the reality of things. It is a most un-Platonic point of view, but it, too, plays a part in shaping Gothic architecture, and Chartres most of all.

The complex accommodation of contradictions at Chartres does not stop with the towers. The Royal Portals, for example, are squeezed between them (figs. 271a, b, c). They do not stretch across the entire facade as they do at St. Denis and more or less everywhere else. They are framed and constrained by the towers. They are not large and are shaped according to a very moderate set of proportions;

271a. Chartres. Cathedral. West facade.

they are rational, accessible, and calm. Their statue-columns are not high overhead; we can touch them. Moreover, they and their companions on the north and south transepts are the whole body of figural sculpture that the building possesses, because, beginning at St. Denis, all the figural sculpture that the Romanesque had lavished on capitals disappears from the interior of the church. It no longer celebrates, as Romanesque sculpture did, the fructifying power of the fabric itself to germinate life, to produce saints and monsters out of its own compressive heat. Now the sculpture steps forward from the fabric, though it is still tied to it by the fiction of the column, to become a rational human population, our more beautiful equals greeting us as we arrive.

Even more than at Suger's St. Denis, all the flamelike ecstasies of Moissac, for example (fig. 252), disappear at Chartres. Christ is brought forward in sculptural three dimensions to teach us clearly, rationally. Even more important is the fact that the Virgin appears on the facade for the first time. She holds the Child in her arms above the southern portal, the side of light (fig. 271b). She is the patroness of the universities, whose liberal arts fill the archivolts above her head. She thus stands for reason, learning, academic achievement. She is not Woman as Force of Nature, or Intuitive Irrational Wisdom, or even as simple Mother Goddess. She is woman as Intelligence, as more than brute force, as Mind. She is not only the patroness of the liberal arts and the goddess who is embodied in every important cathedral—since it is always Nôtre Dame of Noyon, of Laon, and so on, with the Abbey Church of St. Denis the exception that proves the rule—but she is also the protectress of the state, the guardian of the king of France, his Athena, his Wisdom, his guide. So he, too, politically, puts his faith in reason and sides with the universities and the towns in opposition to the dark, traditional, emotional feudal power.

To go further: Romanesque sculpture had been animalistically potent, full of acrobatic physical energy. The statue-columns at Chartres are just the opposite. Their bodies are feeble; they seem to have lost all physical vitality. They dance no more (fig. 271c). However, their faces have become intelligent, civilized, a bit ironic, very gentle. For the first time, they have become utterly French, men and women alike. Their union of intelligence and beauty was to become one of the major glories of France. It is all here for the first time, showing up all at once and

271b. Chartres. Cathedral. West facade. Detail.

271c. Chartres. Cathedral. West facade. Detail.

complete, at least so far as mind, soul, and spiritual beauty are concerned. It was, in fact, to be several generations before the body caught up with these qualities in the physical statue-columns and began to stand out as a muscular being in space.

Above this firm and civilized base at human scale, with the solidly realized Christ sitting in blessing just above it, the scale of Chartres' facade explodes. The big windows leap up, and finally the curiously solid rose, opening like a heavily petaled flower. Our eyes are lifted upward in exaltation; they are carried on farther by the towers, so that the whole lifts together, while for the first time on any facade the little *pignon* of the nave gable is not screened, as it had been at Paris and Laon and, of course, at St. Denis. Its emergence increases the upward burst and pulls the towers closer together. It releases the energies to the empyrean; from their base in human intelligence, they leap to the skies.

We pass under that climactic triumph and enter the church, squeezed between the towers, so passing from the light of the outside into a low, dark place (fig. 272). Those Jungian archetypes so well delineated by Maud Bodkin in terms of the literary arts can be applied equally well here: especially those dealing with movement from dark to light, hell to heaven, death to resurrection.* Because at Chartres, the floor is sloping down toward the entrance, flowing like a heavy tide around the piers (fig. 273). So, upon entrance, we are looking up from below toward the mighty piers, now massive and high, rising up through the space once occupied by the tribune. They lift like giant living bodies, all the more powerfully because we are made to approach them at an

*Maud Bodkin, *Archetypal Patterns in Poetry,* London, 1934, new edition 1963.

angle from below. We are being led toward a physically embodied divinity, much as we were on the Acropolis of Athens.

The best description of that body is Villon's, in the fearful tread of his line invoking the Virgin: "Dame des cieulx, régente terrienne,/Emperière des infernaux palux . . . "* How different those palisades of Chartres are from those of Paris. Now there is no wall, only sculpturally distinct beings standing up ponderously in space. Everything about Chartres involves the diagonal that is rising through it from entrance to choir, a dynamic line of sight that is being carried by the lifting bodies of the piers on both sides of the nave (figs. 237, 273).

When we perceive that vista from the entrance, I think that we also feel two curious contradictions in it. One, as we saw before, involves the fact that the triforium is not glazed. So our eyes are stopped by the zone of darkness in the choir. Moreover, the diagonal is not continued by a vertical tower over the crossing, such as we found at Laon. Such a tower seems promised at Chartres, where, unlike Paris, all four piers are handled in the same way, as if shaping one larger bay of space of greater height between them. Again, at Chartres, this is the opposite of Paris and more like Laon, except that there is no tower. The continuing responds above the vaults show us, however, that one was intended. It was begun, probably inspired by Laon, and then stopped. Like Laon, too, the transept is narrow and deep, not wide and shallow like that of Paris. There is no dematerialization. So the diagonal is arrested at the choir.

There, however, other aspects of the resident divinity make themselves felt.

*François Villon, "Le Testament," lines 873–4, in *François Villon: Poésies,* ed., Jean Dufournet, Paris, 1973.

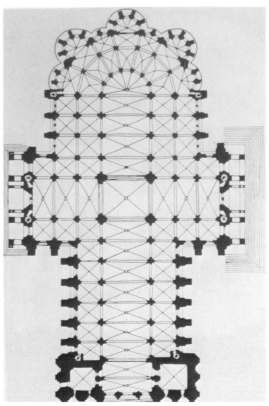

272. Chartres. Cathedral. Plan.

274. Chartres. Cathedral. Choir, ambulatory.

273. Chartres. Cathedral. Nave as seen from the entrance.

This is especially apparent to us when we face the choir (fig. 273). The experience is nothing at all like that at St. Denis and Paris. We remember that at St. Denis the columns were very slender and the radiating chapels hardly projected at all, so that the glass could be brought closer toward the altar and the whole could be as brightly lighted as possible. It is not like that at Chartres. It is dark in the choir (fig. 274). It is a heavy darkness, because, as we noted before, there is not only a deep double ambulatory but also radiating chapels that are pushed far out from it in a plan that again, like the piers themselves, looks back to Romanesque forms (fig. 272). And, like the piers, the chapels involve a subtle alternation, here of shallow and deep.

We know that one reason why the radiating chapels took shape as they did, and probably the major reason, is that there are three distinct cults of the Virgin at Chartres. Down below in the crypt is the most ancient one, that of *La Vierge sous Terre,* the Virgin below Ground. She has the largest crypt of any Gothic church, running as a long cavern throughout the foundation, to whose shapes the radiating chapels of the choir generally conform. There is the sense of a very old, pre-Christian divinity down there. Moreover, when we stand in the crossing and look from that point to the left, to the north, the darker side of the ambulatory, we see, right there in the first bay, the altar of another cult, that of the *Vierge Noire,* the Black Virgin. Here is another goddess, surely pre-Romanesque and connected with darkness. But on the right side, which is the side of the sun, the side of the light, and again in the first bay, directly opposite the altar of the Black Virgin on the other side, is the great window of the *Belle Verrière,* the Virgin and Child in stained glass.

Instead of the usual small scale of early stained-glass figures, this Virgin is over life size, coming in with the light, *as* light, into the choir. She is the third Virgin, the culmination of the cult in Suger's "heavenly windows." It is her light that is penetrating the deep, cavernous choir, which, contrasted with that of St. Denis, is being modeled with an almost baroque chiaroscuro in a play of light into darkness and of chapels shallow and deep. So Chartres is among the noblest of mysteries, a condensation of many different systems of experience and belief. No other cathedral is so complex, or so physical, combining spatial environment with sculptural body somewhat as the Acropolis of Athens had done (figs. 148, 149).

Chartres, like the Periclean Acropolis, entirely redirected the course of architecture. Every subsequent cathedral was affected by her, though none was ever so complete as she. Amiens, for example, picked up the leap of her *piliers cantonnés* and her diagonal line of sight and brought it all to fruition by glazing the triforium in the transepts and the choir (figs. 239, 240). Indeed, at least the eastern wall of the transept must be glazed if dematerialization is to occur when, as here and at Chartres, the transept itself is narrow and deep compared with that of Paris. And now with the glazing, a great transformation occurs. The whole becomes a vast park, a forest, the garden of the Virgin, lifting to the full blaze of glass at the head of the church. Great height is essential to Amiens; it rises spectacularly as the Heavenly City above the everyday city below it. This effect would have been even more spectacular if all its projected towers had been built. The diagonal line of sight is made possible by that height and, indeed, integrates it into a unified experience. It starts right at the entrance (fig. 244). The

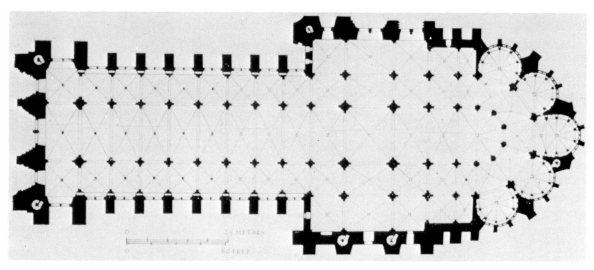

275. Reims. Cathedral. Plan.

statue-columns are high above our heads. The little scenes in low relief below them seem introduced in part to fill that space. So we begin by being forced to look up. Christ holds the central trumeau, the Virgin that of the southern portal, but they are pushed way up, as is the whole facade. The rose, as we have seen, is forced up between the towers to light the high nave behind it. Hence, everything at Amiens is directed by the desire for height.

We remember that Reims totally gave that up. Its builders were willing to bring the rose down and to shake the towers loose from it, and then to skeletonize the towers so completely that the flying buttresses are visible behind them. Reims thus returns to the open aedicula, really for the first time since Laon, and integrates its towers anew by means of it (fig. 245). So the whole exterior is articulated into those skeletal elements that the structural system had suggested from the beginning.

On the other hand, one cannot really believe that a desire for rational integration shaped the major intentions at Reims. That is not, for example, why Reims is lower and why the statue-columns are

brought way down, close enough, as at Chartres, for us to touch, rather than high up as at Amiens (figs. 277, 278). All this, instead, must have to do with the most important function of Reims, which was to provide the ritual setting for the coronation of the kings of France.

Height, therefore, is not the main concern. The nave is lower; the capitals of the nave piers are reasserted and enlarged into a broad horizontal band in a stone of a darker color, which enforces a strong horizontal movement down the nave (fig. 241). At the end, in the choir, the triforium is dark, as triforia always had been. No one at Reims seems to have worried about that, as they were to do at Amiens. The effect they sought to achieve at Reims was of something majestic happening at ground level, surrounded by rather classically conceived piers marching like soldiers, not growing up like trees. And when we turn around in Reims and look to the west, there everything is glazed, the tympani for the first time in medieval architecture (fig. 243). So it is to the west that the climax takes place. That is clear if, once again, we contrast Reims with

Amiens, where the rose is almost meaningless from the inside, pushed as it is way up in the apex of the high nave. Below it, the whole wall is dark. The climax at Amiens was, as we have seen, in the other direction, in the choir.

To go further: The plan of Reims shows enormous extension of the open area around the crossing, an area that we do not quite know whether to identify with the transepts or the choir (fig. 275). The two tend to merge into a space that was obviously intended to contain a great number of people during the coronation of the king. The nave in front of it is very clearly a processional space, much longer and narrower than the nave of Amiens, which is based on the chunky model of Chartres. It is an extended, axial space that leads us from the entrance to the crossing

278. Reims, Cathedral. West facade, central portal, south jamb, Annunciation and Visitation groups.

277. Reims. Cathedral. West facade, central portal.

but that, in fact, is culminated only by the view back from the crossing to the west.

Indeed, after the king was crowned, he walked in that direction, toward the light, and as he did so he was passing beneath the capitals, which carried the fruits and flowers and the laborers in the fields and the vineyards that were the richness of his realm (fig. 243). Here, for the very first time in Gothic architecture, figural sculpture returned to the interior of the church in the broad bands of the capitals of the nave. And this is its theme: the fruitfulness of the vegetable world and the labor of mankind to bring it forth. Deep back in time, all that side of things had been the responsibility of the king; he gave his life to it, and sometimes for it. Now it marches with him as he goes out toward his glory in the west. In order for that glory to be complete, the interior of the western wall, where it cannot be glazed, is completely broken up by a unique checkerboard of figures in niches, so that there is no sense there of a solid wall anywhere. All solids dissolve before the king as he steps out to the western sun, anointed and crowned (figs. 245, 277).

It is one of history's most awesome facts that all this was worked out in the thirteenth century and was there when it was needed two hundred years later, on July 17, 1429. It was on that day that Joan of Arc led her dauphin through those portals to become the anointed king of France, so uniting it anew with the heavenly order and liberating it from subjection to the English king (fig. 276). Reims was not merely the setting for this event; its iconography may be said to have brought it about. It has to do with Joan, the virgin, whose powers touch those of the supernatural. We remember that when Joan first went to Blois, the dauphin hid himself among his courtiers to see whether she could pick him out. The story is that she walked straight up to him and said, "Most noble Dauphin, I have come from God to help you and your kingdom. . . . I tell you from our Lord that you are the true heir of France and the son of the king." "Je te dis de la part de Messire que tu es le vrai héritier de France et le fils du roi."* Then she led him at last to Reims to be crowned, right through the central portal (fig. 277), and on the trumeau of that portal stood the Virgin herself. To her left, Joan's right as she entered, the statue-columns embody the primal scene from Joan's life (fig. 278).

Beginning at Chartres, the statue-columns had been there to greet us at our scale. But at Chartres there had been no conversation between them; they stood stiff as columns. By the time of Reims, which had, of course, the greatest and certainly the most influential body of sculpture of all the French cathedrals, the statue-columns were arranged in dramatic groups. They converse and interact. At Amiens, the Virgin had appeared on the trumeau and among the statue-columns of the southern portal. The columns to the south there embodied two fundamental scenes: the Annunciation and the Visitation, when Mary visits Elizabeth, who is at that time pregnant with John the Baptist, as the Virgin is pregnant with Jesus. At Amiens, all the figures were carved in the way that the figure of the Virgin alone is carved at Reims—in a simple, rather blocky style, at once Classical and vernacular in character. The Virgin herself is a plain, sturdy, peasant girl.

But at Reims, there are three different styles to be seen among the two groups (fig. 278). Again, as with the variation of the crossing piers at Paris, we must not

*Jules Michelet, *Jeanne d'Arc* in *Classiques Larousses,* Paris, 1941, 22.

dismiss this variety by passing it off simply as resulting from the work of different artists. It has to do with the adjustment of form to the meaning it is intended to embody. So the angel is more slender than the others, with a small head and a whole different set of proportions. He is aristocratic, smiling, elegant, a heavenly voice from a court even more rarefied than that of Paris. He speaks to the peasant girl, smiling. It is Joan and her voices precisely rendered. Did this group suggest them to her, peasant girl as she was from Domrémy not far away?

Then, when the Virgin visits Elizabeth, they both become Roman matrons, splendid, noble women who greet each other as sisters: women pregnant, as Joan was never to be. But the Virgin of the Visitation looks out at us as she must have looked at Joan. And she looks out over us to the world, and, according to Luke, she is making one of the most rousing political speeches of all time. Elizabeth, among other things, has just said, "For, lo, as soon as the voice of thy salutation sounded in mine ears, the babe leaped in my womb for joy." And under the Roman robe the sculptor makes us see the child move. Mary replies:

My soul doth magnify the Lord./
And my spirit hath rejoiced in God my saviour./ For he hath regarded the low estate of his handmaiden: for, behold, from henceforward all generations shall call me blessed./ For he that is mighty hath done to me great things; and holy is his name./ He hath showed strength with his arm; he hath scattered the proud in the imagination of their hearts./ He hath put down the mighty from their seats, and exalted them of low degree./ He hath filled the hungry with good things; and the rich he hath sent empty away./ He hath holpen his servant Israel, in remembrance of his mercy:/ As he spake to our fathers, to Abraham, and to his seed for ever.*

God in fact, had helped his servant, France, as he spoke to Joan. What Suger hoped for was fulfilled. His intention to connect the kingdom of France with a cosmic order shaped and called forth the power that saved it. So it came about that in the transepts of St. Denis, under the roses of the Virgin's garden, there were to sleep not only the French kings of the Middle Ages but those of the Renaissance as well (fig. 279).

*Luke 1:44, 46–55.

279. St. Denis. Abbey Church. Tomb of Henry II.

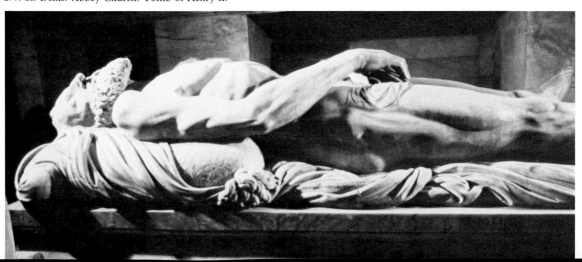

8
ITALIAN URBANISM:
THE TOWN AND THE GARDEN

URING THE LATE Middle Ages, European urbanism, more or less continuous as an architectural environment since antiquity, took on a new burst of life. That revival was in large measure an Italian achievement, though its influence soon radiated, with its banking, to the north. Through it, Italy not only reinvigorated the town but also revived the Classical landscape and eventually reinvented the garden as a major architectural form. We begin with the city of Florence in the thirteenth century, closely packed north and south of the Arno within its high and thin medieval walls (fig. 280). Outside them, the lovely landscape of Tuscany mounds up in verdant hills,

304. Rome. Piazza Navona at night.

turning soft and blue in the distance while, just north of the town, the higher spines of the Apennines begin to rise.

Deep in the body of the city, its most important building was planted like a seed from which all the rest grew (fig. 281). This was the Baptistery, where nameless souls were brought, through baptism, into the Christian community that made the town. The building is a shape that was to become central to all Florentine art. It is a polygonal block, a domed volume, a massive body set in an urban square just large enough to contain it as within a stage. It was built in the eleventh century, but already, by the late thirteenth, the Florentines wished to believe that it was of late Antique construction and had thus been there since time immemorial. Later, early in the fifteenth century, Brunelleschi, the inventor of one-point perspective, was to do what was apparently his very first perspective study precisely of this building as it was seen from the door of the cathedral in front of it and, thus, as a solid body set in an urban niche, a stage of space.

Brunelleschi also finished the dome of the cathedral at that time. This, too, was clearly the kind of form the Florentines liked, a large geometric solid standing firmly in space. The cathedral as a whole was begun by Arnolfo di Cambio in the late thirteenth century, and even then, though the dome was not completed for

280. Florence, Italy. View of city. Circa 1490.

281. Florence. Cathedral and baptistery. Air view.

282. Florence. Cathedral. Begun 1296. With Palazzo Vecchio.

more than a hundred years, it was obvious from the beginning that it was the projected dome that counted. Massive foundations were laid in preparation for it, while the long nave was built as economically as could be, with thin walls and wide spans, as if intended simply to enclose as much of the square as possible, in a totally different order 1of being from the sacred dome. Hence, the big geometric forms of baptistery, dome, and campanile were to shape the cityscape in the heart of Florence (figs. 280, 282). Later, when Brunelleschi finished the dome, Alberti was to say that it was "ample to cover with its shadow all the people of Tuscany."* It is thus seen as a swelling and maternal goddess-mother and a sacred

*Leon Battista Alberti, *On Painting*, rev. ed., translated and with introduction and notes by John R. Spencer, rev. edition, New Haven and London, 1966, p. 40.

mountain all at once, another Mount Jouctas, now lodged in the center of the town.

Already, at the very end of the thirteenth century, the dome, at least the hope of it, was joined by a very different kind of form, that of the Palazzo Vecchio (fig. 283), the town hall. It is a harshly surfaced, sharp-edged castle block, jaggedly crenelated, above which a high, aggressive bell tower thrusts. The tower and the dome were to be the major features of Florence's skyline, rising above it to its setting of soft hills, one swelling and full of peace like them, the other nervous, active, angry, ringing out the horrid tocsins of human culture: aggression, fear, defiance. Already "old," which is always culture's pretension, the Palazzo Vecchio shoves a hard, uncompromising edge of nastily roughened masonry out into an otherwise quite formless square. It does not shape the urban space but challenges it, invades it with its block. Michelangelo's *David* was to stand in front of it later, an image of heroic Florence, as aggressive as the building that rose behind it.

Next to the Palazzo Vecchio, and built later in the fourteenth century, its exact opposite opened to the square. It was a high, voluminous loggia like a great sounding board, from which the edicts of the council were read to the citizens of the town. Later, it acquired an ominous name, the Loggia dei Lanzi, recalling the German mercenary cavalry that was quartered there during the sixteenth century under the Medici dukes. The two buildings together can be taken as an exact image of government: harsh decision in one, announcement and persuasion in the other, one a fist, the other a voice.

These are the shapes of the city that Giotto loved; with them, he shaped the stage sets wherein the monumental actions of his people were framed. At Padua, his meeting of Joachim and Anna (fig. 284) outside Jerusalem's Golden Gate is set most specifically before a condensation of a building something like the new Palazzo Vecchio and a loggia (the Loggia dei Lanzi itself not yet built in Giotto's time) brought down in scale in order to shape an urban environment in which the actions of human beings can be read as large, dignified, and important. Giotto projected the sharp edge of the palace toward us and opened up a round-headed arched volume between the towers, from which a monumental humanity gushes with awesome force. It culminates in the bodies of Joachim and Anna brought together into a single domed figure, a sacred cone, a mountain that comes most alive at its very tip, where the eyes of the old people search each other out and their hands tremulously touch one another and the mountain becomes mankind.

Indeed, all of Giotto's great cycle in the Scrovegni Chapel in Padua, the Arena Chapel, where Dante visited him in 1306, is about human love and how it alone can

283. Florence. Palazzo Vecchio. Begun 1298.

284. Giotto. Arena Chapel, Padua. *Meeting of Joachim and Anna.* Fresco. 1305–1306.

atone, perhaps, for the terrible new sins that living in the new cities entails: the central sin of usury most of all. Dante, with his conservative, aristocratic view of things, most despised the moneylenders, whom he consigned to hell because their purses were marked with the stemma of their noble houses, now turned no longer toward nurturing mankind but toward bilking it, at least in Dante's view. One of them, the roughest of all, in fact, swaggers up to Dante (Vergil refuses to speak to them at all) and demands, "Che fai tu in questa fossa . . ." and later boasts, "Con questi fiorentin son Padovano."* It is Reginaldo Scrovegni, a banker from Padua among the Florentines, and it was in the hope of saving him from the hell to which Dante unhesitatingly assigned him that his son, Enrico Scrovegni, commissioned the building of the Arena Chapel and engaged Giotto to paint it.

So it is with the problem of the new life of the towns that this perhaps greatest of all European fresco cycles deals, with that and with the Virgin of the Annunciation, who alone may save even Reginaldo Scrovegni with her love. So she is planted in the chancel arch at Padua in a deep, illusionary niche (the Baptistery in its square) and receives the Annunciation from Gabriel in a shower of gold like Danaë's. Her aged parents look at each other in love when they learn that she will be born to them, and she and Elizabeth look at each other at the Visitation (the scene at Reims all charming French manners, this one all Italian peasant directness), and she and her child look at each other, poor Joseph asleep, and the infant literally sparkles back at her in his swaddling clothes, as if in delight at discovering what it means to be human.

*Dante Alighieri, *La Divinia commedia: Inferno,* Canto XVII, Rome, Editori Riunite, 1980.

286. Siena, Italy. Piazza del Campo.

285. Siena. Palazzo Pubblico. 1288–1309.

Finally, Christ and Mary Magdalene reach out to each other, though only with a glance, Christ saying to her, "Touch me not," and perhaps Scrovegni, who is right there below Gabriel as Judas with the money for which he sold Christ—a meager man at whom the high priest looks with loathing, while next to him, on the nave wall, Christ is driving the money changers from the temple—in the end perhaps even Scrovegni may be forgiven it all. Giotto's view seems clear: In this new world of money, it is only human directness, teaching love even to divinity, that can save mankind. Giotto's view, perhaps fundamentally Franciscan, represents a true growth in the conception of human nature, seen in the challenging context of the new human environment, which is that of the reviving towns.

It is all very Florentine, worthy of Dante in its piercing honesty, its curiously unquestionable truth, but Florentine, too, in the grand volumes of its human forms and the hollowed-out urban niches of the spaces in which their actions take place. But every town is different. The Palazzo Pubblico of Siena, for example, was being built at the same time as the Palazzo Vecchio in Florence, and there a different kind of urbanism was being shaped. The Palazzo Pubblico is without mass (fig. 285). It does not thrust three-dimensionally out into the square before it but defines it with its flat surface, bent as if responding to the needs of the urban space it contains. The whole Campo of Siena is shaped in that way (fig. 286). The palaces around it are treated as one simple continuous surface to contain it. They are without bulk, defining a miraculous volume of air in the hollow between the spines of the hills along which the solid masses of the town are flowing. They divide just there, leaving the open space itself slanting steeply down toward the Palazzo Pubblico. It is a slope dramatized by its very drainage, directed as it is into the earth near the center of the Palazzo Pubblico just slightly to one side of its porch and its high, thin tower.

So, though tower and portico are there, everything else is different from Florence, where it is all aggressive bulk and hard gray-green stone. Here, it is all surface and the lively colors of soft red brick and bright white trim. Exactly so were the paintings of Giotto and those of his Sienese contemporary Duccio different from each other (fig. 287). Duccio, with glowing reds and gleaming whites, set his figures in stages whose appearance of depth he masked, so that they would never seem to hollow out a niche in the surface of his painting. He was all Sienese, like the flat red and white palaces around the Campo. It was not a lack in him but the operation of a positive principle, the opposite of Giotto's. We see that contrast best in the famous comparison between the two Madonnas by these masters in the Uffizi.

Some of the most illuminating painting of people and towns at this period can be seen at Assisi, a place very different from Florence and Siena. It has to do with another aspect of the new urbanism, one that would lead in the end toward the Renaissance garden. Assisi is a typical Italic sacred site of the kind with which we have become familiar. It is on the slope of the mountains and can be seen from afar across the valley (fig. 288). There, St. Francis may be regarded as having introduced Christianity to nature, opening its attention out toward the landscape in a way that was perhaps more Hellenic than Roman. It is with a medieval, Christian fervor that he preaches to the birds, but he also seems to recognize their brotherhood to man in ways that Christianity had not done before.

So here is nature sacred once again on a windy slope in the Umbrian highlands, with the olives shimmering silver in the breeze and the heavy clouds riding above them, and we can feel the presence of St. Francis in all of that perhaps better than we can feel it in the Church of San Francesco that dominates the town. His followers had developed that basilica into a high-powered organ of Franciscan propaganda by the late thirteenth century, one of which it is doubtful that St. Francis himself would have entirely approved. Still, it has some fine frescoes in it, those in the upper church of the life of St. Francis painted by somebody whom few scholars of recent years have believed to be Giotto but who probably painted a good deal as Giotto may have painted in the years around 1300, before he went to Padua.

In any case, they are supremely contextual paintings, conceived in relation not only to the walls of the church on which they are placed but also to the town outside it, in which some of their scenes were made to occur. For example, in the three scenes into which each bay is divided, the two on the sides were normally painted below solid walls, which they hollow out illusionistically into deep niches, while that in the center, painted below the high, narrow window, encourages that void to slide illusionistically down through the center of the panel. As in Padua, the architecture of the building is enhanced, dramatized, and articulated by the painter.

So is the town outside. In the panel, painted under a solid wall, of the *Simple Man Venerating St. Francis* by spreading his cloak across a puddle before him (fig. 289), the action is augmented by a high tower behind the saint, a broad, open, pedimented colonnade above the cloak, and a palace with overhanging loggia on the right to frame two witnesses to the scene. The tower is there in Assisi, somewhat modified by the painter but close to its actual appearance, and the pedimented

287. Duccio. *Christ in White Robe Before Pilate,* from back of the Maesta Altar. Panel painting, 1308–1311.

288. Assisi, Italy. Distant view.

colonnade is that of the old Temple of Minerva beside it (fig. 290). The painter, Giotto or whoever, thinned out its columns to emphasize void rather than column sequence above the puddle, and its pediment was heightened to frame the action of flinging the cloak more dramatically; here the circle in the pediment helps as well. The palace on the right was inadequate to shape a volume of space for the witnesses to stand in. Hence, the painter endowed it with the porches projecting above. The environment of the town was made not only to frame but also to act with the actions of its citizens.

This was not anything especially new. Buildings had been used to frame and focus figural action in painting at least since Byzantine times, but never with this new flexible interaction and lively reality.

It is once again the new life of the town, the new township, that brings the human act and its environment into a heightened set of relationships. The same kind of interaction and lively modification take place in the panel of St. Francis renouncing his wealth and his father, and in that where he divides his cloak with a beggar (fig. 291). There, painted next to the Simple Man and under a window, the landscape itself becomes the major setting (fig. 292); its slopes and olive trees were painted with a passion that recalls Cennino Cennini's great treatise of the end of the century and can now suggest to us, as well, the technical passions of the years when Cubism was taking form. Both the painter at Assisi and, say, Braque in about 1908, conveyed the excitement of a pioneering way of painting that transforms the environment

290. Assisi. Temple of Minerva.

289. Assisi, upper church. *A Simple Man Venerating St. Francis.* Fresco, 1296–1304.

with its own new possibilities and demands, its fresh objective correlatives for nature's forms. Cubism, though, soon moved toward flat planes floating together in space, but this painter looked at the buildings of the town and made them literally more cubical, blocky, standing even more solidly and three-dimensionally in space than they do in actuality (fig. 291). Again, however, it is the excitement of the town that directed his hand and, here in this panel, not only the town but its olive-bearing hill slopes as well.

Yet what might be called the summa of the late medieval painting of cities was done not by a Florentine but in the Palazzo Pubblico in Siena. There are also some magical wooden panels from Siena showing jewellike towns set in rocky landscapes, all seen as from the heavens, but the frescoes in the Palazzo Pubblico sum up the new urban world. In the main hall, the condottiere *Guidoriccio da Fogliano,* by Simone Martini (fig. 293), rides high on the wall across an empty landscape, silent

291. Assisi. *St. Francis Gives His Coat to a Beggar.* Fresco. 1296–1304.

292. Assisi. San Francesco.

but suggestive of the rumors of war. A towered town crowns the highest hill, and a fortified camp lies lower down in the plain. Ropes suggestive of gallows hang from its walls. Chevaux-de-frise (perhaps inspiring the form of those employed by Kurosawa to shield his musketeers) rise up out of defilade; pikes lean against them. There are no human beings anywhere, only this puffy little god of war, Tolstoy's Napoleon to the life, who rides across the forlorn landscape as if he had cleared it out himself, the skirts of his horse's housing bouncing and flowing as he goes. The new

man has achieved devastation, but who can tell what yelling hordes may not yet materialize from the naked hills around him.

In the room beyond the *Guidoriccio,* a more comprehensive scene is set. It is the fresco sequence of *Good and Bad Government,* by Ambrogio Lorenzetti. One series shows a city and landscape under Good Government (fig. 294). It is much the larger, and better preserved. The other depicts a city and landscape as it is under Bad Government. The painter dealt more summarily with this distasteful theme. Good Government has the citizens dancing in the streets and squares of a city of many towers, below whose crenelated walls a steep road leads down to fields of golden grain and far off, rounded Tuscan hills, striped with vines.

The scene almost exactly reproduces the one that can still be experienced today at San Gimignano, in the hills not far north of Siena itself (fig. 295). The towers are still there, as they once were in Siena as well. The town crowns the slope; its walls are mostly gone, but its confines are sharply defined against the slopes and the vineyards below them. Clearly, the farmers live by choice not on their fields but in the town, in the ancient Mediterranean

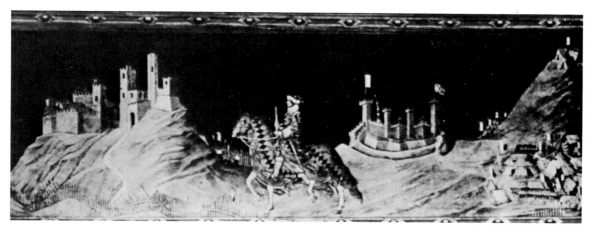

293. Simone Martini. Palazzo Pubblico, Siena. *Guidoriccio da Fogliano.* 1328.

294. Ambrogio Lorenzetti. Palazzo Pubblico, Siena. *The Allegory of Good Government*. Fresco. 1338–1340.

pattern so clear at Athens or Lindos. In the town, they compete with each other for political power or merely for personal advantage and glory. Their strife gives the town its form. It raises up the towers, each trying to outface the others. In his dark and profoundly perceptive novel *Where*

295. San Gimignano, Italy. Air view.

Angels Fear to Tread, E. M. Forster puts himself in the place:

> Close opposite, wedged between mean houses, there rose up one of the great towers. It is your tower: you stretch a barricade between it and the hotel, and the traffic is blocked in a moment. Farther up, where the street empties out by the church, your connections, the Merli and the Capocchi, do likewise. They command the Piazza, you the Siena gate. No one can move in either but he shall be instantly slain, either by bows or by cross-bows, or by Greek fire. Beware, however, of the back bedroom windows. For they are menaced by the tower of

the Aldobrandeschi, and before now arrows have struck quivering over the washstand. Guard these windows well, lest there be a repetition of the events of February 1338, when the hotel was surprised from the rear, and your dearest friend—you could just make out that it was he—was thrown at you over the stair.

"It reaches up to heaven," said Philip, "and down to the other place."*

That competition will go on fierce and bloody until the tower of the town hall rises over the others as it is seen to do

*E. M. Forster, *Where Angels Fear to Tread*, Cambridge, 1905, 1975, pp. 89–90.

today in San Gimignano, thus enforcing the will of the commune over those of the individuals who make it up. It is the fundamental truth of the town, and one that Americans, for example, have been loath to accept: that there can be no peace, no complete town either, until communal values transcend those of individual competition. Still, San Gimignano once used to be compared with downtown Manhattan, where the skyscrapers were clearly in competition with each other, so that perhaps the principle is, in fact, a dynamic one invoking at once competition *and* communal control, like the New York zoning laws out of which some of its greatest set-back skyscrapers took form.

The plan of the town is affected by competition as well. If we start with an ancient forum like that of Pompeii, for example (fig. 296), we find the post-Classical principle of ordered control; the spaces of the town have a positive shape that the architectural solids are intended to define. This suggests a central authority, probably, as was the case at Pompeii, far overshadowing that of the town itself. That authority falls apart in the early Middle Ages, at least on the whole, and the towns are left to fight it out on their own. So the houses press in on the square that contains the fountain; at San Gimignano, a tower rises up beside it to control the source of water if it can (fig. 297). Eventually, the commune manages to stabilize the situation. An irregular open area results. The town space is what is left over when the encroachment of the house masses is halted.

On the uphill side of that same square, near its intersection with the square that opens in front of the church, two towers rise. They are truncated, have been cut off, in fact; the tower of the town hall rises above them (fig. 295). It is a direct record of political events. The family in question tried to control the two squares and impede movement between them. The citizens of the town intervened; the family was overcome, and a loggia called the Loggia del Popolo was opened at the corner of their palace to provide easy public access to both squares. Finally, beyond the strife, opens the public space of the basilica, an ideal interior environment unique in the town and brightly striped with Sienese banded arches.

All of this, except for the interior of the church, is matched in Lorenzetti's fresco (fig. 294). The road slopes steeply down below the towers. Merchants travel on it in safety because above them the winged figure of Security guards the way, and down in the plain the peasants can beat

296. Pompeii, Italy. Civil forum. 1st century B.C. to 1st century A.D.

297. San Gimignano. Piazza della Cisterna. Circa 13th century.

the grain in peace. In the fresco of *Bad Government,* they are harassed by armored soldiery. Within the wall of the city, the painter becomes the first flâneur, like those who were to delight in the streets of nineteenth-century Paris. He leads us through the market square with all its activity; he conducts us with other tourists through the streets of the town. The buildings close in around us; a friend on horseback is just disappearing around the next corner; above him, the palazzi mass up, the loggias and the towers. In the fresco of *Bad Government,* the buildings are all shown in poor repair, haunted like the fields by sinister armed men. Finally, in the big square that stretches all across the foreground, the people dance, like those of the pueblos, while the travelers and traders still go on their way.

The governments that shape these towns are personified in figural form. Bad Government is a cross-eyed tyrant, who rules by brutal force. The vices to which politicians traditionally have been most prone, among them Avarice and Vainglory, hover around his head. Good Government is the majestic figure of the commune itself, to whose preeminence all the citizens of the town contribute. Indeed, they voluntarily grasp a golden cord that leads down from him and binds them all together. Again, communal values override those, very real as well, of individuals. In the center of the whole composition, not the largest figure but the one so posed and brightly colored as to dominate the whole, is in fact the embodiment of Peace, the greatest good the community can bring to mankind and upon which its own existence depends. Seen in its widest historical context, keeping in mind the pueblos of the Southwest, the cities of Mesopotamia, and the Greek polis, the *Allegory of Good Government* is the most complete pictorial representation we possess of the virtues that make the city, within itself and in relationship to the natural setting that supports it.

In the second half of the fourteenth century, the peace of the city was shaken not only by wars of various kinds but also by the Black Death, the deadliest enemy of all. Long before, a hymn to Asklepios

had said of man, "There is only death that he cannot escape from," and the Black Death struck the new urbanism, the new human confidence, a fearful blow. In Italy, when the towns had recovered from the disaster, the Renaissance began. That statement, ridiculously oversimplified on the face of it, is not far from the facts. What happened in Florence, where it can hardly be denied that the Renaissance first took shape, is the very best demonstration of it.

Deep in the industrial, mercantile heart of the city, a late medieval market had been built. It had thick Giottesque walls shaping deep open archways, so creating a monumental loggia for trade. After the Black Death, it was tranformed into a church, called Or San Michele, and the archways were filled in with tracery, so creating a thin, planar exterior masking the space within (fig. 298). Niches of varying depths had, however, been hollowed out of the walls in the first campaign of building. In the early fifteenth century, just at a time when Florence had decisively recovered its political as well as its economic vitality, those niches began to be filled with sculptural figures. One of them was Donatello's *St. George* (fig. 299), whom we may perhaps be allowed to re-

298. Florence. Or San Michele. 1337–1404.

299. Donatello. *St. George*. Circa 1415–1417.

gard as the embodiment of the first modern man.

Unlike the comparable figure traditionally identified as *St. Theodore* (but perhaps Roland) on the south porch of Chartres, Donatello's *St. George* is a nervous, aggressive figure, taut and staring. He plants his feet wide and rocks forward; his head is cocked, his gaze paranoiac. He is tight-strung with anxiety and expects the worst. Originally, his sword struck straight out in space not far over the heads of the passersby in the street below him. *St. Theodore,* by contrast, is wholly unstrained, not aggressive; though he stands firmly on his feet, he is also bound back into the body of the cathedral that supports him. He is part of the environment; it is his strength; he needs no other. *St. George* stands alone. This was especially

apparent when the statue was still in its original niche, where a replica can be seen today. That niche is unusually shallow, so that the figure seems thrust out of it, pushed into the void. Unlike *St. Theodore, St. George* has been liberated to act on his own and is by the same token no longer protected or sustained by the environment (call it that of medieval Christianity) whose constraints he has cast off or which has cast him out.

So the Renaissance, right at its beginning, liberates the individual and leaves him alone in the world. At the same time, paradoxically, and in a very modern way as well, the Renaissance also wished to create a perfect environment for the individual, one wholly controlled, Utopian, and complete. The modern age has continued to aim for both those irreconcilable objectives—liberation and protection—ever since. The Renaissance solution was Neoplatonic, involving the reliable old circle in the square. Its centrally planned churches, such as Santa Maria della Consolazione at Todi, were built around those shapes, still the images of perfect universal order (fig. 458a). They were first used during the Renaissance in this regard by Brunelleschi, at the end of the very decade in which Donatello's *St. George* was made.

Brunelleschi, we remember, is also reputed to have invented perspective. Whatever the case, he clearly enough put one-point perspective together with the circle and the square in his loggia for the Foundling Hospital in Florence (fig. 300). Here, the fundamental Neoplatonic connection of pure beauty with pure drawing, uncompromised by gross matter, is beautifully realized. All the solids, diminishing into impeccable perspective distances, are reduced to pure lines, like those, for example, of Leonardo's drawing. They literally *draw* the volumes of cube and sphere

300. Florence. Ospedale deglie Innocenti. 1421–1424. Filippo Brunelleschi. Arcade.

301. Florence. Santissima Annunziata with colonnade.

in space, so shaping an architecture of air rather than of solid masses. We cannot help but be reminded of Suger and his columns thin as metal tubes (figs. 221, 222), tautly joined to the thin canopy of ribs above them, but there is an important difference. Suger's ideal universe is being shaped inside, Brunelleschi's outside, defining the space of a square. It is the projection of a will to control not merely a single building as an image of heaven but the actual urban environment as a whole— *this* world, not the next. The entire facade of the Foundling Hospital is a space definer, urbanistically conceived, its columns and arches drawn together in one plane by the flat, thin wall above them. It is not intended to project an aggressive mass but to shape the urban space before it.

That suggestion almost immediately was taken up in the piazza as a whole (fig. 301). The facade of the Annunziata was clothed in similar arcades, and that of the building across the way was eventually screened in the same way. The piazza thus became a perspective box. The space was the positive element, a shaped environment, which the architectural solids were intended to serve. The difference between this piazza and the squares of San Gimignano is complete (fig. 297). Here, the piazza is distinguished by a new spatial absolutism rather than by the old conflict between individual architectural masses where the principle of design, if so politically dynamic a process may be called that, was indeed mass-positive, space negative.

The equestrian figure of Ferdinando I, introduced into the piazza by the Medici, completed the new image. Individual authority, embodied in sculptural action, shaped the space. The city had become an extension of the individual will. Beyond that, it seems fair to say that in America, and during Classical Antiquity and the

302. Piero della Francesca. *Flagellation*. Circa 1456–1457.

303. Rome, Italy. Piazza Campidoglio. Michelangelo. From 1536. Air view.

Middle Ages, space, even when directed along an axis or enclosed, was read as the interval between objects or the hollow within them. Now, with perspective, it is the positive, the directing element in any composition, the structure of the field in which solid objects are placed. How reasonable it was that the painters of the fifteenth century, newly endowed with the tool of "divine perspective," should have understood this so well (fig. 302). Now it was they who, through illusion, could create environments more complete than architects could bring about in fact, and could populate them with more awesome images of human action than sculptors could easily realize. From this moment, therefore, the painter became the most powerful artistic force in the visual arts of Western civilization. He became the great experimental artist, normally calling the tune for everyone else. And from that, exacerbated by the painter's embrace of abstraction and by the architect's irrational determination to rival the painter in freedom to abstract and to invent, some of the most important and disastrous developments in twentieth-century urbanism were to derive.

Only Michelangelo, perhaps, was far beyond it all in whatever art he chose to employ. His Campidoglio in Rome is a demonstration far beyond the resources of painting of what architecture and sculpture fundamentally, unequivocally, are (fig. 303). He affirms that architecture is a space, an environment. The buildings are pushed back to shape that space, to bring it into being. But sculpture is in the center. It is active; it seems to push the solid buildings back. It says that the human act creates the environment, shapes the human world. To lift the image of that act to the zenith, Michelangelo drew on his pictorial skills. He designed a pavement that looked illusionistically like a dome rising in the void. It was not installed until after World War II, but now it lifts the sculptural figure into the empyrean that is created when the solids are pushed back on either side.

This is the foundation of Italian Baroque urbanism, wherein the human act in sculpture is seen as shaping the environment, but nowhere else is it carried out with Michelangelo's tragic grasp of the event. Elsewhere, it tends to become fine theater; the figural sculptures are actors on a stage. The whole affair becomes a theatrical extension of Giotto's fundamental unity of action and setting and a normalization of Michelangelo's titanic vision of the creative act itself.

Piazza Navona shows that relationship as well as any Roman square (fig. 304). The figures gesture; the fountains play. Eventually, the artificial illumination of the city, which could rarely be rivaled in the countryside, would enormously extend the day for human beings and make the urban theater the richest setting for their imaginative lives. The famous map of Rome by G. B. Nolli, of 1748 (fig. 305), not only shows us the radiating avenues of Sixtus V, which seek to unify the city, but also presents the quarter around the Piazza Navona as a new kind of manmade landscape (fig. 306): no sidewalks yet, but streets like paths flowing between the building solids and then opening out into

stony bosquets of courtyards and church interiors. There is the Pantheon's universal hollow, hidden behind its Greek colonnade; there is Borromini's St. Ivo, modeling space like one of Hadrian's pumpkins at the end of a long court; there is St. Agnese flinging up its towers near the center of the great piazza (fig. 304), its dome pushed forward enough so that all three elements can seem to play a counterpoint of act and environment with Bernini's fountain before them.

Within, the special grandeur and release of domed space offers itself as a Roman climax to the urban experience as a whole. It is the city made as much fun as the city was ever to be. Only Paris was to rival it, and Rome and Paris are, curiously enough, the most "natural"—let us say the most like gardens—of all great cities in their own entirely different and wholly manmade ways. In both of them, the basic work of shaping the spaces was done by palazzo blocks, and these are a supremely Italian form. At Piazza Na-

306. Giambattista Nolli. *Pianta Grande di Roma.* 1748. Piazza Navona and environs.

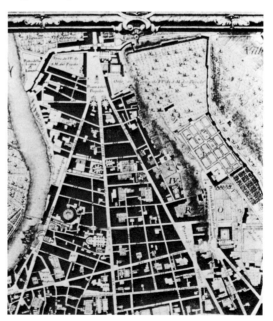

305. Giambattista Nolli. *Pianta Grande di Roma.* 1748. Piazza del Popolo to Piazza di Spagna.

vona, they are like those of Siena, one long, flat backdrop defining the space. But *palazzo* also means an urban block in Italian, so that *fare un giro del palazzo* means to go around the block.

The Palazzo Medici-Riccardi in Florence was, with Brunelleschi's Pitti, one of the first of all Renaissance palazzi, and it was wholly expressive of the new banking age, of power in money rather than in communal government or even in arms (fig. 307). Compared with the Palazzo Vecchio (fig. 283), it does not gesture. It closes solidly in upon itself, though its corner arcades were originally open, and it is capped by one of the first and most boldly conceived of Renaissance Classical cornices, shaping a powerful horizontal gesture defining the street. Outside, the palace is closed and rusticated in horizontal layers, weighty and keeping their own counsel, while, within, the court is a melody of delicate columns, derived from those of Brunelleschi.

The Medici-Riccardi received additions later and was, in any event, always asymmetrical in conception. The Strozzi may be said to have regularized the type. And the palazzo block was to become, in fact, the basic urban type in European architecture, far transcending changes of style and, indeed, challenging the nineteenth-century idea of the dominance of style in human art. It is a building unit with which dense, firmly defined streets and squares can be built. So, like Greek temples but for a totally different reason, each palazzo block is much like all others, so that they can all get along with each other to shape the city. But each can be decorated differently for individuality and variety. Here is another way in which the individual can remain individual but still submit as necessary to communal requirements. Hence, the traditional architectural

307. Florence. Palazzo Medici-Riccardi. Begun 1444. Michelozzo.

308. Rome. Palazzo Farnese. Begun 1515. Antonio da Sangallo the Younger, Michelangelo. Air view.

aphorism that one should decorate construction, never build decoration, is a sound one in urbanistic terms. It simply means that individuality should be subordinated to type, as should style.

In the twentieth century, the International Style of modern architecture, especially in its later phases, was to forget that sound advice, and it helped tear the traditional city apart by trying to make each building individual in massing as well as in surface detail. Soon everything but the work of Mies van der Rohe, which had other problems, was standing on one finger and kicking its legs in the air. The Renaissance knew better. So the Farnese (fig. 308) flaunts its great cornice and draws its sharp horizontal stringcourses and sounds a variety of notes with the pediments of its windows, but it remains a block, *the* building block that makes the city as a whole.

That block could be decorated in many different ways without injuring its fundamental urbanistic role. Alberti traced a thin and elegant web of pilasters and entablatures across the surface rustication of the Rucellai. Palladio in Vicenza was especially adept in variety of treatment. His Palazzo Iseppo Porto (fig. 309) supports robust engaged columns and heavy balustrades on an arcuated and rusticated base suggested by the work of Raphael and Giulio Romano. In the Palazzo Thiene (fig. 310), Palladio permitted a much rougher rustication to take over the whole surface, turning the palazzo into a brutal presence suggestive of the daimon of the countryside but wholly urban at the same time in respecting the city's communal laws, as the otherwise somewhat similar Brutalism of the 1950s and 1960s was not able to do (fig. 490). Moreover, the decorated facade for house or palace is special to European civilization; it does not occur

309. Vicenza, Italy. Palazzo Iseppo Porto. Begun circa 1550. Andrea Palladio.

310. Vicenza. Palazzo Thiene. Circa 1545–1550. Andrea Palladio.

311. Vicenza. Palazzo Valmarana. 1566. Andrea Palladio.

312. St. Louis, Missouri. Wainwright Building. 1890–1891. Adler & Sullivan.

313. New York, N.Y. Lever Brothers Building. 1952. Skidmore, Owings, and Merrill.

314. St. Louis. Wainwright Building. Restoration and annex. 1974.

at all in the Far East, for example. There, everything is private, hidden from the populace. But the Western Facade, pompous or silly as it may sometimes be, is an effort toward communal dialogue; it wants to tell the rest of the city about what its owner is or thinks. Most of all, it enriches the communal experience as no blank wall can do.

Touchingly, Louis Sullivan's Wainwright Building in St. Louis, his first steel-framed skyscraper, seems almost to have been modeled on one of the richest and most complex Renaissance facades that remains to us, that of Palladio's Palazzo Valmarana in Vicenza (figs. 311, 312). Colossal pilasters seem to push the base down and the attic up in both buildings, causing them to stand out from the buildings on both sides of them while remaining respectful of them and, indeed, depending on them for their urban context on the street. The International Style was to despise that traditional urban context and so cut holes in the street in order to show off its buildings as anarchic individuals. Lever House, as we noted in the first chapter, began the process in New York (fig. 313). When, as it were, the International Style caught up with the Wainwright Building in 1974—when, that is, the buildings around the Wainwright were torn down—Sullivan's building lost its presence, because it had been designed in the traditional way, with the buildings around it in mind (fig. 314).

The principle that Sullivan understood was one of the essential principles of urban

building that the Renaissance explored, that of individuality tempered by context or, perhaps better, of context as a spur to individuality. The latter phrase surely characterizes the work of Robert Venturi at the present time. His Wu Hall at Princeton (fig. 315) enhances the presence of the two preexisting Tudorish buildings on the site but at the same time stretches its own mass to a new, lively tautness. Similarly, Venturi's addition to the National Gallery in London (fig. 316) picks up the best feature of the old building, its colossal colonnades, and distributes them at ever-increasing intervals and decreasing density

317. Philadelphia, Pennsylvania. Institute for Scientific Information. 1978. Venturi, Rauch & Scott Brown.

315. Princeton, New Jersey. Wu Hall. Completed 1983. Venturi, Rauch & Scott Brown.

316. London, England. The Sainsbury Wing: An Extension to the National Gallery. Begun 1986, completed 1991. Venturi, Rauch & Scott Brown.

across its own facade, nudging his cadenza of pilasters with smaller pilasters from behind, while the last becomes a column, calling to the big one, Nelson's Column, that stands in the middle of Trafalgar Square before it. At the same time, Venturi's Institute for Scientific Information in Philadelphia (fig. 317), largely housing computers, seems at first almost dumbly International Style in form. Why? Clearly because of its context of International Style office buildings and garages, in which a Tudorish or Classical building would have looked absurd. But Venturi then decorated his building's facade as no International Style architect would have done. The principle remains constant: contextuality, not a jealous style, is literally the determinant of the design, which is, however, enlivened by human wit, by decoration, in every instance. Each existing environment is made just a little better, and livelier, than it was before, and on its own terms. This is the way the city renews itself but keeps its form.

It is true that the Renaissance was by no means guiltless of Utopian dreams. It,

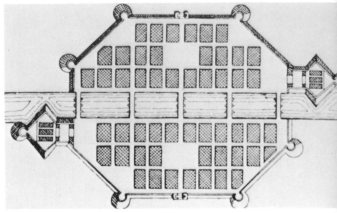

318. Francesco di Giorgio Martini. Ideal city. 15th century. Plan.

too, sometimes yearned for vast open spaces, all new, that would blow the dense fabric of its cities apart. True enough, most ideal city schemes, such as those by Francesco di Giorgio (fig. 318), respected the solid definition of streets and squares by palazzo blocks. But some ideal views, such as that attributed to Laurana in the Walters Art Gallery (fig. 319), perhaps intended as a stage set, ripped the solid geometries of palace, colosseum, baptistery, and triumphal arch wholly out of

319. Luciano Laurana. Architectural perspective. 1450–1475.

context and set them in an enormous perspective space. It seems only one step from
that to the blasted environment of the
modern urban connector (figs. 423, 424),
and we are perhaps fortunate that the
means of the Renaissance were normally
more limited than our own, so that its
most ruthless schemes were rarely carried
out.

We have, however, the lovely and very
restricted sketch of such a scheme constructed in the town of Pienza, sited along
a high ridge south of Siena. There the hu-
manist Pope Pius II, Pio Piccolomini, who
called himself Aeneas Silvius, opened out
a little square in the center of his home-
town, with the triumphal arch of a new
cathedral on its axis (fig. 320), the small
palace of the bishop on one side and his
own big palace on the other. Both palace
blocks are set along expanding diagonals,
so that there is the sense of opening to a
distant view (fig. 321). A major feature of
that view is Monte Amiata, a conspicuous
landscape feature on the road between
Siena and Rome and one of the few Italian
mountains that seems to stand free of the
chain (fig. 322). Aeneas Silvius had
climbed Amiata, as no medieval man before Petrarch would have done, and he
directed the view from his palace in Pienza
toward it. The building progressively
opens from the tight little square of the
town through its own columned courtyard out to an open loggia facing the
mountain on the horizon. From the loggia, one looks across a strictly contained
medieval garden down below to the vastness of nature itself, with the body of the
mountain climaxing the view. In this way,
the sacred mountain was brought back
into human focus once more, and when,
almost immediately, the new gardens of
the sixteenth century began to be built, it
was the archetypal sacred mountain, the

320. Pienza, Italy. Cathedral. 1460–1463. Bernardo
Rossellino.

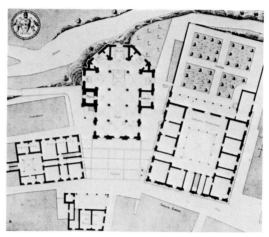

321. Pienza. Plan.

322. Pienza. Palazzo Piccolomini. View of the Val d'Orcia
and Monte Amiata from loggia.

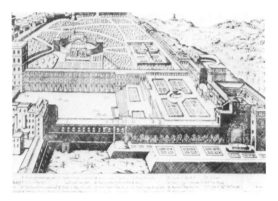

323. Rome. Vatican. Courtyard of the Belvedere. Donato Bramante. Engraving by Ambrogio Brambilla, 1579.

Temple of Fortuna Primigenia at Praeneste, that served as their inspiration.

Bramante, in the very years when he was building the new basilica of St. Peter's, with its vast projected dome, literally brought that sacred mountain into the Vatican and set it down at the end of his courtyard of the Belvedere, directly opposite the rising body of the church itself (fig. 323). Praeneste's steep face, its ramps, and the hemicycle were all there (fig. 183). It was a blatant and wonderful declaration: Antiquity, pagan or not, was alive again. The old open landscape, sacred once more, was made to balance the interior world of the dome of heaven across the way.

From this time on, the garden became a major program of Renaissance architecture and in many ways perhaps its most original, intellectually stirring, and important one.* Praeneste remained the model. The Villa d'Este at Tivoli (figs. 324, 325), by Pirro Ligorio, was also based upon it. But in Antiquity, Tivoli itself might have looked a good deal like Prae-

*For its documentation see now: Claudia Lazzaro, *The Italian Renaissance Garden,* New Haven and London, 1990.

326. Tivoli. Villa d'Este. View toward Rome.

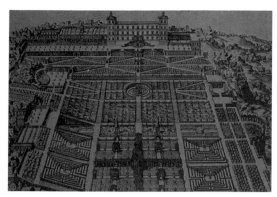

324. Tivoli, Italy. Villa d'Este. Begun 1550. Pirro Ligorio. Engraving by E. Dupérac, 1573.

325. Tivoli. Villa d'Este. Garden facade.

neste. There were two sanctuaries of Hercules nearby at least, and Hercules still holds the hill slope at Tivoli; he is, after all, the demigod who cleans up nature for mankind and so makes the garden possible. The creation of gardens thus became a very special kind of human activity. Human beings began to shape na-

327. Tivoli. Villa d'Este. Garden, water organ fountain.

ture itself once again, and in so doing could hardly help but endow the landscape with their own characters. Indeed, they set out to do just that, and the garden architects of the Renaissance believed that their clients could be personified in the garden more richly and truly than was possible in the villa or the palace itself.

At Tivoli, for example, the climactic line of a hundred fountains leads us toward the Rometta, professing to be a model of Rome, and there the goddess Roma is joined by the stemma of the Este with its eagle and fleurs-de-lis. The client signs the garden. It is himself, and it is linking him, humanistically, like Aeneas Silvius on Monte Amiata, with the Antique world and its divinities in the landscape. So at Tivoli the viewing pavilion at the summit of the climb is canted just a few degrees off the axis of the villa behind it in order

to focus on two conical hills rising out in the plain (fig. 326). Ancient sacred presences are being consciously invoked. Behind the slope at Tivoli, the body of the Appenines is rent by the Grotto of the Sybil, above which the Romans erected a tholos temple and in whose depths the waters of the earth can be heard roaring like Poseidon deep underground.

Therefore, in the garden of the Villa d'Este, water once again is called upon to play the central role (fig. 327). It is being pumped up from below, in fact, but the effect is of its gushing abundantly out of the earth, out of Fortuna Primigenia herself, the nurse of the god. Water jets from the hundred fountains and the breasts of sphinxes, and it roars out from below the water organ, rusticated, dark, and cornice-horned, that is the dominant feature of the northern slope. Again, as in Rome, it is the mountainside and the water that count. The garden is evoking the ancient Roman sacred site to the life, and it is using it as a vehicle for attitudes and emotions that can only be described as Romantic, calling up as they do a delicious terror of the wild earth and a profoundly emotional enthusiasm for its powers. As such, the Italian garden is the direct ancestor of English Romanticism and of its "Poetic" and "Picturesque" gardens.

But the English garden, for all its many charms, was to remain a pallid reflection of the Mediterranean passion. There is no true fear in the English garden, in its soft, domesticated landscape, under its wet and gentle skies. Nor was there any strong tradition in English culture that traditionally feared nature and insisted that the only life for human beings was the life of the towns. In Italy, the terror of nature was far older than Christianity; it was built into the structure of Mediterranean culture as a whole. Only in the polis, in the po-

329. Titian. *The Death of Actaeon.* Oil on canvas. Circa 1559.

litical life of the town, could a human being be truly human. Nature, the very embodiment of ultimate divinity, was terrifying not only in its absolute power but also in its lack of intent. Only mankind, the political animal, intended something.

Christianity seized that archetypal instinct. Baptism makes the citizen. Joachim is banished from Jerusalem because he has failed to produce a child. In wild, hard nature, thorny, rocky, and sunstruck, the citizen might well become a *bestia,* an animal, something far less than a man. Giotto shows Joachim as unresponsive as

the rock behind him when he is greeted by men and animals at his farm, to which he has been driven in exile from the town. Later, at his sacrificial fire, he crouches like a beast. The gardens explore that fear of regression, loving it.

The Villa Lante at Bagnaia (fig. 328), by Vignola, is probably the most eloquent on this theme. We start in the town at the foot of the mountain: the good, proud, sharp-edged, manmade town. From there, we enter a gate in a mythical wall. What can lie behind it? In fact, it opens upon a broad, geometric parterre with a deep basin

330. Bagnaia. Villa Lante. View from the garden toward the town.

328. Bagnaia, Italy. Villa Lante. Begun 1574. G. B. Vignola.

of water lifted in its center, above which the stemma of the Montalto is flaunted in the air. Beyond the parterre, the villa is divided into two pavilions, one on the left, one on the right, with the ramps of Praeneste and Tivoli mounting between them toward a dark, heavily wooded garden. This climbs the mountainside toward secret pools and springs and is continued by a wooded park that climbs farther up the slopes—who knows, perhaps into the unknown heart of the mountain itself.

With what sinister courtesy the villa opens up to invite us into the wild. How dark it is under the trees. As we press onward, the shaggy shapes of forest beings and river gods, water-worn, emerge, half human, half animal, covered with moss. Human shapes are merging back into nature, perhaps beyond the animal to the vegetable world. We are reminded of Titian's *Death of Actaeon* in London (fig. 329), where Actaeon, having penetrated too far into virgin nature and come upon Diana unclothed, is changed by her into a stag and is set upon by his own hounds. As Titian paints him he is literally dissolving into the thickets of the forest, a *bestia* and worse. Then, ideally, we are meant to know the truth of the wilderness, which is panic fear.

Water is running down through the center of the garden, running as if in flight off the mountain and sometimes leaping

331. Bomarzo. Sacro Bosco. Hercules killing Antaeus.

333. Bomarzo. Sacro Bosco. Fame with the Orsini Palace.

332. Bomarzo. Sacro Bosco. Woman on Tortoise, an Image of Fame.

over the crouching water gods, sometimes rushing in narrow channels as down long, grooved stone tables set in the ground. Now at last, we are *of* the water. We run with it, leap with it, branches whipping our eyes, until suddenly the villa opens into its two parts once again, this time, miraculously, to let us out, to let us see the civilized parterre, but more than that, far more than that, to show us the city out there in the light beyond the forest, the work of man, our refuge and our only home (fig. 330).

The Italian Renaissance garden was sometimes able to explore human culture, memory, and primal fear even more disquietingly than that. At Bomarzo, in deep Etruscan country, Vicinio Orsini built himself a garden in the valley below his ancestral castello on the hill. He had volunteered for service under the French king and had been captured by the ancient Imperial enemy from across the Rhine. For some reason, he had been at least psychologically mistreated as a captive and went in fear of his life for a time. Eventually released, he returned to this valley and built his garden as a kind of haunted grove, embodying his hopes and fears,

334. Bomarzo. Sacro Bosco. Pegasus.

perhaps even what he had felt and seen.

It is a sacred wood, full of disquieting monuments, some seeming to grow out of the rock itself. The original entrance and axes of movement along its slopes can only be conjectured. The intended sequence of experiences is therefore not clear, perhaps was never meant to be so. The path through the modern entrance is perhaps as good as any other. It leads downward toward the trees, crossing a little watercourse leading farther into the depths of the forest. Directly ahead, stand-

336. Bomarzo. Sacro Bosco. War Elephant.

ing in the light across a gentle open field, a good, rationally abstract chapel can be seen, columned and domed, but the path does not lead toward it. Instead, it turns away from it down the darkening slope. Soon, hewn out of the natural rock, Hercules rises before us, tearing the giant Cacus to pieces in his hands (fig. 331). He is guarding the garden for us but is markedly alarming, nonetheless. Finally, we come to the deepest part of the forest, and the darkest. There the stream runs into a cleft in the earth and disappears with a gurgling sound like a cut throat. The horrible gargle is surely enhanced by the whale's mouth, all teeth and gullet, into which the living rock at the mouth of the crevice has been carved.

Right there, looming over the cavern, an enormous round-eyed tortoise has been

335. Bomarzo. Sacro Bosco. Amphitrite.

carved out of the rock (fig. 332). On its back, the figure of a woman, apparently sounding a trumpet, is placed. We know from the emblem book of the Cavaliere Ripa that she is an image of Fame—Fame lost down here in the depths of the wood, sounding her trumpet in the wild, while high above her the Orsini Castle can be seen shining in the sun (fig. 333). There is no connection between the two, no apparent route from this place to that. The effect is again bestial—the woman is, after all, right out of the Apocalyptic Vision of St. John, mounted as if in ecstasy upon a beast. The heir to the palace of the Bears is lost in the wood. But just beyond Fame, in the darkness of the forest, a bright light gleams. It is Pegasus, the winged horse, symbol of hope, touched by a ray of sun, rearing up in the darkness (fig. 334). He shows us the only route to follow out of here. It is a sinister-enough path through the wood: "Nel mezzo del cammin di nostra vita / mi ritrovai per una selva oscura."*

As we follow it upward, we are led further into dream. Goddesses of earth re-

*Dante Alighieri, *La Divina commedia, Inferno,* Canto I, lines 1–2.

338. Bomarzo. Sacro Bosco. "Tempietto." Attributed to Vignola.

cline like Etruscan matrons in the rock, heavy and somnolent, bearing urns upon their heads (fig. 335). A house appears before us in a sunlit glade. It is leaning steeply into the hill. We mount ever higher beyond it. A war elephant looms up: A castle crowns its back, and a mahout sits upon its head (fig. 336). It is lifting the broken body of a soldier in its trunk. An enormous lizard flares beside it. We are climbing out of the depths, but the images around us are becoming more alarming all the while. At last our dream, the guardian of our sleep, is broken by a figure of true nightmare: a colossal screaming face, as big as a house, demolishing the censor, awaking us as if to our own scream (fig. 337). And then, awake, we are out (fig. 338), standing in the sunshine beside the mercifully abstract chapel we saw before and looking beyond it toward the palace, bathed now in clear white light, but remembering still the woman on the beast deep in the wood and pondering the meaning of our unaccountable yearning for Fame.

337. Bomarzo. Sacro Bosco. "Gate of Hell."

9

THE FRENCH CLASSIC GARDEN: THE ART OF *POURTRAITURE*

THE ITALIAN GARDEN OF the Renaissance is personal. It explores the character of the individual and celebrates his newfound, fundamentally Romantic relation to nature and to the pagan past. The French Classic garden is personal, too, but it comes to be profoundly political as well, and revolves at last around the person of the king.

In an earlier chapter, I tried to show that Gothic architecture was from the first the symbol of the king of France, its forms the very hallmark of his kingdom. In fact, it did a great deal to create the image of being French and to give body to the idea of French nationality that enabled France to withstand the terrible

355. Vaux-le-Vicomte. Air view from entrance side.

strains of the later Middle Ages, especially those of the Hundred Years War. Joan herself is a direct product of the Gothic program, the virgin who saves France. So the kings of the Renaissance, too, could be laid to rest under the heavenly light that linked them with a cosmic order. In Gothic architecture, that order was conceived in terms of interior space, as had

been the case in the West since the time of Rome. It was through the creation of an ideal interior universe that the connection of human beings with the cosmos had been conceived throughout the Christian centuries.

By the seventeenth century, however, when the kings of France wished to create a new image of cosmic order with which they and the realm could be identified, it was no longer with interior space that they were primarily concerned but, for the first time since Antiquity, with the space of the natural world, and with that kind of architecture— the garden—that connects the manmade and the natural at the scale of the entire visible environment. Hence, it was once more the exterior rather than the interior program that became the basic vehicle of meaning. In that program, buildings became incidents in, or ways to define, exterior space. Behind it, of course, lay the example of the Italian Renaissance garden, which, however, the French drastically reshaped and transformed.

342. Versailles. Palace. Louis Le Vau and Jules Hardouin-Mansart. Garden side.

221

340. Versailles. Palace. Forecourt.

None of this has as yet been written about very well in terms of form and meaning. Writing about Gothic architecture, one could refer to those scholars who have explored its fundamental shapes and meanings in different ways: especially Viollet-le-Duc and Jean Bony in terms of structure and Otto von Simson in terms of symbol. No such reference can be made in quite the same way about the French Classic garden. There are some reasonable books of various sizes about French gardens,* but serious modern exploration of

*Ernest de Ganay, *André Le Nostre 1613–1700,* Paris, 1962; William Howard Adams, *The French Garden, 1500–1800,* New York, 1977; Kenneth Woodbridge, *Princely Gardens,* New York, 1986.

339. Versailles, France. Palace and environs. 1662ff. Air view.

the meaning of the French Classic garden simply does not exist. A recent book about Le Nôtre ascribes the whole vast series of programs to a simple love of "display," apologizes for its grandeur, and says nothing whatever about iconography.*

The young scholars who are now working in the archives may soon change all that. In my opinion, however, the best book yet written about French gardens in terms of an analysis of meaning is Lucien Corpechot's of 1910, which he called *Les Jardins de l'intelligence.* It was republished

in 1937 by Marguerite Charageat, who stands, I think, with Corpechot as the best writer on this subject and on gardens in general.* Corpechot insists that the basic quality of the French Classic garden is that it bends nature to the laws of human intelligence. But he does more than that. His analysis also connects the garden with the army, and with war. He says of it, and I translate: "From hours passed in a crowd, we leave with our souls broken, twisted, while from a military review, where trained and well-commanded regiments have passed in review in a perfect order, we draw renewed moral comfort, a quiet

---

*Franklin Hamilton Hazlehurst, *Gardens of Illusion: The Genius of André Le Nostre,* Nashville, 1980. But see now: Thierry Mariage, *L'Univers de Le Nostre,* Brussels, 1990.

*Marguerite Charageat, *L'Art des jardins,* Paris, 1962.

without equal."* It is the same, he says, for Versailles, "where Le Nôtre knew how to make a disciplined army of the crowd of trees and plants of all kinds, [and] wherein, with the waters and the earth and the sky itself, he subjected all imponderables and bent them to the laws of human intelligence."†

So in 1910, in the first modern work of scholarship about French gardens, a parallel is drawn between them and the military art; and in a later chapter I will try to consider the fortifications of Vauban in this connection. But from the very beginning, and certainly in the seventeenth century itself, gardens and fortifications were considered as closely related arts for many obvious reasons having to do with their common command of topography. In the early twentieth century—largely because of the French obsession with *revanche* after her defeat by Prussia in 1871—the parallel drawn was even more specifically between Classic gardens and the military virtues. It is quite clear that by 1900 France was trying to gird herself again for what Le Corbusier, himself a product of this phenomenon, was later to call "*La Grande Epreuve.*" She wanted to destroy the nineteenth-century Offenbachist image of herself as a superficial and decadent civilization and to call up some stern national characteristics—and not of a kind associated with the Middle Ages, which she tended to assign at that time to the irrational, "oriental," Germans.

The connection that the French hoped to make in 1910 was with Classic Antiquity, especially with Greece and most particularly with Sparta. Therefore, Corpechot goes on to say that only the French

understand how to make Classic gardens. The Germans, he says, do not understand this kind of order, where divinity is seen in "a civilized parterre." They, on the contrary, worship their gods by burning people alive in wicker cages. He says that what the French are after is much more like what the Greeks wanted, except that "the stern lines of Greek temples found their natural prolongation in the shapes of the landscape,"* while the French had to turn to landscape architecture to create that relationship. Aside from his chauvinism, he is not far wide of the mark.

The resurrection of the garden also involved the beginning of an attempt to rehabilitate the reputation of Louis XIV. The royalist historian, Bertrand, as late as 1924, was writing that Louis "at least knew how to deal with the enemies of France."† Still, the best that can be said about the reputation of Louis XIV is that, throughout history, he has had a very mixed press. Directly after his death in 1715, his reputation was at its nadir, but it was no less a figure than Voltaire who first tried to rehabilitate it. Voltaire entitled his history of seventeenth-century France *Le Siècle de Louis Quatorze,* and he pointed out that Louis had organized France as a modern state in a way that no ruler before him had been able to do. In the nineteenth century, colonial-minded historians tended to dwell on the theme that Louis had injured France by caring more about the loss of a fortress on the Rhine than about the liquidation of the colonial empire. Today, of course, one is not so sure that they were correct, in view of the fact that France, like all other European nations, has lost her empire but remains a viable modern state in large part

---

*Lucien Corpechot, *Les Jardins de l'intelligence,* Paris, 1910; 2nd ed., Paris, 1937, p.33.

†Ibid., p. 81.

*Ibid., p. 22.

†Louis Bertrand, *Louis XIV,* Paris, 1924.

because of the continental conformation that Louis engineered for her.

One act by Louis that everyone has found sympathetic was his writing and re-writing of a little treatise on how to show the gardens of Versailles to visitors. He called it *Manière de montrer les jardins de Versailles.** He tells us that we must begin by entering through the Court of Marble that faces the town of Versailles. That court was the heart of the château of Louis XIII, Louis XIV's father; and Versailles as rebuilt by Louis XIV always respected the shape and character of the old building, especially as it was seen on the entrance side, where Louis would never permit his architects to rebuild it in any substantive way. He simply wrapped vast new con-structions around it and made the garden facade the more important one. The ad-ditions were fundamentally one room deep, though eventually of considerable lateral extension.

*Published with a preface by Raoul Girardet, Paris, 1951, and commented upon extensively since and now in a delightful new edition, beautifully illustrated: Si-mone Hoog, *Louis XIV: Manière de Montrer les Jardins de Versailles,* Paris, 1982.

However, when we approach the Court of Marble today, we see a good many things on the entrance side that were not there in Louis' greatest days. To our right, for example, rises the rather Gothic profile of the chapel (fig. 340), which breaks the horizontality of the main building mass behind it. The chapel with its verticality was built by Louis only very late in his reign when, under a variety of influences—Madame de Main-tenon, church politics, and failing diges-tion—he became more religious than he had been before. Nor were the two pavil-ions with their columns commissioned by him; he stubbornly resisted all the importu-nities of Jules Hardouin-Mansart to build a monumental facade on this side. The pavilion on the right is by Louis XV; it destroyed a very beautiful staircase inside. The one on the left was built in the nine-teenth century at the time when the palace was turned into a museum. The equestrian statue, too, is nineteenth century.

What was to be seen originally was, in fact, a very low and, in that sense, quite modest building that was approached up

341. Versailles. Palace. Louis Le Vau. Center block and Court of Marble.

343. Versailles. Parterre d'Eau. André Le Nôtre.

the contour lines and culminated in a tiny enclosed court straight ahead. A small fountain played where the statue now stands. Behind it, the old entrance court of Louis XIII's château was enriched with marble pavement, trophies, and marble busts, some new and some Antique (fig. 341). Otherwise, it remained a mansarded building of moderate size around a court-yard of domestic scale. Louis sends us first to that courtyard, and then tells us to go on through the narrow volume of interior space behind it to exit at once in the center of the garden facade.

Immediately, we are in a totally different world; all containment by buildings falls away; we are released to the vastness of space. Before us are only the great and simple elements of earth and sky; sand like

344. Versailles. Fountain of Latona. Tapis vert and Grand Canal.

a desert, water stretching out in two great lakes, a low mass of trees, and the sky that sails free above it all. Two urns stand out in space (fig. 342). They define the space without populating it, as human figures

would have done—indeed, as they do in the squares of Baroque Rome. That was not what was wanted here. The king is the major actor and piece of sculpture in this garden, abetted by his crowd of courtiers and most of all by the great dances of the Ballets de Cour taking place around him. These are the sculptural actions that populate the space, which is itself wholly environmental, avoiding all intrusive sculptural masses. All its elements must simply define it as a place. Out there on the big Parterre d'Eau (fig. 343), the rivers of France lie down like bathers around the great pools; they do not interrupt the space by standing up in it. Through nominally embodiments, they remain environmental elements. We are the actors, and as we go forward, the great urns swing toward us, and the goat faces peer at us from their sides (fig 342).

We go forward under them, down the few stairs. And Louis tells us to go forward, admiring the Parterre d'Eau and walking across it toward the head of the staircase, which is as yet invisible beyond it. We progress, then, toward what seems to be a void with an indefinite sort of avenue suggested in the distance, and we cannot see what is directly ahead until we arrive at the top of the stairs. Then it all bursts out before us (fig. 344): the Fountain of Latona just below us, the *tapis vert* that slants gently down through the trees that are brought tightly in to focus the view, the Bassin d'Apollon, the Grand Canal, and, most of all, the overriding sky. Louis tells us to admire it all. He was quite aware that it was a moment of vast release. The oval of Latona opens up and surprises us, releasing us to the burst of velocity that explodes up the middle of the garden. Our gaze moves rapidly down the *tapis vert,* but when it hits the water it literally takes off. It no longer adheres but slides—slides across the water to the sky reflected in it.

We are released to infinity, or at least to indefinitely expanding space. One recalls the experience at the crossing of Nôtre Dame in Paris. At Versailles, however, it seems, as it did to Charageat, a directly Cartesian expansion. The optics of reflection were analyzed by Descartes, who also described space as "indefinite," not "infinite" but seeming to expand without limits like something real in itself.* That is exactly the effect of this view. We might note one of many subtleties in plan (figs. 344, 353), this one surely Le Nôtre's, which helps us to experience that Cartesian expansion. The far end of the Grand Bassin opens in plan into a curious dumbbell shape that seems incomprehensible until we look at the view itself and realize that it dissolves the edges of the far end of the canal, so that our eyes can be released from it to the sky. If the two edges went on straight to the far bank, they would trap our view and prevent that expansion. What we have, in fact, is water and sky, bursting through the trees beyond the canal and opening up and out together, focused at the very last instant by the two plane trees that are set on the horizon like sights at the end of a rifle barrel, aiming us toward far space.

Pre-Columbians, Pueblos, and Greeks all looked out across the space of the earth from one object to another, from temple to mountain. Now the human brain, led on by the human two-eyed vision that Descartes analyzed so well, shapes every inch of space to the horizon and, by impli-

cation, far beyond it. A human absolutism rules the world at last. So the garden becomes the setting for the great royal fêtes, whose significance Roy Strong and M.C. Moine have interpreted for us.* It was the ritual function of those vast entertainments to embody in the king those cosmic powers and virtues, those ideas, of which he was normally simply the terrestrial reflection. In them, for example, Louis XIV was presented as the Sun King. In his youth, Louis had, of course, danced the Sun King himself in the early Ballets de Cour. At Versailles the whole canopy of sky spreads that Sun in majesty over the garden, while the fountains themselves dance the cosmic nature of the king. The iconography is simple. It is the mother of Apollo, Latona, whom we see at the foot of the stairs; it is Apollo himself who is rising out of the water in the distance (rising out of the west, unfortunately, but that can't be helped). So Louis is, in fact, the whole sky and Apollo as well (fig. 347).

It is when the fountains go on that we can feel a little bit how those great masques must have worked, those illusionistic festivals with their boats, their floats, their fireworks, and their *jets d'eau,* translating the elements into the king. Because, as the fountains rise up, Apollo really seems to be moving. The powerful white jets leaping up before him are a narrative or sculptural embodiment of his action. They make us feel him moving forward in space; they embody his resolution and his power. At the Fountain of Latona, the ballet begins as the jets of water start up out of the mouths of those unfortunate Boeotian peasants who were ill-advised enough to deride Latona and

---

*René Decartes, *Discours de la methode . . . Plus La dioptrique,* Leyden, 1636; Paris, 1668.

*Roy Strong, *Splendor at Court Renaissance Spectacle and the Theater of Power,* Boston, 1973, Idem, *Art and Power: Renaissance Festivals 1450–1650,* Suffolk, 1984. M.C. Moine, *Les Fêtes à la cour du roi soleil,* Paris, 1984.

345. Versailles. Fountain of Latona beginning to play.

346. Gianlorenzo Bernini. Louis XIV. 1665.

her son and were punished by Zeus by being turned into lizards and frogs (fig. 345). They are the citizens of Paris, who insulted Louis and his mother during the disorders of the Fronde. The water is their cry, and it rises as their anguish mounts to surround Latona at last in an aureole of light like fire. All the elements of that typical four-part, simplified iconography that was used over and over again at Versailles are present: Louis becomes, in fact, earth, air, water, and fire.

If we imagine him standing at the head of the stairs where we left him, looking out across that view that is himself, we realize that, despite everything, it was the Italian Bernini who understood him best. His portrait bust was made in 1665 (fig. 346), just at the time when Louis was deeply involved with Le Nôtre, Le Vau, and Lebrun in the first great program of building at Versailles, which had begun in 1662. Once more we can imagine him at the head of the stairs, carried in this bust on his *gloire,* on what seems like a cloud in the cloak that bears him up. So the bust avoids the solid foursquare mass that all the French busts of Louis possess. Instead, it dematerializes him into pure aspiration, where water and sky and fire all merge in the flowing, flaming, windblown locks of the great wig, and the eyes are looking up to the sun, of which he himself, radiant, is the embodiment, looking up into the blinding light like the great hawk of Egypt who stared unwinking with the Pharaoh at the sun.

Ancient images are being embodied in Baroque optics to associate the power of the universe with the realm of France. Rising above the clouds, Louis is wholly the Sun King. Irving Lavin pointed out what Bernini did with Louis' eyes, which were, in fact, rather small. Around them, he carved a flat, smooth plane that

347. Versailles. Fountain of Apollo.

reflects the light, so making the eyes seem bigger and shining. The whole bust conveys a wonderful sense of the aspiration of the young king, dreaming of a larger France and carried on his glory across the continental space before him. Far out in that view, Le Nôtre makes that optical adjustment to the end of the Grand Bassin which we have already noted. Like Bernini's eyes, it makes us see more, makes us believe in the reality of the idea, believe in the young king and in the nation of which he believed himself to be the embodiment. Again, this is ancient kingship, employing Cartesian tools.

350. Versailles. Garden side.

348. Versailles. Fountain of Latona and facade of the palace from the *tapis vert*. Garden side.

The king still stands above his realm as surely as Gilgamesh had done on his ziggurat. Indeed, the first important French Classic garden had been that at St. Germain-en-Laye, modeled on the Villa d'Este, where the king, like Louis in his youth, surmounted the ramps high above the Seine and looked back toward Paris, exiled from it by the events of the Fronde. At Versailles the sacred mountain has almost disappeared. It is simply high enough to give the king a clear view across his great, flat, verdant kingdom. The garden is no longer a mountain slope but an expansive national terrain under the regal sky (figs. 347, 348). Hence, the whole gar-

den is the embodiment of Louis and of his France with its centralized authority, its continental scale, and its straight canals. But it is also more than that, and the cosmic order to which it refers is more than its elements of earth, air, fire, and water.

Louis himself wants to show us more. He tells us rather sternly to turn around at the head of the stairs and, looking back along the way we have come, to admire the facade of the château. As we actually see it from this point today, the chapel is largely masked, and the very late roof of the theater to the north projects only a little (figs. 348, 350). Now we realize that with the suppression of the mansard roof, which is elsewhere used over and over again during the seventeenth century, the whole building becomes flat, as if it were only one plane deep. It avoids any hint of three-dimensional volume or bulk.* It becomes, in fact, a fence to define the sweep of sand and water that lies in front of it.

This facade has not always been admired by modern critics for those characteristics, and it offers an excellent example of how the preconceptions under which all of us labor can often make it impossible for us to see what is really there. For example, in 1953, when Anthony Blunt was writing his fine book about French art, it was the fashion among art historians to admire the Baroque, especially the Italian Baroque, and to be rather stern with the French because they tended to call the Baroque "le style Jesuite" and to avoid it. So Blunt preferred the earlier state of the château, by Le Vau, which he regarded as more Baroque because the central portion was cut deeply

*In this it vividly contrasts with, for example, Dampierre, whose mansard makes it a solid chunk, seen on entrance from above and filling a narrow valley defined by chunky hills.

349. Versailles. Parterre d'Eau and garden facade. Painting, 17th century.

back above the ground floor, pulling the eye into the building and holding it there, so creating an effect both centralized and hermetic.*

At the same time, a number of designs for the Parterre d'Eau were being tried. At first, before Le Nôtre's time, it apparently had a circular *bassin* with four plots of *broderie* around it, so that it, too, was closed in upon itself and centralized. There were a number of other proposals or fantasies; in one of them there is a long pool that leads our eyes right into the center of the building's hollow. The effect is, again, the opposite of expansive (fig. 349). Therefore, when Jules Hardouin-Mansart inserted the Galerie des Glaces into the hollow in the middle of the building and the rest of the facade was adjusted to it, he probably was doing exactly what was needed (fig. 350).

When we walk through the Galerie des Glaces today, we find that the side away from the garden is all mirrors that are reflecting the garden on the other side, so

*Anthony Blunt, *Art and Architecture in France, 1500– 1700,* Harmondsworth, 1970.

that we still seem to be in the vast space of the garden. All the other major rooms at Versailles, none of them very large or deep, also try to focus our attention on the garden, though none are as successful as Mansart's Galerie. On the outside, it fills up the centralized void in the château and turns it into the long, gently articulated fence we noted before (fig. 350). It has just enough in the way of colonnades to modulate its rhythm musically, and it wholly fulfills its function of acting as a definer of space for the vast order opening to the sky that the final version of the Parterre d'Eau achieves.

The long facade stretches north and south but carries our eyes especially in the southern direction. And Louis tells us that, having admired the château, we should go south to the Parterre du Midi until we come to its southern parapet and see below us the Orangerie and the Pièce d'Eau des Suisses (fig. 351). Here, yet another circle, like that of the Gothic rose, opens before us. Once more, we experience the sense of release that comes from the unexpected springing of a great circular form. Beyond it, our eyes are carried to the vast rectangular *bassin* with its expansively curved end.

We are in the presence of shapes which had been fundamental to the French conception of order since Suger's St. Denis: the Neoplatonic shapes of the circle and the square. Most of all, they are embodied as drawings rather than as physical mass: tightly stretched and weightless on the thin surface of the parterre, as dematerialized in their own way as any rose window (fig. 352). The Neoplatonic idea that ideal beauty was to be found only in essential shapes uncompromised by matter, and which the artist could therefore hope to capture, if at all, only in drawing, had of course been central to Renaissance aes-

thetics since the very beginning. Moreover, those shapes were regarded as the most perfect expressions of that order of the universe which also manifested itself in harmonic proportions in the visual arts and in music.*

The drawing by Leonardo I have cited so often must now be recalled once more (fig. 201). The perfect shapes are as close to pure Idea as possible. They are pure *disegno,* here pure line, tight-drawn as wire. That is what Neoplatonic "beauty" is, and it had posed a problem for Renaissance theory from Alberti onward. If beauty is pure idea, how can it be embodied in a building, which has to have some mass, which has, in fact, to compromise the perfect idea by its involvement in gross matter? Brunelleschi had tried to make the loggia of his Foundling Hospital pure line, but the Renaissance could hardly hold to that ideal. The French garden resolves the dilemma. For the first time, it is possible to eliminate all compromise, because it is not the building that counts, not built matter, but the whole plane of the earth reduced to a drawing. The *broderie* is cut so tightly and the circular *bassins* are so tautly designed that the effect is, in fact, pure *disegno:* pure surface, no depth, no mass. It is the ideal order of the universe made visible upon its face (fig. 352).

It is also as close as one can get to subordinating the building and designing, as it were, only with nature: not with the ephemeral appearances of nature but with its underlying order embodied in the circle and the square and, by extension, in the person of the king who stands in the center of it all. If we can think of the Platonic image as at least analogous to that of Christ in the twelfth century, I think that we can think of it in direct relation to the

*Rudolf Wittkower, *Architectural Principles in the Age of Humanism,* London, 1949.

351. Versailles. Orangerie et Pièce d'Eau des Suisses.

king in the seventeenth. Indeed, Roy Strong writes that "The world of the court Fête is an ideal one in which nature, ordered and controlled, has all the dangerous potentialities removed." Actually, it is even more than that, I think: It is not so much a question of "removing" as of "revealing." It is making us see with our own eyes what perfect order is, and the effect of that vision is in actuality a liberating, exalting one. Again, I say, the French garden does not "impose"; it releases, as Gothic architecture had done. It makes us apprehend a cosmic idea at the full scale of the world. This is its "intelligence." It makes the world make sense.

But it goes further. It extends its image of mind and action in great Baroque diagonals (fig. 353). It breaks out of the circle and the square. It becomes modern, explosive, overriding all previous divisions and static boundaries within the closed shapes. The contained power of the individual now explodes across the landscape, which has become the image of his liberated will. This is the plan of Versailles. It is the culmination of all the historical phases of the Classic plan. We might trace its ancestry very briefly, in part through our earlier chapters. It evolves as human beings grow into the belief that they can control the environment. So the lineage is: Delphi with its purely sculptural, competitive action (fig. 94); the Acropolis of Athens with its balance between sculptural and environmental modes (fig. 134); Lindos and Praeneste with their firmer axes and primacy of space (figs. 178, 183), coupled with the Classic Greek and Roman grid plan and the radiating avenues of Baroque Rome (figs. 174, 183, 186, 305, 306).

Finally, here at Versailles, it all bursts loose at regional scale, or perhaps we should say at cosmic scale, since the ra-

352. Versailles. Parterre du Midi.

diant shapes of the avenues were called, in fact, "*étoiles*" (fig. 353). Many images are in it, in one sense that of the new France most of all. There are the long canals, the forests, the fields, and the new territories. There is the administrative focus on the person of the king. There is the king's will most of all, which makes it all possible. He is the released individual who imagines this command of the world and whose *gloire* the nation is.

Here we should leave Louis, I think, standing on the Parterre du Midi with his guidebook—in which he goes on to lead us through all the bosquets of the park, supplemented by a side trip to the Trianon if we choose—in order to return to Versailles later and in other contexts. The idea I would like to pursue now is that central one of the liberated individual who images his control of the world through the shapes of the Classic garden. The man who first grasped that possibility wholly, much as Suger first imagined the possibilities of Gothic architecture, was, like Suger, not the king but one of the king's most important subjects, probably his most intelligent one. That was, of course, Nicolas Fouquet, *Surintendant des Finances* under Mazarin.

It was Fouquet who first integrated the garden image of the world bent to the human will, which Louis was to develop into an image of the state. At his château of Vaux-le-Vicomte (fig. 354), which he began in 1656 and (almost) completed in 1661, Fouquet first assembled the team of artists Louis was to employ at Versailles: Le Nôtre the landscape gardener, Le Vau the architect, and Lebrun the painter and apparently the administrative director of the group. Fouquet was without question the greatest patron of the arts in seventeenth-century France other than the king. And he was well ahead of Louis in his

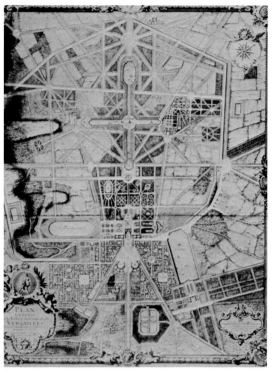

353. Versailles. Plan drawn by P. Le Pautre. 1714–1715.

perception and his capacity to recognize young talent and to back it. He was the beloved patron of Molière, La Fontaine, Puget, and Poussin, as well as of the incomparable architectural team that was his own creation. He had the vision, the will, and the money because, in the manner of Mazarin, he had enriched himself from the public treasury. He was not a noble; his purchase of Vaux brought the title with it; hence: le Vicomte.

The first thing Fouquet did there was to plant a forest. That was the very stuff of nobility, its ancient setting. We can trace the pattern all the way back to Charlemagne's time. The nobles and the king try to preserve the forests for their hunting, for the exercise of their manly virtue and warlike arts. The peasants want to cut the forests down, burn the wood, plant farms, build villages. There were, in fact, three villages on this site when Fouquet

354. Vaux-le-Vicomte, France. Château and gardens. 1656–1661. Louis Le Vau, André Le Nôtre, and Charles Lebrun. Entrance side.

bought the land. He moved them away (now it all sounds like the American Re-development of the 1960s) and planted the forest, and he had Le Nôtre design the garden to look as if it had been hollowed out of the woods.

Somewhere not too far from the center of the open space, the château is placed (fig. 355). The first thing we notice about the building is that it is separated by a moat from the flat planes of the garden. It weighs heavily upon its foundations, weighs heavily within the moat and thus not on the ground. It is like the phantom of a *château fort* that has been cut away to become only two rooms deep, but whose

basement is still heavily bastioned and massive. It therefore becomes essential that the mass does not seem to rest heavily on the surface of the earth. If it were doing so, we would feel in our bones that the ground was solid and thus inert, and Le Nôtre did not want that. By separating the mass of the château from the earth, he was able to transform the surface of the garden into thin planes that are apparently floating on water and are therefore free to be manipulated dynamically, a little like the free planes of the French Cubist painters later on. So Le Nôtre (Le Vau? Fouquet?) separated the château from the ground and made that plane as thin as

drawing paper or as a mirror reflecting the sky, all of it seeming to push back the forest away from the château itself (fig. 355).

The way all that looks in plan should be fairly familiar to us already, and I compare it with Suger's plan for St. Denis (figs. 218, 356). We see the long axis running up the middle of both, with the château looking a bit like Suger's entrance facade. The axis of the garden recalls that of the nave, where, when we arrive at the crossing, a cross axis of transept opens left and right, largely hidden until we arrive at it. The canal that acts as the transept at Vaux is well below eye level until the moment of discovery. Beyond it, as in the

Gothic church, we are looking at a new facade, that of an apselike hemicycle that contains the image of divinity. At Vaux, it is Hercules who, as at Bomarzo, is the Classical god of the garden. It is he who clears out nature for human habitation and in accordance with a human sense of order. So Fouquet set up a replica of the Farnese Hercules at the end of his garden, with radiating avenues behind it that recall the radii of Suger's choir. Indeed, the plan of St. Denis could almost be laid down upon that of Vaux. The château itself becomes Suger's narthex, an entrance to lead us out to the nave of the garden, which is the shaped space as a whole. So, speaking in a way that the French a few years ago might have called "structuralist," we can suggest that similar structural principles underlie the plans of French Gothic churches and those of French Classic gardens—especially those plans that came first and were the inspiration for future work.

Another point is that Suger designed his facade with two balancing towers and an entrance in the center that pulls us toward it. That is exactly the way Vaux is designed, but in very subtle ways. As we aproach it, the elevation seems quite medieval; there are the towers gesturing on either side. We note that Le Vau designed those side pavilions—incorrectly, in a Classical sense—with a pilaster right in the middle of the bay. He clearly did not wish to suggest a void in any way. He wanted impenetrable side pavilions to anchor the pull toward the center that he intended to exert upon us. Everything gives back in the middle to pull us into it. So we cross the moat and walk through the phantom of the old *château fort,* which exists only in plan. We feel that it has been swept away; all that mass of matter is gone, opening everything to the sky and setting up the pull through space.

We know there is something beyond the low, pedimented entrance; we have already seen the cupola rising above it over what is, in fact, a large elliptical room. When we look at the plan, we see how we are intended to be pulled right through into that room (figs. 357, 358). It is pushing out on the other side of the château just as the entrance is pulling in; it is pushing us out to the garden. Its high windows are dark on the entrance side, where it is embedded in the body of the château, but they open out in light toward the garden.

At present, a model of Girardon's equestrian figure of Louis XIV from the

355. Vaux-le-Vicomte. Air view from entrance side. See also p. 221.

360. Vaux-le-Vicomte. View of the garden from the château.

356. Vaux-le-Vicomte. Plan of the gardens.

357. Vaux-le-Vicomte. Plan of the château.

Place Vendôme stands on the central axis facing the garden, but it is possible that this was the spot where Fouquet intended to place Pierre Puget's image of the young, seated, brooding Hercules (fig. 359), which is now in the great (rarely visited) Puget gallery in the Louvre. This Hercules is fat, double-chinned, rather vulgar. It is not an aristocratic image. He was probably intended to look out toward the garden, as if he were contemplating his labors not yet begun. If so, he would somewhat resemble the young Herakles in the first metope of the Temple of Zeus at Olympia (fig. 119), where Herakles is shown young, unmarked, but wholly exhausted and, indeed, daunted after his first labor, in which he had killed the Nemean lion. It is only as he gets wholly into his trials that he becomes a fully committed, mature man. Puget's heavy, inert Hercules looks out upon his destiny with the kind of loutish lassitude that only untried youth can know.

Puget's bust shares the gateposts of the Beaux-Arts in Paris with Poussin's. This is very apt, because if Poussin embodies the Classic side of French character, Puget may be said to represent the wild, Romantic side. Frank and Gaulois, the French would say. Puget was, of course, a decidedly Baroque sculptor who worked in Italy with Pietro da Cortona. He loved Fouquet; just before Fouquet's disgrace, the king sent Colbert to Italy, literally to plead with Puget to stop working for Fouquet and work for him. And Puget, with the impeccable political sense that characterizes so many artists, refused to do so. He would remain with Fouquet. Because of that decision, Puget spent most of his life in the naval shipyard at Toulon. There, he carved wonderful sculptural embellishments for the galleys of the Sun

King that roamed the Mediterranean with a truly barbaric image of his splendor—a radiant painted sun—on their sails.

Such naval carvings, of which we can see an example in the Musée de la Marine in Paris, were the ultimate Baroque pieces of sculpture, because in them Poseidon and Amphitrite and all their train would emerge from the waves and go down again into the sea and come up dripping water, sparkling in the sun. All this marvelous art was destroyed by the English, simply by the fact that they stopped doing it. They took the sculptures off their ships and so made them much faster: Thereafter, the French and everybody else had to stop carving, too.

The scholarship of Vassanti and Yates has shown us that Hercules was associated with the king of France; he is the Gallic Hercules.* Hence, Fouquet intended to install an image of Hercules in his house, presumably as a compliment to Louis XIV, but the image is proletarian, hardly royal. One senses in this something of the curious relationship Fouquet had with the young king. In a way, he was constantly jousting with the royal house, as if testing it. Fouquet, too, was the liberated individual after all. How could he bear a master? In any event, his Hercules was probably intended to look out toward the Hercules that crowned the garden at the far end. And he, the Farnese Hercules, was just the opposite: the aging Hercules who has been exhausted, even brutalized, by his labors. He leans heavily on his club and looks back over what he has made. (fig. 382).

Toward that image, the whole facade on that side of the château projects. It swells out toward it; the classical details are barely pinned on. It is the interior space that is ballooning out toward the garden.

Then, as we come through those doors, we see it all: an unprecedented burst of energy to the horizon (fig. 360). All at once, we realize that everything we have experienced so far has been only a prologue to the great architecture that opens before us. It is an architecture of space.

One important thing about it is, I think, that it was conceived according to the 180-degree arc of vision of the human eye. Here again, it recalls the cathedrals. The seated sculptures to the left and right of the stairs help define the arc (indeed, are set well within it) and frame the experience. The human eye focuses on only one percent of its half circle (White's book is, I think, the best on this),* but it is aware of the wide area on both sides, whose forms syncopate more and more toward the edges. The camera cannot normally catch anything like that in one frame, but Le Nôtre's gardens were designed according to that arc.

Here, it is all focused on Hercules far out in the light in the center, but it also stretches left and right to the forest barrier. That definition is not, as the English were later to assert, the same on the left as it is on the right. Here, as elsewhere in almost all of Le Nôtre's gardens, there is the great burst of energy up the middle and then varying degrees of expansion on both sides, secondary to the power of the axis. At Vaux, the forest comes close on the right but gives way to the left, so that we feel a wonderful lateral expansion in it. It moves right through our bodies, pulling toward the left, toward the heart, even while the high-velocity view toward Hercules is running up through the center. The whole vista is organized with only a few pieces of sculpture, balustrades, and stairs. Everything works with a spectacular economy of means.

*In general: Frances Yates, *Astraea, the Imperial Theme in the Sixteenth Century,* London, 1975.

*John White, *The Birth and Rebirth of Pictorial Space,* London, 1987.

359. Pierre Puget. Hercules.

358. Vaux-le-Vicomte. Grand Salon.

It seems obvious why the *broderie* developed as it did. A comparison of Vaux with the Villa Lante (figs. 328, 363) or with modern gardens planted in the Italianate manner such as that at Villandry, near the Loire, shows that in Italian practice the evergreen is treated sculpturally in hedgelike masses and is disposed in geometric figures that are separate and discontinuous one from the other. The eye tends to get trapped inside each deep group; it is all very sculptural. Soon, however, the French cut the Italian evergreen hedges right down to ground level. Then, with the *broderie,* large asymmetrical elements took shape and cut through the old static geometric forms so that the eye could be carried rapidly across space, across the surface of the ground (fig. 360). Again, the earth is made weightless and taut. Attention is dynamically directed into the distance. The whole garden becomes one thing, one unit of released energy.

In its thin surface, too, there is just a touch of that curious presence that is always there a little in Classic architecture—and that I mentioned briefly in relation to the plans of Gothic cathedrals—an anthropomorphic image, here in some sense of a mask (figs. 355, 384). One cannot help but feel in the symmetry of the whole something of eyes, mouth, and brow. And it is central to this connection that French garden treatises of the seventeenth century refer to the process whereby geometric shapes are transferred in scale to the ground as *pourtraiture*.

From, for example, Boyceau de la Barauderie of 1638, to the Mollets of 1651 and 1652, and to Dezallier d'Argenville of 1709–1713 or thereabouts* there runs a very clear strain of theory and method, which goes something like this: The most important thing of all is geometry. Geometry is at the very center of the garden art. Secondly, Boyceau writes, as early as 1638, that through *échelle,* scale, comes what he calls *pourtraiture,* which may be directly translated as "portraiture," a "portraying." Through scale, that is, geometry is transferred to the garden itself and so puts things into their proper relationship to one another, which is, after all, the fundamental art of the portrait itself. But the word, like *colonnette-en-délit,* clearly means more than one thing. Its Latin root, *portrahere,* means to draw forth, to reveal, to expose, so that it may legitimately be connected with that revelation of the fundamental order of the universe with which we have already been concerned.

In this process of *pourtraiture,* geometry may be seen as Ideal and Neoplatonic, but the scale is pragmatic, scientific in a Cartesian sense. It is, indeed, professional, and it is the major professional tool of the landscape architect's art. Claude Mollet is nothing less than violent on this point. He writes that those who do not understand the science of scale, through which the geometric concept is fitted to the actual size of the landscape itself, cannot be regarded as landscape architects. Clearly, scale is the professional's pride, its command the very hallmark of his professional status. It transforms him from a gardener into an artist, from a man who digs to a man who designs. In fact, that overworked modern word *design* is very cogent here; it had real meaning as *disegno,* drawing, which is Ideal and Neoplatonic and scientific and optical all at once, hence the ultimate medium of *pourtraiture.*

Here we have a theory and a method together. It is an amalgam of the Real and the Ideal. Because of it, because of geometry and scale, these new garden architects indeed were able to draw a "portrait" of the order of the universe which is of enormous graphic power. But that portrait is also in part a portrait of the client, a symbolic embodiment of his character, but in a more literal sense sometimes just a breath of the human shape, the human face itself. Again, it is the man of perfect proportions in the circle and the square, bound up in the world's order. So smiling Vaux is also the portrait of Fouquet as Nanteuil shows him to us, sparkling and urbane (figs. 383, 384). We have seen that Italian gardens had also embodied the character of their clients, and sometimes deep and disquieting states of mind, involved with a sense of something terrifying in the earth itself. There is none of this awe or psychological depth in the French garden. It thins out the earth to cultivate it and skim across it. It is in one sense a supremely

---

*Jacques Boyceau de la Barauderie, *La Traité du jardinage selon les raisons de la nature et de l'art,* Paris, 1638; André Mollet, *Le Jardin du plaisir,* Stockholm, 1651; Claude Mollet, *Théâtre des plans et jardinages,* Paris, 1628: published 1652. Antoine-Joseph Dezallier d'Argenville, *Théorie et pratique du jardinage,* Paris, 1709 and ff., cf. Also F. Hamilton Hazlehurst, *Jacques Boyceau and the French Formal Garden,* Ann Arbor, 1966; Elizabeth MacDougall and F. H. Hazlehurst, eds., *The French Formal Garden,* Dumbarton Oaks Colloquium, III, 1974.

modern view, a liberating one.

Le Nôtre's plan for the Tuileries, for example (fig. 361), became the image and the frame of modern urbanism itself. In his youth, Le Nôtre inherited the direction of the Tuileries from his father, who had been the landscape architect of its parterres, and Le Nôtre's plan owes a great deal to Mollet and the others who had worked on the Tuileries before him. But it is Le Nôtre who gave it that characteristic burst up the middle which was soon to climax at Vaux. There is a new velocity in Le Nôtre's axis; it traces an urbanism of movement rather than of static mass and was to culminate in the Champs-Elysées, which continued Le Nôtre's axis at the Tuileries into the far distance. So the principle is already at work, and it is there in Vaux: an architecture that leaps across space, that is, in fact, earth-space rather than building mass.

Another great difference from the sculptural, deeply Romantic Italian garden can be seen in the use of water, fundamental to sacred sites since time immemorial. In the Italian garden, water is the awesome gift of the earth (fig. 327); in the French garden, water becomes primarily the optical medium by means of which the sky is reflected. There are, of course, Italianate cascades at St. Cloud and elsewhere in France and something like them, as we shall see, even at Vaux, and jets of water will always leap upward into space. These are reflections of Italy, but the image the French discovered for themselves was that of the flat *bassin* (fig. 362), designed with a rounded rim that seems stretched so that the whole is a taut surface. When the water inside it is calm—which in most, though not all, gardens is most of the time at present and a good deal of the time in the seventeenth century—it reflects the sky and further de-

361. Paris, France. Tuileries. Garden. Engraving after Israel Sylvestre.

materializes the earth's surface. In the Italian garden, water is always sculptural, either active or lifted in a tub (fig. 363). It is always weighty. The French pictorialize it into the heavenly light of the sky.

This intention was not new in seventeenth-century France; the circular *bassins* resemble rose windows clearly enough, and the principle of dematerialization is very Gothic indeed. But even back in the early Bronze Age, we find much the same kind of thing. In the Mediterranean, as on Malta, megaliths were used to build temple images of the goddess of the earth,

hollows deep in the earth, where the initiates slept and from which they came forth, reborn (fig. 192). If we follow the tradition of megalithic building northward along the Atlantic Coast of Europe to Carnac in Brittany (fig. 364), we find that the megaliths are soon liberated from the earth, and indeed from containment, and stand forth in what the French so appropriately call *alignements* under the sky. As the clouds roll in across Brittany from the Atlantic, these march with them, so evoking not primarily the earth but a religion of the sky. They also suggest mil-

itary formations, and their battalions at Carnac are graded in height in the military manner from tallest to shortest as they breast the hills. At present, they are described locally as the army of the local saint. And we do feel them march up and halt and touch the sky and, indeed, pull the sky down to them as the clouds roll along.

That is much like what Le Nôtre did at Vaux (fig. 365). There is an enormous length of parterre: so long that later printmakers were sometimes to chop off one section of it in order to produce a change of level much closer to the château, as Le

362. Paris. Tuileries. Bassin.

365. Vaux-le-Vicomte. Parterres and château.

364. Carnac, Brittany. Bronze Age. *Alignements.*

Nôtre himself was to do at Versailles. Here, it is all wonderful sky as we progress down the parterre to arrive at last at the rectangular reflecting pool at its end (fig. 366). The way that pool is used seems to derive directly from Descartes. He writes, as Charageat pointed out, that the angle of reflection is the same as the angle of sight.* So if the pool of water is large enough and the position of the viewer can be controlled, one can reflect not only the sky but objects that might have been thought to be far out of reflective range. When we arrive at the critical spot beyond

*Marguerite Charageat, "André Le Nôtre et l'optique de son temps," *Bulletin de la société de l'histoire de l'art français,* 1955, 66–78.

that rectangular *bassin* and look back at the château, we find that it, which seemed so far away, is miraculously reflected in the water. This is exactly the moment when the transept, the cross axis of the great canal, opens before us.

We find ourselves standing above the famous Cascades of Vaux, an Italianate feature (fig. 367). They are, or are intended to be, flowing with Italian generosity down below our feet, so that something exciting, lively, and unexpected happens just as we first find the great canal and see the full sweep of the climactic hemicycle on its far shore. We look at it across a flat parterre of sand that is designed with flat stone rims to seem as

363. Bagnaia, Italy. Villa Lante. Parterre with fountain.

thin as a plank spanning the water, which appears to be flowing under it from the pool below the Cascades. Beyond the broad canal rises the apse of the garden, with its figure of Hercules. It is the last memory of the sacred mountain at Vaux, and, as later at Versailles, the king, here as Hercules, occupies it, not Fouquet's château. At Vaux, it is the Gothic choir as well, while Italian river gods recline in the niches of its rusticated facade. To arrive at it, though, we first must cross the canal.

The crossing of water has, of course, marked a fundamental rite of passage from Teotihuacán onward. But the great French canals were something new. There was nothing like them in Italy. Dutch gardens employ canals, but not nearly at this scale. On the one hand, we feel that they are in part referring to the medieval moat. On the other, as Neil Levine first suggested to me in conversation, there seems to be a reference in them to the outstanding French engineering achievement of the seventeenth century: the building of the network of commercial canals. Indeed, the greatest accomplishment of thc rcign of Louis XIV has often been regarded as his building of the Canal du Midi, cut through the south of France to link the Atlantic with the Mediterranean. It was completed in 1681, largely through the efforts of Vauban. Jefferson visited it when he went to France.

The apparent reference to such commercial canals at Vaux and afterward can

366. Vaux-le-Vicomte. Reflecting bassin.

well remind us of the Pop Art of the mid-twentieth century. One takes a common industrial element, not previously regarded as art, puts it into a new context, and perhaps blows it up to a larger size. By this device, it is infused with the reflective and allusive character of conscious art. It becomes symbolic. Its use as such surely seems intended at Vaux, where it is not only the major surprise but is very large indeed. There is also a big canal at Sceaux, designed by Le Nôtre for the Marquis de Seignelay, Colbert's son and the Minister of Marine at that time. The greatest one of all is the Grand Bassin at Versailles, where the king himself tested landing barges for Vauban and sailed warships cut down to manageable scale. So the canal should be regarded as related not

368. Vaux-le-Vicomte. View of château across the canal.

only to the industrial waterways but also to the development of the French navy, a major event of the early years of the reign of Louis XIV and one of Colbert's greatest achievements.

Beyond all that, however, the canal was the place where the dematerialized evocation of the sky and of a cosmic unity could be brought about most fully. One could look into the canal and drown in the cosmos (fig. 368). Le Nôtre himself loved Netherlandish painting, and he was one of the first of those many Frenchmen who collected it and, in many cases, wrote about it so beautifully: about the clouds piling in from the North Sea, heavy and full of rain and reflected in the shallow seas and canals. A painting by Salomon van Ruysdael (fig. 369), not in Le Nôtre's collection but very much like a number of paintings owned by him, can show us that.

To go further: When we look into those canals today (fig. 370), we cannot help but think of the greatest landscapist among the French Impressionists, Claude

367. Vaux-le-Vicomte. View across cascades and canal toward hemicycle.

369. Salomon van Ruysdael. *River Scene.* Early 1630s.

Monet, who was obsessed with the phenomenon of reflection (fig. 371). He spent the last decades of his life painting the water lilies in his garden at Giverny, in paintings that are always water and sky alike, endlessly reflective and mysterious, always dealing with the whole of things. We recall that later, during the darkest days of World War I, Clemenceau would visit Monet at Giverny and look for hours into those reflecting pools, drawing a special refreshment from them.

All that is already at Vaux, in a magic of light and color as engrossing as that created by the stained glass of Gothic cathedrals. Still, Le Nôtre contained his body of water in a classic way, not with the Romantic looseness of the English garden or of Monet's paintings (fig. 372). It is very much the way Claude Lorrain handles it in his more architectural paintings, especially those of seaports. Claude, too, was one of Le Nôtre's favorite painters. He owned two splendid seaport views by Claude, which he gave to the king and which are now in the Louvre (fig. 373). The sun comes in very low across the water and is reflected in it. That scene can be almost matched on autumn days at Vaux. Le Nôtre did not have all the wonderful baggage of architecture and ships that Claude employed, but he could do a great deal with those elements I referred to earlier: a few moldings, stairs, urns, and balustrades.

370. Vaux-le-Vicomte. View down canal.

371. Claude Monet. *Morning on the Seine.* 1897.

It is a fine demonstration of how an artist can suggest a great deal with very little, so long as there is a style, like that of Classical architecture, which makes use of elements that can be read as parts of a recognized language. It can be eloquent in a few words, and wholly understood. The modeling around that beach of sand by the canal is instructive; it is not rounded like those of the circular *bassins,* which look stretched. It is flat-planed and rectangular, and makes the parterre look like a thin plank spanning the water. Then the urn stands out against the light, defining an architecture, an ambience as Classical as Claude's. A great deal is suggested; the mind builds the rest. It is a city; the garden lives by allusion.

There is even more of the greatest French Classical painting involved, or intended to have been involved, at Vaux. Poussin was also admired by Fouquet, who commissioned him to design a number of herms to be set up somewhere in the garden. Unfortunately, they did not arrive in time to find a place there and were eventually installed at Versailles, where

372. Vaux-le-Vicomte. Stairways and canal.

we can still see them and their descendants. The herm, as we observe in paintings by Poussin himself, such as the *Realm of Flora* in Dresden (fig. 375), is the god Terminus, who marks boundaries. He is the god of the edges of things, especially of that critical boundary between the garden, the sown field, and the wild. As shaped in Antiquity and enthusiastically revived in the Renaissance, he is, of course, a Classical statue-column. He is partly architectural, partly human. And he

373. Claude Gellée, Le Lorrain. *Seaport at Sunset*.

performs that role of standing at the boundary of things which the Gothic statue-column had filled as well.

In fact, the way the Classical herms are used at Versailles directly recalls the position of the Gothic statue-columns. They stand not in the middle of the space but at its sides, facing toward it, with the high facade of the trees behind them (figs. 374, 375, 377). We go past them at Versailles to enter the world of the trees that contain the green rooms of the bosquets, the hidden city of fantasy—of vanquished giants, La Fontaine's talking animals, Apollo's marsh and his metal tree (fig. 377). Originally, the trees defining the bosquets were shaped *en charmille,* as hedges, but quite soon, during the early eighteenth century, they were allowed to come up to great crowns and eventually to their whole natural masses. So it is not unfair to show them as they are now, rising up behind the statue-columns exactly like the high, dark, movemented masses of Gothic cathedrals behind their own statue-columns at human scale (figs. 276, 278).

At Reims, we remember that the Virgin is shown in a number of her aspects as Virgin and Mother on the central portal and that the nineteenth-century equestrian statue of *La Pucelle* stands before it (fig. 276). The Virgin is still important in the Classic garden, but now she has yet another aspect. She is Artemis (fig. 376) and she is still essential to the meaning, because she is the embodiment of the wild, of the forest and the hunt. Louis XIV shared with his ancestors a consuming passion for the chase; it was the ultimate aristocratic and kingly art. The Assyrian kings can be seen on their reliefs killing lions in their gardens. It is kingly ritual. So at Versailles, and in all the great French parks, the darkness of the forest comes to be treated as an intended contrast with the

377. Versailles. Statue columns and the trees of the park.

375. Nicholas Poussin. *The Realm of Flora.* 1630.

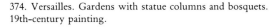

374. Versailles. Gardens with statue columns and bosquets. 19th-century painting.

376. Versailles. Fountain of Diana.

rationality and civilization of the parterres. Artemis survives, embodying at least the memory of the wild. Sometimes her chase spills out upon the parterre, and the kill takes place right there.

As we go past the statue-columns into the trees, we cannot help but feel that we are moving into a world that the Gothic architects would have understood. Corpechot, whom I cited at the beginning of this chapter as writing about the gardens in relation to the military arts, also compares them to Gothic architecture. Indeed, if we look at Amiens, with its glazed triforium, we are struck once more by its forestlike character (fig. 240) The piers can only be read as rising up, growing rather than pushing down, and the tracery opens into twiglike elements between us and the light. Finally, the branching canopy of the ribbed vault arches over all. It looks a lot like the forest at Versailles, especially when the latter is clothed in autumnal colors (fig. 378). Corpechot writes about "galleries of greenery which are as regular as vaults of stone." Or he says:

The avenues are like tunnels for light; they illuminate the intersections where the nymphs of Girardon will come to dance. Under the cathedrals of greenery that they construct, the architect disposes spots of light and dark. He plays with chiaroscuro with the mastery of a Rembrandt, under vaults which seem to let in the light only as if through the most sumptuous of stained glass windows.*

Corpechot might equally have said "with the mastery of a Monet"—who at Rouen built up the light in the rose with pigment in a way that reminds us both of the reflecting *bassins* under the trees at Versailles and of the luminous wheels of Suger himself (figs. 255, 379). So the connection with Gothic architecture, again a "structural" one, is very strong.

Finally at Vaux, we come to the apse of the garden. Two river gods derived from Michelangelo's on the Capitoline are set in niches in its rusticated facade (fig. 380). The Tiber is one of them, and Vaux's own little stream, the Anqueil, is the other. Here we find another side of Neoplatonism, which deals not with dematerialization but with its polar opposite: the giant in the building who is strapped and bound into the heavily rusticated mass of the wall itself. That rustication was developed by Raphael and Guilio Romano

*Corpechot, *Les Jardins de l'intelligence*, p. 94.

378. Versailles. Fountain of Autumn (Bacchus)

379. Claude Monet. *Rouen Cathedal*. 1894. Detail.

381. Vaux. The stairs. Fouquet and the King. (Jeannie Baubion-Mackler)

together, then by Serlio, through whose publications the French came to love it, and then by Palladio himself.

Heavily rusticated grottoes were very much a part of the Italian garden and were universally adopted in France. Later, though, La Fontaine was to remark to Le Nôtre that the water games played in such grottoes were fine for German tourists but not quite the kind of thing one did in France. And the importance of the grotto and the heavily rusticated wall does in fact dwindle in France throughout the later years of the seventeenth century.

But at Vaux, it is right at this point, where the ramps begin to lift toward Hercules, that Fouquet signed his garden. He did so by installing sculptural groups that show his royal protector, the king of France, as a lion who steps on Fouquet's cold-blooded enemies, like Colbert, personified by a serpent (fig. 381). Fouquet himself, in a play upon his name in the patois of his region, is the squirrel in the lion's paw who is eating the nuts of the realm, refreshing himself on the fruits of France under the protection of his royal master. Then, nearby, with indescribable effrontery or reckless courage he inscribed

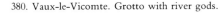

380. Vaux-le-Vicomte. Grotto with river gods.

his famous motto, couched in the third person: "How high will he not rise." This signing of the garden by the patron had also been done in Italian gardens. The Villa d'Este was signed by the Este at the Rometta, near Roma and the Wolf; their eagles and fleurs-de-lis crown the parapet around it. They affirm that they, like Hercules, can shape the world according to their own desire.

Fouquet went further at Vaux. He was able to shape the world almost literally according to his own image. When we come at last to the Farnese Hercules (fig. 382), leaning heavily on his club and looking back across the world he has made, we are struck by how much that world actually resembles Fouquet himself as he was when he imagined it. The beautiful portrait of him by Nanteuil was made just at the moment he was completing the garden (fig. 383). Across his face shimmer those fugitive expressions of intelligence that are the lights of the soul. His eyes are gleaming with wit and a touch of malice. He is alive with that wonderful French sense of irony and manner that we saw embodied with hardly more sweetness and no greater charm in the faces of the statue-columns at Chartres. He is a lovely man; it is no wonder that the artists he backed were so loyal to him. His garden itself is like that, a masterpiece of *pourtraiture* drawn on the surface of the ground, civilized and mannered in the very best meaning of those words (fig. 384). So Vaux is courtly and what might correctly be described as positively superficial (fig. 382). It is the thin, taut skin of the ground, as thin as paper, under which the water seems to slide and which can therefore embody in itself much of the mobility of feature, the play of intelligence and wit, and the ironic *adresse* of Fouquet, who created it.

383. Robert Nanteuil. *Nicholas Fouquet*. Engraving. 1661.

384. Vaux-le-Vicomte. Air view from above Hercules.

We all know what happened next. In his notorious fête of August 17, 1661, Fouquet pushed Louis just too far. Louis attended—he had clearly had his eye on Fouquet for some time—pretended to be infuriated by the expense involved, left in a rage and, three weeks later, caused Fouquet to be arrested and charged with treason. He clearly did not want a man of Fouquet's parts around, and he put every kind of pressure on the court to find him guilty and to sentence him to death. Bravely, the court refused; it would sentence him only to banishment. Louis intervened (one of the few times in history that a French king has done so in order to make a sentence more severe) and sentenced him to incarceration for life in a cold *château fort* in the Haute-Savoie. Taken all in all, it was a truly terrible irony, which Fouquet bore, we don't really know how, for too many long years. Most of his staff, including his physician, pleaded to go with him.

A few years later, La Fontaine, who had been one of Fouquet's first discoveries and whose bust can be seen at Vaux today, published his poem *Le Songe des Eaux de Vaux,* in which he calls upon the nymphs of Vaux to weep now that their fountains play no more. What happened is that they rose up at Versailles. The king took everything over; he brought Fouquet's *équipe* of Le Nôtre, Le Vau, and Lebrun to Versailles, and he shaped the image of his realm upon the principles that Fouquet had worked out at Vaux, through which it was now possible to draw a portrait of the new continental France and its Sun King. Touchingly, of course, the process recalled Suger and his king, except that Fouquet had not intended it to turn out quite that way. Yet, how much their works of art shared and alike gave to France: the great circle in the square, the

382. Vaux-le-Vicomte. Farnese Hercules.

heavenly light, the axis and the crown. In his masque of 1668, *The Loves of Psyche,* performed at the greatest fête ever held at Versailles, La Fontaine put it all together when he wrote:

> Tous parcs étaient vergers aux temps
>   de nos ancêtres.
> Tous vergers sont fait parcs. Le sa-
>   voir de ces maîtres
> Changent en jardins royaux ceux des
>   simples bourgeois,
> Comme en jardins des dieux ils
>   changent ceux des rois.

It is a fact that the great and most characteristic days of the Classic garden came to coincide with the greatest days of Louis' reign itself—from about 1661 to 1690. Its dominion over space and its conquest of nature were the objectives of Louis himself and the very stuff of his *gloire.* So we may legitimately return to St. Germain-en-Laye. We recall the sacred mountain of its Renaissance garden. Higher up is the irregular shape of the old castle with its thirteenth-century Sainte-Chapelle. In front of it, on the plateau and looking toward the park, Le Nôtre laid out a splendid parterre, which has since been truncated by the suburban railroad line. Finally, on the military crest above the Seine, he built his famous terrace over-

385. St. Germain-en-Laye, France. The terrace.

386. St. Germain-en-Laye. Terrace, detail.

looking Paris (fig. 385). It has at present one great joint in it, and then stretches out along the height almost as far as Maisons, where the sternly Classical château by François Mansart overlooks the Seine in its turn. As Le Nôtre drew it, he broke the terrace again at another circle, so enlivening its otherwise interminable axis, but that break was apparently never built. Today, there is just one great circle (fig. 386), with its urns and balustrades, and then the long terrace with the crowns of its trees behind it, to direct us to the royal view across the Ile-de-France.

This is the view that Louis symbolically left behind in his youth; here, later, he framed, commemorated, and monumentalized it. It is, indeed, about confidence and power, about the city and victory, and as we look across it toward St. Denis, we can feel the whole structure of French kingship from the twelfth to the seventeenth centuries lock together. Everything is in plain sight except, out beyond St. Denis, the garden that, with Vaux and Versailles, most tellingly embodies the theme. It is Chantilly (fig. 387). Louis XIV himself believed that it was the greatest garden of all.

Chantilly was designed by Le Nôtre at about the time he was first employed at Versailles, and he worked on it for a good

twenty years. It was for Le Grand Condé, who was France's greatest general during Louis' minority and the early years of his reign. Le Grand Condé eventually succeeded to the title of Prince de Bourbon, whose major seat Chantilly became after it was taken over by Richelieu from the Montmorency family, which had built the château. It was an irregular, late Medieval, early Renaissance building. We see it today as it was rebuilt after the Revolution of 1789, when it was destroyed down to the basement. But it always remained irregular in plan and massing, despite a rather top-heavy addition by Jules Hardouin-Mansart.

To understand Chantilly properly, we have to know something about Le Grand Condé. During his youth, he had been the Duc d'Enghien and, hardly out of his teens, had defeated the Spaniards at Rocroi in 1643. Voltaire, whose attempt to rehabilitate the reputation of Louis XIV I mentioned earlier, begins what he calls *Le Siècle de Louis Quatorze* with the victory of Rocroi itself. It took place on the borders of Belgium, and it enabled the reign to begin that push for a frontier on the Rhine that became one of Louis' fixed objectives. Rocroi was thus the critical French victory of the century, and a myth goes with it, suggested by the fact that on

388. Chantilly. View across bridge toward equestrian statue of Anne de Montmorency, Constable of France.

387. Chantilly, France. Château and gardens. 1663–1673. Air view.

the day it was taking place, Louis XIII lay dying in the Louvre. As he awoke from what was to be his last living sleep, he saw the father of the Duc d'Enghien, the then Prince de Bourbon, in the room, and is supposed to have said to him, "Monsieur le Prince, I dreamed that your son won a great victory." That victory began the reign of Louis XIV, and Le Nôtre's Chantilly may be said to commemorate it.

When Le Nôtre took over the garden, he inherited an axis of entrance that ran out of the woods in front of it directly to its gate. On that axis stood an equestrian statue of Anne de Montmorency, once Constable of France. Using that statue as a pivot, Le Nôtre changed the axis of approach by ninety degrees, so that it now

389. Chantilly. Approach to château.

ran directly across the face of the château rather than toward it (fig. 387). It is, in fact, directed past it. Today, if we start at the railroad station and walk directly through the woods with the racetrack of Chantilly on our left, we come out of the trees on the new axis, and we see the château to our left front, dominating the view, with the equestrian figure rather lost below the crest of the woods that lie behind it.

The present statue base is slightly different in height from the way it was in the seventeenth century, but the principle is the same. As we approach it, it begins to stand out against the sky and to balance the irregular mass of the château (fig. 388).

As we get closer, it stands out even more and seizes our attention. We cross the bridge over the moat and mount the slight but increasing slope that leads toward it. Our view is now developing a wonderful velocity as it is directed rapidly up the slope toward the figure on horseback. When we finally come up below it, it seems much more important than the château, which is now deploying in complex profiles off to the left of our arc of vision (fig. 389).

This is especially so because as our eyes go to the statue, we see for the first time that there is a break in the parterre beyond it, through which a gleam of water now appears fairly far off and down below.

This offers a new objective for our eyes, and we are led to move in its direction. As we do so, the water enlarges *toward* us, literally step-by-step, to show us a broad canal emerging (fig. 390). At last, when we get to the top of the stairs, a great circle appears directly below us, and we see a whole parterre, of which we had not previously imagined the existence, opening out generously before us (fig. 391). Its new, grand, clear shapes instantly obliterate our memory of the château. The building no longer seems of much interest. A vaster order and a more releasing architecture than that of mere buildings has been revealed to us.

The effect is staggering because, while

390. Chantilly. View beyond equestrian statue toward the garden.

391. Chantilly. The parterres.

392. Chantilly. Air view, floating on the water.

393. Chantilly. The Connetable from the parterre. (Jeannie Baubion-Mackler)

we are first shown the canal, which extends along our axis of movement, the ultimate expansion is unexpectedly lateral, and the distance straight ahead is, in fact, comparatively restricted. The staircases and their urns give scale to that lateral breadth. The release is on the diagonal, to the corners of the parterre, with the circle in the center spinning out to them. Of all the gardens, this is the closest to the climactic experience of the choir of Nôtre Dame in Paris, but here it all happens on the surface of the ground. In every way, though, it says "Victory," and it makes us feel a grandeur of soul, a generosity of action, and an expansion of space far beyond anything we had imagined before.

It is very different from the long view down the path to the sky that we saw at Versailles (fig. 344). There, we noted that the trees were closed in to focus our view because there was potentially too much lateral space, which might well simply have vitiated it. Here it is the opposite. We are in a volume, an enormous room, one that the circle tells us is as big as the world and in which the little stream, the Nonette, never ran dry, so that the fountains could run night and day. Of all the French gardens, it is the most perfect. Architecture as buildings is literally pushed to one side; the whole earth becomes architecture. It is also the ultimate celebration of the circle and the square. The Neoplatonic Idea of universal order is inscribed here as in a mirror, floating on the waters (fig. 392). Here, finally, the old moat becomes more even than a canal. It becomes the void upon which the thin earth floats.

It is that which releases us from the normal scale of the earth to something vast and grand. It is surely the cosmic order we talked about before, but it also Condé,

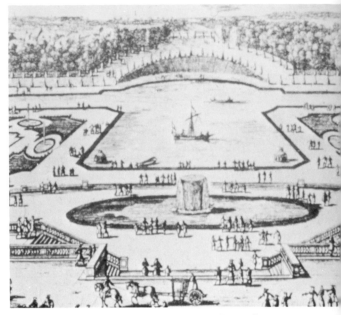

394. Chantilly. Parterres. 18th-century engraving by Perelle.

the Duc d'Enghien, and Rocroi: the *furia francese* and the victory of France, the expansion of France to the Rhine (fig. 393). All smaller conceptions now give way before this one, exactly as they had done before Suger's vision long ago. The shapes that embody the two are much the same, as a comparison between a print of Chantilly and a photograph of the facade of Nôtre Dame in Paris can show (figs. 394, 395). There are the twin towers in both, the sky between them, the reflecting *bassin,* and the rose. It is the central, constant image. Its endurance must make us realize that our identification of styles—Gothic, Renaissance, Baroque—can be limiting and misleading. As Henri Focillon pointed out, there are other styles often transcending these.* There are families of form that endure across time, and this family is French.

*Henri Focillon, *Vie des formes,* Paris, 1934.

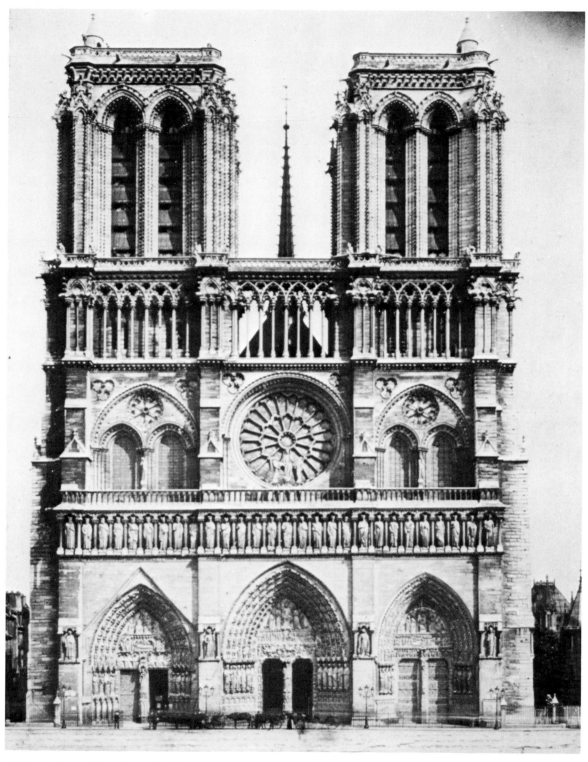

395. Paris, France. Nôtre Dame. Facade.

10
THE SHAPE OF FRANCE: GARDENS, FORTIFICATIONS, AND MODERN URBANISM

I N THE LAST CHAPTER, I discussed the word *pourtraiture* as it was employed in the garden treatises of the seventeenth century and suggested that, through the methodical adjustment of geometry to scale that it was intended to describe, garden architects did draw, in fact, a "portrait" of the order of the world upon its surface. At the same time, the word *pourtraiture* may be thought to have a double meaning, since each of the gardens was intended to portray the character of its client and to embody his own intentions. At Vaux, it was clearly the will of Fouquet as an individual that was portrayed and embodied in landscape. At Versailles, it was the realm of Louis XIV, his *gloire,* which was the new France. And at Chantilly, it was surely Victory itself in the person of Le Grand Condé, especially his decisive victory, as the Duc d'Enghien, at Rocroi, in 1643.

Chantilly is the garden everyone loved. It is the one even Louis most admired and, indeed, wanted for himself. We know that he hinted to Condé on more

416. Mont-Louis, France. Fortifications. Vauban. Air view.

than one occasion that he would be glad to receive it from him, but that gift was never made. Perhaps Louis wanted it so much precisely because it embodied what he, despite his *gloire,* had never really experienced firsthand: direct military victory, its special release and incomparable satisfactions. As a field commander, Louis was never quite able to close with the enemy. The one chance he had to do so he let slip through his fingers. Unlike the Duc d'Enghien, who won his victory at Rocroi through reckless personal daring, Louis, despite his often-demonstrated physical courage, was never quite able to let himself go in that way. So all his victories were in a sense secondhand. And before we despise victory as a theme, we should remember that the Periclean Acropolis was about exactly that, the victory of Athens over everything. The Parthenon is hubris embodied, and so is Chantilly, but the fierce joy and the grandeur are no less for that.

These concepts may also be associated with the intention to "*forcer la nature,*"

401. Lucca. Fortifications. Curtain wall from flank of bastion.

which surely played a part in the creation of the French Classic garden. Yet it was Louis and his advisers who employed the term, never the landscape architects. It is a political phrase. So the English, as they developed their Romantic gardens in the decades to come, tried to make them look natural in part for political reasons, as a widely recognized criticism of French absolutism—though the gardens themselves are no less works of human artifice and the manipulation of growing things than the French gardens are.

On the other hand, the French landscape architects, though they were serving the concept of "*forcer la nature*" to a certain extent, clearly did not think of their work in those overbearing terms. Their view was better stated by Boyceau de la Barauderie when he named his treatise *La Traité du jardinage selon les raisons de la nature et de l'art*. Both are reasonable and they work together. We noted earlier that *pourtraiture* itself involved a similar conjunction—in its case, a cooperation between the ideal, in geometry, and the real, in scale. We have found a similar union of the Real and the Ideal before, most particularly in Gothic architecture, and the integral relationship between cathedrals and gardens has constantly made itself felt.

Here we encounter one of the many reasons why art historians have to study works of art directly, and afresh in each generation, and cannot depend upon what others, even when they are contemporaries of those works, have written about them. The deepest, most persistent visual images often remain nonverbal, precisely because they *are* deep and persistent. They deal with experiences that are in part outside verbal discourse. Not one of the landscape architects of the seventeenth century would have said that he was working in a Gothic order, even though from Phili-

bert de l'Orme to Blondel there is some suggestion that the idea of a continuing order, embracing the Gothic, may well have been present.

It is, in fact, their mixture of Neoplatonism with rationalism, even with scientism, that links the cathedrals and the gardens. They are both very French, and it is, therefore, no wonder that their most important forms bear family resemblances. Moreover, we must not assume that because the landscape architects did not write about symbolism they were any less concerned with it than were the Gothic architects—who did not write about it either. But they were Cartesians after all; they wanted to show us, make us *see,* not merely allude. So they threw out almost all the old iconography and came down to how things look. In a sense, the word *pourtraiture* says it all, and in the hands of Le Nôtre it becomes one of the great vehicles for the expression of human meaning. It is, in fact, one of the greatest to be created by any age. Through it, and through the program it serves, the Classic garden, all Cartesian optics, becomes the cathedral of the seventeenth century, celebrating the Virgin's garden of France, the cosmic order, and the rationality of the human mind.

Another thing that the landscape architects and theoreticians did not talk about much, but which they knew perfectly well, was the art of fortification. They were contemporaries of the greatest military engineer of all time, and one of the most admirable of human beings: Sébastien le Prestre de Vauban, who became marshal of France. We know that Vauban was a special friend of Le Nôtre. He and Le Nôtre were almost the only people at Versailles about whom the poisonous Saint-Simon had little but good to say, despite the fact that their pedigrees were

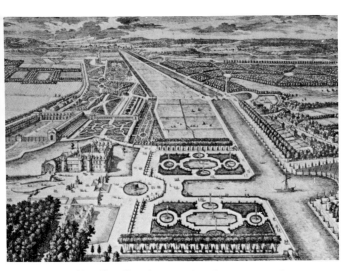

396. Chantilly. Château and gardens. Air view from west. Engraving by Perelle.

not noble enough to enjoy his approval. We are told, too, that Vauban and Le Nôtre were collaborators at Chantilly. Vauban was supposed to have designed balancing bridges to span the great moat and connect the island of the château with the mainland. We do not know whether or not they were ever built. We do know, however, that Vauban's work was closely connected with the gardens in contemporary thought. A letter recently found in a Venetian archive by Mirka Beneš describes a certain parterre as laid out "in the manner of Vauban."

The idea that the arts of fortification and of landscape architecture were almost the same was quite a logical one in the seventeenth century. Together, they shaped a new architecture, an earth-moving art in which, at the scale of the landscape itself, the human will reached out to control the environment farther than human beings had ever been able to reach before. So the treatises written about fortifications are much like those about gardens. They begin with geometry and go on to scale, because they are expanding their conceptions to landscape size, and it is fascinating to watch the great new forms take shape step by step, logically and with obsessive passion.*

How did it all come about? Again, we can begin at Chantilly (fig. 396). If we look at the courtyard in front of the château, we see that it looks like a citadel with bastions at the four corners, and we can compare it for a start with a fort at Nettuno (fig. 397), built by Giuliano and Antonio da Sangallo in 1502. This is a citadel with a bastion at each corner. Each bastion has a face (the outward face) and a flank. In the flank is at least one gun that was meant to fire across the curtain wall of the citadel and the opposite face of the bastion across the way. That face takes its angle from the siting of the gun, or rather, the two are coordinated so that the shot can rake the bastion's face. Then, in order to protect the gun, to shield its flank, the bastion is "eared," so becoming a *bastion oreillonné*. In this way, all the forms take shape according to the intersection of lines of sight and the trajectory of missile weapons. The form, therefore, is beginning to open out in a series of intersecting diagonals, moving out across the countryside as the gardens, too, eventually would do.

These shapes were invented because of the development of cannon during the fifteenth century, which necessitated a total reassessment of the way fortifications had to be made. It is worthwhile to look back at that development for a moment.† The beautiful walls of Montagnana (fig. 398), which is in the Veneto and has a couple of villas by Palladio nearby, can show us what the walls of medieval Italian cities gener-

*Especially in Blaise François de Pagan, Comte de Merveilles, *Traité des fortifications,* Paris, 1645; and L'Abbé de Fay, *Véritable manière de bien fortifier de M. de Vauban,* Paris, 1694.

†It is briefly traced in Horst de la Croix, *Military Considerations in City Planning: Fortifications,* New York, 1972.

398. Montagnana, Italy. Medieval fortifications.

ally looked like. The wall had to be high, because the thing most to be feared was assault by scaling ladders. So the high wall is supplemented by towers that are even higher, and there are crenellations at the top that were meant to protect the archers. The wall can be fairly thin, as those of Montagnana are, because the heavy stone balls that were projected against it from various kinds of machines took a long while to break through it. This gave the defenders time (and Viollet-le-Duc has marvelous drawings of this) to build some kind of structure behind the wall at that spot to trap the assault if and when it broke into the breach. The same principles hold good for mining. The wall does not have to be very thick; it has to be high.

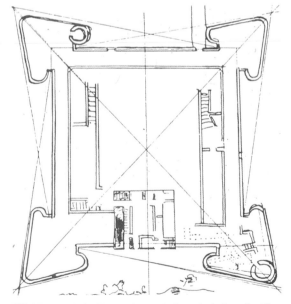

397. Nettuno, Italy. Fort. 1501–1502. G. & A. da Sangallo. Plan.

With the introduction of cannon in the fifteenth century, firing first a stone ball and soon one of iron, a breach could be made rapidly. Hence, the wall had to become thick. Ideally, it should be built up not of stone but of earth; though generally it consisted of two faces of stone packed with earth. Similarly, for one's own cannon, low raking fire was infinitely preferable to plunging fire. The latter is especially ineffective for a weapon, like the Renaissance cannon, of comparatively flat trajectory. With the arrow, which was a weapon of lower velocity and therefore higher trajectory, it did not matter quite so much, but it was essential to bring the batteries of cannon down to sweep the ground before them.

All through the fifteenth century, the builders of fortifications struggled with these new problems. At Soncino, of about 1473 (fig. 399), every ancient instinct told them to keep the wall high and to retain the crenellations for its defenders. At the same time, they thickened it and slanted it back to encourage the cannon balls to ricochet off it. They lowered and broadened the towers as platforms for the guns, but in so doing, they were clearly fighting their preconceptions every step of the way. By the time of Nettuno, in 1502, of which we have already mentioned the plan, they had it all worked out except that they refused to come down. They wanted the height, and with it they needed and wanted the masonry revetment. Otherwise, it is all rationalized. There is the smooth face of the bastion, and its ears. The mouth of the cannon gapes from the flank, protecting the curtain and bastion beyond it. The whole is totally without projections that might shatter under bombardment. It is bound together with one strong stringcourse, of a kind that Vauban and Le Nôtre were both to employ later.

Finally, by the time of Lucca, toward the middle of the sixteenth century, it was felt possible to lower the wall considerably (fig. 400). It stretches out to enclose the whole of that beautiful Tuscan city. The great curtain walls, and the flanks, ears, and faces of the enormous bastions, are all there before us. We can stand at the critical spot, in the flank with the cannoneers. At Lucca, there are spaces for two of them side by side (fig. 401). Their responsibility was not to worry about their own flank but to fire across the front of the curtain wall and the far face of the bastion on the other side. We begin to feel that it is a long way across, a long curtain to defend. Even worse, what if the attack indeed were to come in on our flank, scaling the face of our own bastion? How do we know that the cannoneers

400. Lucca, Italy. Fortifications. 16th century. Curtain wall and bastion.

across the way will keep it off?

One thing we do know is that "they" ("the other") will come in overpowering force, with more men than we have, flooding in toward the curtain wall, and we cannot bring them under fire until they are terribly close. What can we do? The answer to that always was to push the defenses farther out into space. First came a good broad ditch full of water in front of curtain and bastion alike. Then, out in front of the curtain, a *demi-lune* appears (fig. 402), a half-moon, though it is basically triangular, whose own slanting faces can be covered by fire from the bastions and whose own lines of fire will intersect theirs. But that is not enough; the instinct is to get more defenses farther out yet and to fill them with troops to take the first brunt of the assault. This creates the covered way, the most forward position of all. There are traverses in it (like those in the trenches during World War I) so that if the enemy breaks in at one point, he cannot roll up the whole line too easily. For counterattacks, there are *places d'armes* from which we, ourselves, can attack suddenly across the glacis beyond the

399. Soncino, Italy. Fortifications of castello, 1473.

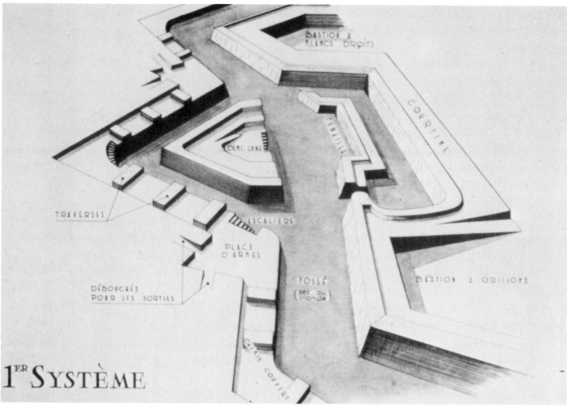

402. Diagram of *demi-lune* and other elements, 1st system, after Vauban.

covered way. This has a gentle slope so that the counterattack can erupt all of a sudden, flooding out upon the attacker in its turn.

Having reached out so far, we then look back and note a disquieting gap behind us between the curtain and the *demi-lune.* We must fill it in, and so create the *tenaille,* stretched taut between the bastions in front of the curtain wall. But the major thrust is outward, and once that is started, there is theoretically no end to it, because there will always be anxiety about the massive force that might be coming. "The other" always threatens to overwhelm us.

Just as the gardens created their great stars, the *étoiles,* so too, by the seventeenth century, did the military art. As Le Nôtre assimilated everything that had occurred in garden design and used it to leap into space, so, too, did Vauban. He was the great engineer of the *dehors,* the outside. He, too, conquered the earth's face. The great *étoile* of the citadel of Lille is an outstanding example (fig. 403): It is still the headquarters of an infantry regiment today. We can see them all there: curtain, bastions, *tenailles,* and *demi-lunes.* (How beautiful the words are, more like drums than bugles, embodying in themselves the stately ritual of the siege.) Beyond the *demi-lunes,* all is doubled. The covered way is repeated, then repeated again. It could go on forever; indeed, it goes beyond practicality into art, to become the ultimate expression of our common anxieties.

It is an obsession, an image of the self and the adversary, as the lovely book about Vauban by Parent and Verroust makes abundantly clear.* The authors publish a beautiful drawing that shows what the new construction means (fig. 404). It means moving the earth; it is like making a garden. Everything is slanting out on a continuous line of sight so that, from the bastions and the curtain, the view is never impeded, and it goes out along the gentle slope of the glacis into space. The revolution the cannon began is com-

plete. It has changed the human view of the city, and of the landscape, too. We have brought our batteries down; we are defending in echelon, in depth rather than in height. The high wall has disappeared: How terrifying that the age-old image of security, as old as Sumer, no longer applies. The wall of Gilgamesh is nothing; security involves interdependence. Therefore, no individual ever feels wholly safe again. Ideally, even the stone would go; now we have trenches, deep earthworks, and we defend in depth, extending horizontally across the landscape. Our entire

*A luminous work: Michel Parent and Jacques Verroust, *Vauban*, Paris, 1971.

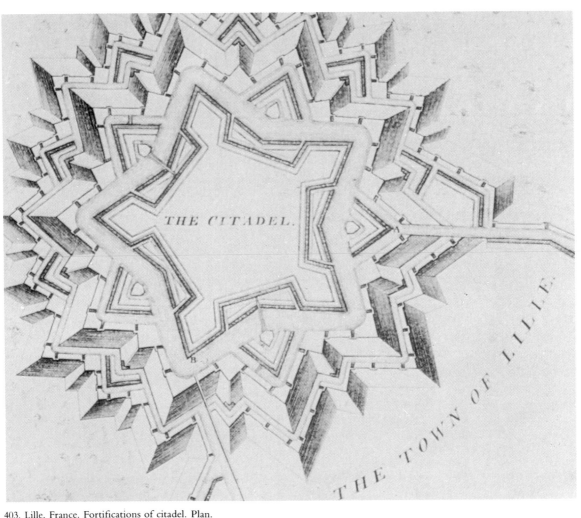

403. Lille, France. Fortifications of citadel. Plan.

404. Construction of fortifications from a treatise by a collaborator of Vauban.

frontier becomes a garden, traversed by cannonballs of iron.

There is one touching footnote to this. In 1527, the thin walls of an ancient town were threatened by the invincible army of the world's most powerful empire. It was Florence. In 1527, when the troops of Charles V sacked Rome, the Florentines took the opportunity to revolt against the Medici Pope and proclaim the republic. Vaingloriously, they inscribed the Palazzo Vecchio with a new motto: *Jesus Christus Rex Florentini Populi.* They had, however, to prepare themselves for a siege. They knew that it would come, as indeed it did before the end of the decade. But they had only their old, thin medieval walls with their high, proud, fragile gates to protect them (fig. 280). So they put Michelangelo in charge of remodeling the fortifications.

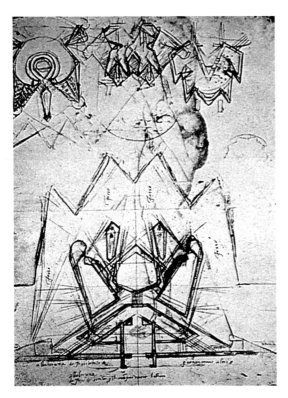

405. Michelangelo. *Fortification Drawing #27.* Casa Buonarotti, Florence.

Michelangelo was clearly moved by this trust and instantly went to work on a series of studies for the fortification of the gates. There was no time to rebuild the curtains, but there was a chance that if the gates could be rebuilt, Francesco Ferrucci (the only partisan leader Florence was to produce between 1529 and World War II) might be able to harass the Imperial troops seriously enough to cause them to break off the siege. In order to do so, he needed to be able to sally forth and to retire under the protection of covering fire from the gates. To achieve that result, Michelangelo devised, indeed invented, methods of fortification a hundred years before their time.

The state of the art in 1529 was much as we saw it at Nettuno. Michelangelo, though, made use of the *demi-lune,* with lunettes, and he studied the relationship of the glacis to the ditch. His drawings are passionately felt; some of them overlie studies of the human figure, an older passion superseded by this new need (fig. 405).* It is remarkable to watch his mind working. He clearly was trying to lower the walls and to tear them apart into their essential components, each element taking its place in relation to intersecting lines of fire, so that the old solid forms are already becoming *étoiles.*

A model owned by Vauban (fig. 406) sets out to show all the variations in fortifications that had developed by the late seventeenth century. There are the big bastions, the *demi-lunes,* with the outer works deploying beyond them. There are also bastions with casemates, of a kind

*They are exhibited in the Casa Buonarotti in Florence, where they first opened my eyes to the splendor of Renaissance fortifications and the genius of Michelangelo, as I tried to describe them in "Michelangelo's Fortification Drawings: A Study in the Reflex Diagonal," *Perspecta* I, 1952, 38–45.

Vauban developed, and there are gigantic hornworks that reach out to deny a landscape feature to the enemy. On another side, the horns are doubled by further outer works, so that a great crown burgeons in the landscape. Michelangelo already had sensed that necessity for considerable extension in front of some of the gates, and for that he imagined a figure that already resembles Vauban's horn and crown types (fig. 407).

406. Vauban. Model of fortified town.

Most moving of all are Michelangelo's drawings of the angle where the thin walls of Florence came down to the Arno at the point where the Mugnone Creek flowed into it (fig. 408). To Michelangelo, it seemed to be the critical angle; he did his most passionate drawings for it. Some, as de Tolnay once wrote, reach out like the claws of crustaceans to crush the foe.* But it is the diagonals of the integrated fire plan that govern the shapes. One of them is, in fact, like a bursting grenade as it literally articulates itself out into space along its intersecting lines of fire. We can almost hear the rattle of its musketry as it bursts itself apart at the angle.

*Charles de Tolnay, *Michelangelo: Sculptor, Painter, Architect,* Princeton, 1975, p. 136.

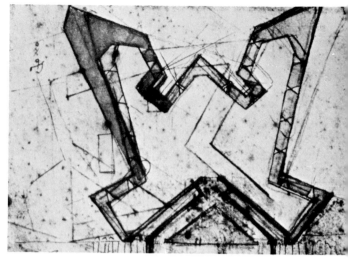

407. Michelangelo. *Fortification drawing #28.*

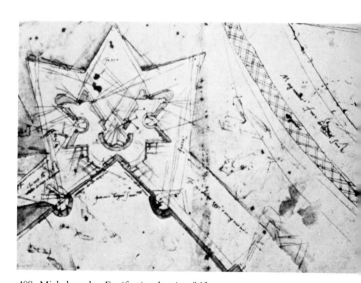

408. Michelangelo. *Fortification drawing #13.*

The other thing about the drawings is that they are dealing with fortifications as a whole landscape art, and Michelangelo developed long spatial diagonals in them, diagonals that he would exploit later in his plan for the Capitoline (fig. 303) and in his Pauline Chapel frescoes, precursors of the Baroque and, in that sense, of Le Nôtre and Vauban. They were already at the new, vast landscape scale that the gardens

410. Rocroi. Town as rebuilt and refortified by Vauban.

eventually were to attain. Michelangelo's drawings for the Mugnone angle can be compared with the general plan of Chantilly and with aerial photographs of it showing the abstract, earth-sculpture shape of the parterre and, indeed, of the whole island on which the château sits (fig. 396). Gardens and fortifications now do seem like one art, and the climax of their relationship comes with the gardens of Le Nôtre and the fortifications of Vauban.

We should go, for example, to Rocroi. Long after Condé's victory—and Condé was one of Vauban's first commanders—it was refortified by Vauban. A beautiful drawing, which may be by the master himself, shows us the fortifications as he developed them (fig. 409). The town has a radial plan, but that is not Vauban's, who preferred, as we shall see, the static discipline of the rectangular grid. Our photograph was taken from the casemate that Vauban built on top of the southern bastion (fig. 410). It looks out across the *demi-lune* that guards the main gate to the bastion on the other side. If we swing the camera around, we see how this art of the whole landscape is totally different in kind and scale from that of the old architecture of houses gathered together behind

walls in cities, and we cannot help but recognize the grandeur of the new conception. As we swing around farther, we see Vauban's church, a kind of simplified engineer's architecture. Although built of stone, which only a minority of American Colonial buildings were, it can still remind Americans very much of their own seventeenth- and eighteenth-century architecture, which was also a kind of simplified and regularized variant of the European type. But as we swing the camera even farther to get the full arc of the horizon, we more fully grasp how the small scale of the old world has been transformed into the enormous scale of the new.

Then, if we can imagine the ditch full of water, we see that Vauban's Rocroi and Le Nôtre's Chantilly are products of a single art, one that seems to owe nothing to the past or to tradition. Far more even than the shapes of the modern architecture of the twentieth century, these shapes are profoundly themselves, having little to do with memory or association. We are tempted to call them "abstract," as we call those of modern architecture, but they are not really that, because they grow out of an inner dynamic which, while geo-

metrically embodied, is still optically, even scientifically, directed. This is their own "scale" and "*pourtraiture.*" They are Cartesian, too; they owe their confirmation to the way the human eye works.

We remember that Vauban collaborated with Le Nôtre at Chantilly and apparently designed *ponts à basculer,* which have since disappeared. Yet the monumental half-round stringcourse with which Le Nôtre bound his island citadel is the twin of the stringcourse that Vauban invariably used, running like a cannon shot along his walls. It is there in the beautiful work at Gravelines (fig. 411), in the magnificent, swelling block of a building that can remind Americans once again of their own architecture, here especially that of Henry Hobson Richardson. It is there in Vauban's unique Tour Dorée at Camaret (fig. 412), where a specialized function was fulfilled in a form that recalls that of the medieval keep.

In his use of towers, Vauban comes to remind us a bit of the architect of Chartres, who had been strong-minded enough to reject the slender columns, which all the up-to-date architects of his generation had come to regard as essential, in order to return to an outmoded Romanesque type,

the compound pier. In fortification, it was the tower that had been discarded. Vauban took it up again and redesigned it as the *tour bastionné,* lowered and compacted like a bastion but also covered, and as such the

409. Rocroi, France. Plan.

direct ancestor of the casemates of modern times. Vauban used such tower-bastions along the extensive walls of Besançon, which, since they border the river, could not properly be enfiladed through the normal bastion system. Vauban's new casemates, part tower, part bastion, not only deal with the problem but are also beautiful, and are as beautifully reflected in the water as any château (fig. 413 and p. *IV*). Behind and above them at Besançon, one of Vauban's greatest citadels guards the heights of this first and most durable of Louis' territorial gains, the Franche-Comté, that marvelous piedmont behind the mountain frontier.

I have alluded to Louis' grand design for the shape of continental France and the criticism that colonial-minded historians of the last century leveled against it. Now, however, when colonies everywhere have been irretrievably lost, we are confronted with the image of a France which seems all the better and stronger for that fact, precisely because of the European shape Louis gave it. We remember, too, that the question of France's shape also played a central part in the creation and spread of Gothic architecture in the twelfth century.

The Ile-de-France, the king's own country, lay under the shadow of Normandy, and the northern and eastern frontiers were only a few miles outside Paris (fig. 210). Suger built in response to these conditions and in defiance of them. In so doing, he shaped the essential symbol of a new nation, which then grew as Gothic architecture itself grew. Each brought the other along with it, two new shining ideas full of light, until everything was held firm by them from Flanders to the Pyrenees, from the coast of the Channel and the Bay of Biscay to the Rhône. All of this survived the Hundred Years War, at the end of which most of its interior parti-

tions, like its humiliations, were swept away by Joan at Reims. Yet the northern frontier still lay only just beyond Amiens, hardly outside Reims. Paris always lay open, almost on the edge. The Imperial enemy, still the more puissant heir of Charlemagne, perennially threatened from the near banks of the Rhine. Louis XIV changed all that. France pushed her boundaries out to the river and the mountains, seizing and, finally, holding Franche-Comté, Lorraine, Alsace: Nancy, Metz, Strasbourg.

Now, at last, the shape that France assumed was at once full and geometric and of an appropriately modern scale. That terminology is intended to recall the art of the garden, the art of *pourtraiture*. Indeed, Louis drew his portrait of France in so authoritative a style that it continues to convince us of the correctness of its likeness. It is a shape that in every way holds together functionally no less than visually, since the frontier provinces that Louis incorporated into the state were also to become the great industrial districts, rich in coal and other sources of power. They made France workable as a self-sufficient nation, as in fact the first modern nation-state at fully continental scale. Other states had surely preceded France in their modernity, England and Holland among them. But England was hardly continental, and Holland, which was Louis' constant annoyance and, in a sense, his nemesis, was simply not as large as France and, in the course of the centuries, especially after the common loss of empire, was surely fated to become the lesser of the two. Again, we are caught up in the big, single shape, like one of Le Nôtre's parterres: The *pourtrait* of France, impressing the nation itself with a common character that sometimes countered, most often overrode, its many serious regional

411. Gravelines, France. Fortifications. Vauban. Detail.

differences in Louis' time as in our own.

The maintenance of that shape was Vauban's responsibility; he was the gardener of the frontiers, and he defended them in depth. The splendid map published by Parent and Verroust shows the conformation of completed France and stresses Vauban's essential contribution to it (fig. 414). His forts, his fortified cities, ring its borders like the bastions, the *demilunes,* and the *tenailles* of a single citadel. Each relates to all the others and to the topography like the outworks of one great *étoile,* the nation as a whole. They push out as bridgeheads across the Rhine, like Huninque's bursting bomb (fig. 415). Others, like Ville Franche-en-Conflent, push down through the boulder-strewn torrents of the Pyrenees, stretching out and deforming in response to the moun-

tains' pressures. Beyond, on the borders of Andorra, the broad, eared bastions of Mont-Louis grip the high slopes above an alpine meadow full of flowers (fig. 416). Its barrack square still gleams white in the mountain sun, clear, clean, cool, disciplined. It is the very image of the new army Vauban did so much to retrain, re-equip, and re-form, and which in the new century was to be uniformed in white, its white columns maneuvering in the white parade.

Finally, we should turn to Neuf-Brisach, lying in wait behind the Rhine (fig. 417). Brisach beyond the Rhine having been lost, Neuf-Brisach was designed by Vauban all complete and in his most developed manner. The bastions are pulled in and become very small, while the curtain wall between them takes on the set-

413. Bensançon. Tour Bastionnée. Vauban.

ban also avoided the radial plan when he could do so, even though it, too, had be come a major canonical element in all ideal schemes for fortified cities. With the radial plan, reserves of men and guns could be most rapidly and directly dispatched to threatened bastions from the central square—but at the expense of stability and calm, since the square so pierced by radial avenues became the hub of whirling, centrifugal forces. Whatever the reason, Vauban wanted none of it. He preferred the rectangular grid. This might delay reinforcement from the center by a matter of a few minutes, but it provides in return a sheltered, well-defined central square, the image of discipline and confidence I referred to earlier.

It is *servitude et grandeur militaire* made visible, made into a city, and it preserves

414. France. Towns fortified by Vauban under Louis XIV. Map.

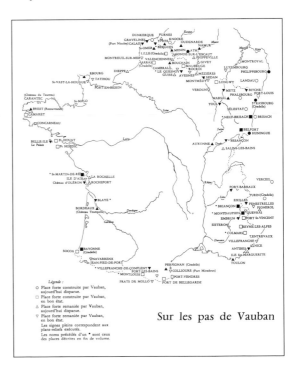

Sur les pas de Vauban

backs of the old *tenaille* itself. But then, beyond the ditch, everything is repeated at larger scale, with what amounts to second bastions connected by another *tenaille,* before which a *demi-lune* is thrown out into space. Each unit of two bastions and *tenaille,* with its expanded outer works, takes on a winged shape, as if, in fact, it were lifting to the horizon. The *dehors* thus seem to reach their definitive expansion, but behind them everything is pulled in, retracted, calmed down. The combination of small bastion with indented wall enormously reduces the final perimeter of defense, so that the tendency toward centrifugal dispersion, which had been building itself into the sytem since the fifteenth century, is drastically reduced. A more stable order is gained.

It is probably for this reason that Vau-

412. Camaret, France. Fortifications. Vauban. La Tour Dorée.

ancient traditions, recalls ancient virtues, in ways that the forms of the new fortifications themselves do not normally do. It does not explode into the centrifugal hysteria that most treatises of fortification had prescribed and which Palmanova, for example, exemplifies—although there every other radial avenue is forced to detour to the central square in order to preserve the stability of that space to some extent. But Vauban's unhurried, orthogonal grid has its own special Roman measure and dignity. An unshakable calm lies at the heart of his *étoiles*.

But, if Vauban avoids radiating avenues, the gardens embrace them, especially those gardens that most try to reach out across the countryside, through parks and over meadows, to seize terrain and to control expansive topographical space. Versailles is the major example (fig. 418). Here, again, as we have seen, there was Italian precedent, especially in the radiating avenues of Baroque Rome, deriving from the urbanistic schemes of Sixtus V (fig. 305). Once again, however, the Italian form is sculptural, the French environmental. The Roman avenues are comparatively narrow and are cut through the solids of the old city. The French reach out toward continental scale, laying out the idea of a new kind of city, region, or nation. It is an affair of space, rapid movement, and expanding powers rushing unimpeded across a void.

As such, Versailles becomes the model not only for all of absolutism's kingly palaces in the last years of the ancien régime everywhere but also, and more cogently, for the capitals of the two emerging nations of wholly continental scope. Russian St. Petersburg is more French than Italian, with its endless open spaces and imperial skies, white all night on a midsummer's eve and frosty with stars in December.

But Washington, D.C., follows the model even more closely (fig. 419). L'Enfant's plan sends out radiating avenues from the Capitol and the White House. They cross the grid of streets upon which Jefferson insisted. By the time of the Civil War, the dome of the Capitol found its own appropriate scale, high enough to control the wide spaces below it. By the 1880s, Washington's obelisk stood on the bank of the Potomac. It is miraculous that so spare a design could have been chosen at that period to balance the Capitol's dome. It may well be that the final decision to build it in that form was affected by the visual relationship between the obelisk in the Place de la Concorde and the dome of the Invalides, as it seems at that angle to be rising above the pedimented portico of the Chambre des Députés.

There, until the early twentieth century, the matter rested, until the World's Columbian Exposition in Chicago, of 1893, brought Versailles forward once again, adapting the forms of the Grand Bassin to shape a new Court of Honor. It is the Classic garden literally translated into a city center. That is one reason why the forms of the buildings around the great basin in Chicago seem so ghostly. It is as if the woods of Versailles had taken one giant step toward the water and turned into white columns, porticoes, and domes. The instinct was correct, because the Classic garden "wanted" to be a city and was, indeed, already the skeleton of the city to come. The City Beautiful movement took shape out of that instinct. It produced Daniel Burnham's plans for Chicago and San Francisco, where the Acropolis of Athens was welded to San Francisco's Twin Peaks and to the major axis of Versailles.*

*Described at greater length in my *American Architecture and Urbanism,* New York: 1969; rev. ed., 1988.

Most of all, it brought about the Park Commission Plan for Washington, of 1901 (fig. 419). Now, at last, Washington surpassed the scale of Versailles. The Grand Bassin became the reflecting pool beyond which the Lincoln Memorial was to rise. It is Versailles developed iconographically according to memories lying far deeper than those embodied in seventeenth-century absolutism alone. Its conceptual structure supports a profoundly Classical imagery in which Lincoln broods in his temple like Zeus and Washington points with his obelisk to the sun, calling up kings far more ancient than those of France. In that setting, all political acts take on the trappings of Classical literature and so attain their most universal dimension. The Kennedy

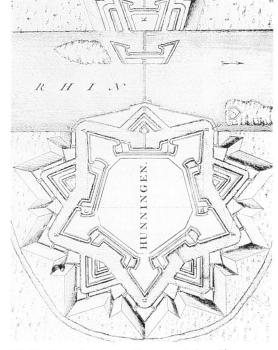

415. Huninque, France. Fortifications. Vauban. Plan.

417. Neuf-Brisach, France. Air view of town showing fortifications.

416. Mont-Louis, France. Fortifications. Vauban. Air view.

418. Versailles. Air view.

funerals become those of the Gracchi; Classicism is Memory and Sorrow, all carried on a cosmic axis from dome to obelisk to temple, and to the burial ground across the water. It is all a garden.

But the ultimate garden is modern Paris; Haussmann's *étoiles,* as finally built, are even more direct descendants of those of Versailles than the avenues of Washington are. Around the Arc de Triomphe de l'Etoile they incorporate Le Nôtre's grand axis from the Tuileries, now become the Champs-Elysées (fig. 420). They are related to the solid blocks of buildings that define them, as the *allées* of Versailles are to the woods through which they are cut. We remember that the trees at Versailles were originally *en charmille,* so that they resembled Italian palazzo blocks, flat-topped masses defining the streetlike *allées.* Then the trees grew; the crowns filled out. The effects became those of Romantic-Naturalism and most specifically recalled the character of Gothic architectural forms. The buildings of Haussmann's Paris bring the opposites together, the Classical and the Medieval, the Mediterranean and the North. The shop windows twinkle with light; above them, a Classical order controls the flat facades, while the high roofs of medieval Paris are adapted to cap the whole with a rounded shape as bursting with organic life as the forms of nature herself. So the mansarded buildings along the streets of nineteenth-century Paris came to create their incomparable building clumps, like clumps of trees (fig. 421). They are not stiff blocks but burgeoning masses, fully crowned. Through them, and defined by them, the avenues run, teeming with life, diverted by every storefront but always reaching on toward some new epiphany on the urban horizon. So Paris becomes the modern garden, the con-

419. Washington, D.C. Mall and central area. Circa 1938. Air view.

summate work of modern art.

Like all living things, the garden carries the seeds of its own destruction within it. In Haussmann's Paris, despite the criticism, surely justified, that may be directed against Haussmann's social aims and effects, mass and void were still in balance. Buildings still, and preeminently, defined and shaped the street. The dynamic principle of open space that we traced from the Tuileries was still in tension with the sense of variety and place, and was in the end controlled by such considerations. In 1922, however, the Classic garden became the model for Le Corbusier's Ideal City for Three Million Inhabitants (fig. 422). It all looks a good deal like Washington. Le Corbusier brings his *jardin anglais* in at one side, like Washington's Mall, and he has two sets of radiating avenues running from the two *étoiles* in the middle of the city, again very much as in Washington. But then, from the outer perimeter inward, he progressively destroys the definition of the grid and its blocks of buildings. He obliterates the traditional relationship of building to street, of the avenues as *allées* penetrating solids and firmly defined by them. Therefore, while in the outer ring he uses more or less traditional buildings with courtyards, like those of contemporary Amsterdam or Vienna, he moves inward to a building type that is a bit like Versailles itself. It is

420. Paris, France. Arc de Triomphe and Place de l'Etoile. Air view.

421. Paris. Rue Turbigo.

a long slab like a fence, stepping in and out, *à redents,* running through a long *jardin anglais* that obliterates the grid of streets. Finally, in the center, there are enormous superblocks with cross-axial skyscrapers set in vast open spaces; here the old definition of the city is utterly destroyed.

In 1925, when he presents his "Voisin" plan for the center of Paris, Le Corbusier violently condemns the traditional street, the *rue corridor*. He says that it forces us to look into the faces of other human beings, which is very unpleasant; it cuts off the sky, denying us air, space, and light. And he specifically calls for a green garden in which the buildings of the city can stand well apart from one another. He shows us what that would look like, with each skyscraper alone in its superblock of *jardin anglais* (fig. 485).

He invokes the garden but has, in fact, destroyed it by eliminating its definition and its scale, so creating a *pourtrait* thoroughly blank. He does so most of all through his obsession with the introduction of the motorcar into the city. He had

already contracted and was to become the major carrier of a peculiarly modern sickness, wherein the automobile is seen as a mythic vehicle, directed by pseudoheroes through the center of the town and destroying civilization along the way (fig. 423). Le Corbusier says, though, that he, too, is Cartesian. He calls his skyscrapers *Gratte-Ciels Cartésiens,* claiming that they are supremely rational because they are all cut off at the top and of the same size, and are therefore not romantic, aspiring, and competitive like the skyscrapers of New York (figs. 1, 2). Most of all, his is an urbanism of open space, and of an especially wide space through the center.

As we have seen, Le Nôtre had imaged that, too, but at a different scale. Still, if we approach one of the great *bassins* of the Tuileries, we feel a vastness of space which is prototypical of that of Le Corbusier (figs. 361, 362). If we look up from it toward the Etoile, we are looking along Le Nôtre's axis, and if we continue out on the Avenue de la Grande Armée to La Défense, we find ourselves in Le Corbusier's world, where the skyscrapers (here not very Cartesian) stand out with shapeless, empty spaces between them. At La Défense, of course, the cars are directed around at a lower level, but the principle is otherwise the same, and it is out of that principle—that puristic, cataclysmic Neoplatonic principle—that everything that had made the city a garden, and worth living in, came to be destroyed. The French resisted it on the whole, and for a long time, though not long enough. It awaited a very naïve culture to put it first into practice.

Such was eventually found in America, North and South alike. In Brazil, it produced the desert of Brasília, but that was a brand-new town. In the United States, it was embraced in the Redevel-

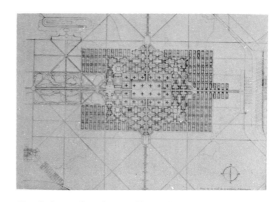

422. Ideal City for Three Million. Plan. 1922. Le Corbusier.

velopment. Bossuet, the greatest of the chaplains at Versailles, once attacked its reason for being by thundering in the presence of the king, "The city of the rich

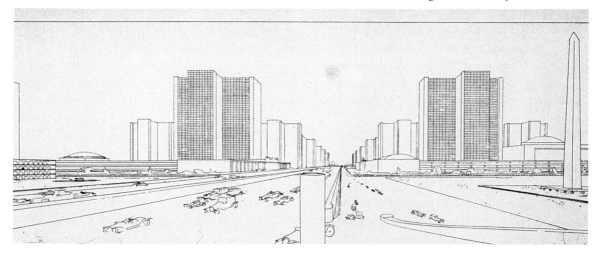

423. Ideal City for Three Million. 1922. Le Corbusier. Perspective along main boulevard.

opment of the 1950s and 1960s and so destroyed cities that existed already. The Oak Street connector in New Haven, for example (fig. 424), with its eight lanes of traffic and corporate skyscraper towers, might well have been modeled upon Le Corbusier's drawing of 1922. In the larger sense, it was, indeed, so modeled.

Sociologically, too, there is a broad avenue that runs from Versailles to Le Corbusier and on to American Rede-

cannot long endure!"* Le Corbusier, *en revanche,* tells us that his Ideal City will be a city of managers, a Cité d'Affaires, and that only those who can speak the language of the city will be allowed to live in it. All others will be banished to the farms or the industrial linear cities of the "Four Routes." American Redevelop-

*In general, see Nancy Mitford, *The Sun King,* New York, 1966.

424. New Haven, Connecticut. Oak Street connector 1960s. Air view.

ment worked out in much the same way. In its attempt to build up the city's tax base and to induce suburbanites to shop in it, it gave everything over to superhighways and luxury housing, while low-income neighborhoods were destroyed. Their inhabitants were pushed out of the center of the city, usually with nowhere to go, and empty space, punctuated by skyscraper images of corporate order, of business at large scale, came to dominate the whole. It may therefore be said, I think, that Louis XIV also presides over American Redevelopment no less than over Washington and Paris.

On the other hand, by the 1970s, the Classic garden was being taken as a model with which to heal the wounds that Redevelopment and the urbanism of the modern movement as a whole had inflicted upon the city. The best image of that was intended for Paris itself, in a project—unfortunately never built—by Leon Krier (fig. 425). It was a competition scheme for a quarter called La Villette, which is bisected by an existing canal running down toward one of the few surviving customs houses by Ledoux. Krier uses it, not a superhighway, as his central axis; he also makes it fairly difficult for automobiles to get into his streets. So once more, as at Versailles, water runs down

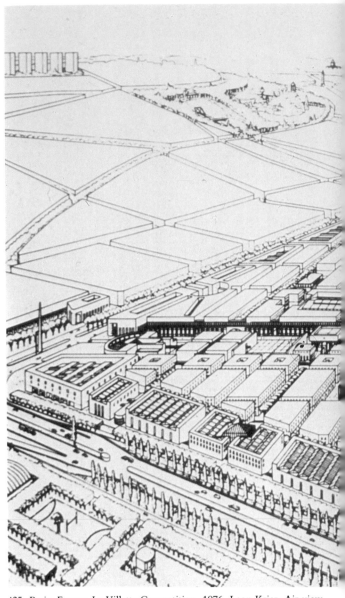

425. Paris, France. La Villette Competition. 1976. Leon Krier. Air view.

the middle, and the fundamental structure of the Classic garden begins to be restored. Krier's perspective drawing should be looked at in that connection. It seems almost directly inspired by an aerial view of Versailles. The buildings are drawn in clumps, like the trees in such photographs, with the *allées* of streets running through

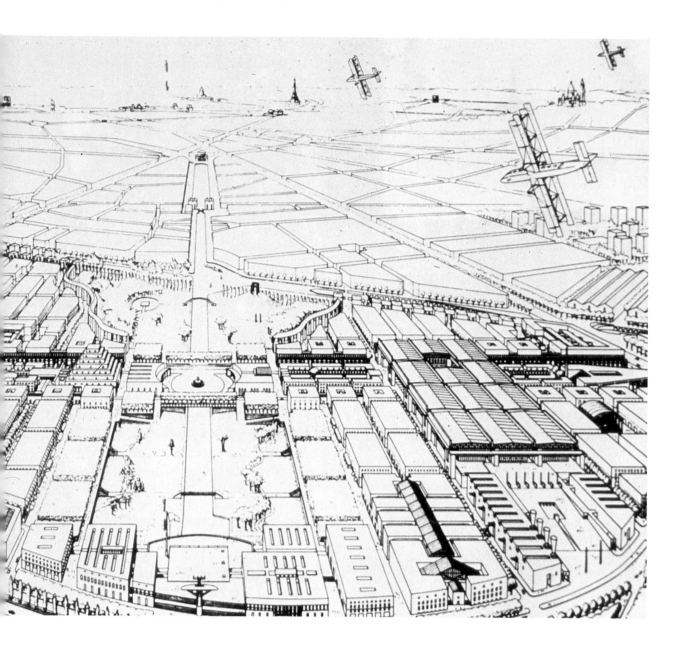

them. In that sense, Krier's scheme reclaims the structure of Paris and of the traditional European city as a whole. It reestablishes the Classic garden, and its debt to Le Nôtre is massive and fundamental. An aerial view of Vaux coupled with Krier's plan for the government center at La Villette shows us forms that are much the same: clear, abstract, unashamedly symmetrical. It is the *pourtraiture* of Boyceau once again, while the patterns themselves remind us of many of those published by Dezallier d'Argenville.

It is equally instructive, even touching, to compare the park at La Villette, which was intended to be surrounded by artists'

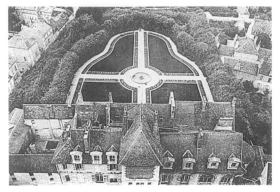

426. Meaux, France. Bossuet's Garden. André Le Nôtre.

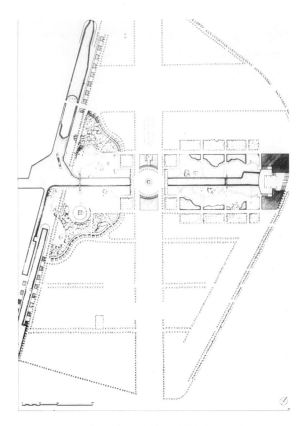

427. Paris. La Villette Competition. 1976. Leon Krier.
Plan of park area.

studios, with the garden that Le Nôtre built for Bossuet himself at Meaux (fig. 426), for Bossuet was the critic of Versailles as Krier is of Le Corbusier, and Krier's garden is clearly based on Le Nôtre's. Bossuet became the bishop of Meaux; his Episcopal Palace was situated close to the city walls, so that there was room for only a small garden of rather irregular shape between the two. Le Nôtre designed one in the shape of a bishop's miter and, as in his Jardin de Sylvie at Chantilly, succeeds in creating impressive scale through the use of one big shape in a confined space. Krier closely adapts even the little *rondpoint* at Meaux, as well as much of the detailing around the edges of the garden (fig. 427). It is therefore obvious that Krier's critically important and influential "Post-Modern" work owes an enormous debt to the French Classic garden, as does that of architects like Ricardo Bofill, whose grand housing groups around Paris have now, like Krier's work also, revived the whole Classical language of building as well.

Earlier, we left the young king looking out over the main axis at Versailles, the Sun King carried on his *gloire* toward his destiny, which for good or ill was to be that of France. We know all too well what happened toward the end of his reign. It is best symbolized, I think, in the portrait of Louis that Rigaud painted in 1701 (fig. 428), during the darkest days of a war, highly avoidable, in which the very existence of France was threatened. Louis is toothless and old; his cheeks have fallen in, but, like a Roman emperor, he is presented as an icon of the state. He stands with the heavy sword of France at his side, the hilt swung well forward. His robe with the fleurs-de-lis, like those worn by Suger's king and Joan's dauphin at Reims, is pushed back to show his marvelous legs in the first ballet position. We remember that Louis had danced the sun-king in the Ballets de Cour when he was a boy. Historians of ballet are fond of saying that modern ballet began when Louis XIV finally was induced to give up dancing. This is clearly a slander. He could at least strike a fine balletic pose, perhaps like Balanchine in old age. He is there in his red shoes in Rigaud's portrait as a figure both female and male: the paternal ruler calling up, as he invariably does, the complementary goddess image to aid him in time of need.

He surely compares more than well with the portrait of Louis XV that Rigaud painted in 1730, a generation later. We see, for example, that Louis XV had terrible legs, all knobbly and knock-kneed; apparently he doesn't want to show them and droops the kingly robe of France over them like a dressing gown. All the glory of the grand monarch is gone—of that obsessed, anointed being, that were-king, who defies the enemies of France with the sword of his fathers at his side. Despite everything, the splendor of his gardens and his citadels is in him, a figure both obdurate and very brave. But brave or not, he suffered monumental defeats during the early eighteenth century.

One of Louis' worst adversaries was Prince Eugène of Savoy, who had been an officer in his army and, despairing of rapid promotion, had taken service with the Holy Roman Emperor and beaten Louis in a couple of bloody campaigns. He might well have taken Paris except that a last army of French peasants, hardly trained, stood up and fought him to a standstill at the battle of Malplaquet. At the conclusion of peace, Prince Eugène's grateful sovereign gave him a fine new palace, the Belvedere, looking out across the city of Vienna. There is a seventeenth-century painting of Vienna as it looked during the Turkish siege of 1683, at which time, it must be said, Louis XIV did not behave very well. He could not resist the opportunity to embarrass his Christian colleague by encouraging the Turks just a little. The siege almost succeeded; the sin-

gle tower of St. Stephen's, the great Gothic cathedral, served as watchtower and command post during it. The contemporary view shows that the Turks had neutralized two bastions, flooding right over the *demi-lune,* and were about to take up the assault of the curtain wall when an army of cavalry, some of it Polish, drove them off. Prince Eugène's Belvedere (fig. 429) was so sited as to commemorate that victory. It is fundamentally Vaux. One enters on the side away from the city and comes through the building,

428. Hyacinthe Rigaud. *Louis XIV.* 1701.

which, like Vaux, bulges out and releases the viewer to the garden view, here of the city that Prince Eugène, like another Hercules, had done so much to save. Only French garden architecture could have so honored one of France's deadliest foes.

In France itself, the plan of Versailles became the plan of France. When the administrative center was moved to Paris and, in the 1840s, the railroads were pushed to the frontiers in one great campaign of building, all of France achieved a centralized, radial plan (fig. 430). It became an "*étoile,*" in fact, and, perhaps more than that, one city, a polis like Athens and a nation as well. Garden and fort, its interior articulation is that of the Classic garden, while Vauban guards its frontiers in depth. Along those frontiers, the fighting hardly ceased for more than two hundred years. The northern border, for example, the old frontier with the empire, was violated at least six times between the death of Louis XIV and World War II. Each time, there was only that little cushion of landscape space that pushes up from Paris toward Rocroi to absorb the shock.

Sometimes the assault was turned back, sometimes not. There is a monument at Maubeuge, where the church bells play the "Sambre et Meuse" at noon, that commemorates the victory of a ragtag revolutionary army that Louis and Vauban might not have recognized as representing France (fig. 431). It was able to regroup after a defeat behind Vauban's fortifications at Maubeuge and to win a spectacular victory shortly thereafter. In 1914, the attack on France failed in large part because Vauban had laid out a network of canals running northeast of Calais to the frontier, and had designed them to flood the countryside in time of crisis. In fact, they were flooded in 1914, so that the German flank was never able to advance along the Channel, thereby in large measure saving England but also saving Paris, because with that flank hung up, the German commander was forced to edge to the east. In so doing, he eventually ex-

429. Vienna, Austria. Belvedere Palace. J. L. von Hildebrandt. 1721–1724. Garden, view from palace.

posed his right flank to the taxicabs of Paris and invited the counterattack that became the victory of the Marne.

In 1940, however, the ancient enemy did break through. One of the places that held him up a little was Le Quesnoy, a bit to the northwest of Charlesville-Mézières, and fortified by Vauban. Le Quesnoy was taken by the Germans in World War I and liberated by the Australians in 1918. In 1940, a breakthrough occurred right near it, but not easily. If we look in the lower right of the plan of Le Quesnoy, we see a large hornwork that crosses the wide moat and culminates in an important gate, near which there are two slabs of white stone fixed to the wall. One celebrates the armored combats that took place there in May 1940. The other honors the colonial regiment that held Vauban's fortifications for four days and was finally allowed to march out with the honors of war. So the Wehrmacht lost four days there. When it fianlly broke through, it avoided the mistake of 1914 and circled back toward Calais, trying to cut off the English and French armies that had advanced into Belgium. As it broke through to the coast north of Calais, it hit another city fortified by Vauban, a place called Gravelines. It was and is still an impressive fortification. We see it in a seventeenth-century view right on the edge of broad tidal sands stretching far out into the sea (fig. 432). Here the Wehrmacht was held up for four days more.

It was then that Goering asked Hitler to allow him to use the Luftwaffe to reduce the bridgehead. The way the story is sometimes written, Hitler did allow Goering to try to do so, and it was because the Luftwaffe failed that the British army was able to get away. But it was not all quite like that. It turns out that Hitler gave Goering only a day and a half, and when

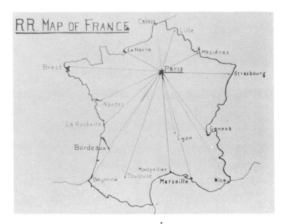

430. France. Main railroads of 1840s. Plan.

432. The capture of Gravelines, France, by Archduke Leopold as depicted by Snayers.

it was seen that this was one more promise Goering could not make good on, Hitler resumed the ground attack; but he held back his tanks. It sometimes has been said that this assault, too, failed only for that reason, but that again is not the whole story.

431. Maubeuge. Battle monument.

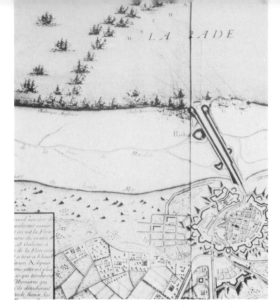

433. Dunkirk. Fortifications and sea defenses. Vauban. Bombardment in 1695.

It is true that Hitler wanted to save his tanks for a massive attack on the French army to the south, but he could not have used them anyway, because the whole area was one great canal-ditch-tank trap around the port of Dunkirk. That fated city had been the base of the revived French navy under Louis XIV, the home of the great corsair Jean Bart. Vauban had fortified it, employing some of his most spectacular innovations. Because of the sands and the tide, he had to design several kinds of experimental fortresses extending out into the water (fig. 433), as well as a wonderfully bursting *étoile* around the town itself. It is ironic that the English forced the French to dismantle some of those fortifications early in the eighteenth century. It was, in any case, toward Dunkirk that the bulk of the British army was withdrawing.

Just seven kilometers inland from Dunkirk, about at the first contour line, and where all the canals were brought together by Vauban, lies the town of Bergues (fig. 434). It is linked with Gravelines in French army tradition; there is a dour army song of the seventeenth century that goes: *"De la peste, de la famine, des garnisons de Bergues et de Gravelines, pré-*

servez nous, Seigneur." Bergues is, indeed, far away and very wet; it also has some of Vauban's greatest fortifications, with big *demi-lunes* and broad ditches connected with the general system of canals (fig. 435). It is the key point, and it was here that the Germans had to attack—without tanks, but with their very best divisions: the Leibstandarte Adolf Hitler, their best Waffen SS assault divison, for one. And they could not take it for a week. French infantry, dug in around the forts and behind the ditches, held them long enough for most of the British army and some of the rest of the French army to get away,

435. Bergues, France. Ditch and *demi-lune* by Vauban.

so that, in fact, the Wehrmacht stumbled over Vauban's forts and lost the war. Not bad for a marshal of France dead two hundred years.

It is clear that the gardens and the forts are linked. The garden symbolizes and, indeed, creates the image of the new, centralized modern France. The fortifications, employing many of the same forms, especially those deriving from projected lines of sight, defend that France in echelon behind the frontiers. In those fortifications, we can read the hard, intelligent, devoted service of the men who created the nation—of whom the gardens drew the portraits and embodied the characters, especially those of Fouquet, Condé, and the king.

434. Bergues, France. Memorial to World Wars I and II.

11
PALLADIO, THE ENGLISH GARDEN, AND THE MODERN AGE

THE ENGLISH ROMANTIC soon triumphed over the French Classic, even in France, and may with some justice be said to have swept the ancien régime away with it. In its fully developed form, as the Picturesque, that English sensibility dominated the period of democracy and industrialism that followed, a period that on the whole preferred "Naturalism" to all other modes of expression in all the arts. But the Picturesque had its limits.

The Classical garden, for example, could function as a model for cities, and continued to do so throughout the nineteenth century, because it was fundamentally architectural and urbane itself. The English Romantic garden, on the other hand, was intentionally rather antiurban, and its "landscaping," culminating, say, in the work of Repton and Loudon and that of their followers in Europe and America, could shape its own kind of nineteenth- and twentieth-century suburb, like Le Vésinet or Riverside, Illinois, or urban park, like Central Park or the Bois de Boulogne

443. Bagnolo. Villa Pisani. River front.

(fig. 436), along with thousands of golf courses (fig. 436a), but not more: These furnished relief from the new metropolis, and were its necessary complement, but they were not its central structure. Even Camillo Sitte's optical irregularities and surprises, which helped produce some outstanding mass housing in Vienna after World War I, required a regular urban fabric to set them off, while Le Corbusier's attempt to combine the *jardin anglais* with the high-rise slab turned out in general to be a true urban disaster. Indeed, Le Corbusier used the English garden as he used the French: to destroy the traditional city (fig. 485). Even the English Garden Cities of the later nineteenth and early twentieth centuries, much more successful as places to live in than the offspring of Le Corbusier's *Villes radieuses,* were in fact based on what Howard called a "Diagram," which was French-classical and radial, and whose frame clearly underlay the Garden Cities of Letchworth and so on as they were built. Their streets, though curving, also "radiated" and were,

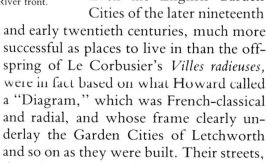

504a. Thiepval. Names of the war dead and their graves. Detail.

313

moreover, closely defined by trees and buildings, so that the Garden City, like Haussmann's Paris, was nearer to the Classical models in conception and effect than Le Corbusier's own impatient diagrams came to be.*

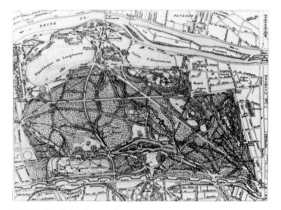

436. Paris, Bois de Boulogne after 1870. Alphonse Alphand. Plan.

*A note on these developments: Camillo Sitte, *City Planning According to Artistic Principles,* Vienna, 1889, trans, edited, and annotated by George R. Collins and Christiane Collins, 2 vols., New York, 1965, provides some of the many lessons Andres Duany and Elizabeth Plater-Zyberk have drawn from history in the traditionally conceived towns they are now building all over the United States, of which Seaside in Florida was the first example. There is also one for Prince Charles at Poundbury, England. In this connection, it is estimated that in 1991 more than thirty million people were playing golf in Britain and the United States, in which case the golf course has to be taken as the ultimate popular manifestation of the English garden and park. In Florida, for example, hundreds of new communities have been laid out around golf courses. But in the new group of Windsor, at Vero Beach (fig. 436a), now in building by Andres Duany and Elizabeth Plater-Zyberk, with Scott Merrill as resident architect, eight out of ten new buyers are choosing lots in the traditionally planned, narrow-streeted town rather than around the golf course. Windsor, with its beach and polo fields, may be regarded as a paradisal setting offering maximum freedom of choice, making the popularity of the town grid especially striking. Developers everywhere seem to be taking note of this revival of traditional urbanism. It is hoped that someday soon it may find its proper employment at the popular level where it is most needed.

This book can add very little to the vast literature on the English Romantic garden and the Picturesque that has been accumulating for almost three centuries. Nor can it pretend that the English garden needs to be seen with fresh eyes, as is so manifestly the case with the gardens of France. The English landscape garden has been seen very well indeed, and richly appreciated—sometimes, unnecessarily, at the expense of France and often as if it represented the only way in which nature could possibly be experienced or conceptualized. It is hoped, of course, that this book helps redress those imbalances, but it does not seem possible or necessary to review the mass of Picturesque theory and practice that brought them about. It can be taken as given that the wonderful English art of producing eloquent "natural" effects, as it was developed throughout the eighteenth and early nineteenth centuries, has generally shaped and, indeed, limited the cultivated modern conception of the relationship between the natural and the manmade—when, that is, any such conception can be said to have existed at all in the modern period. But there are elements in that relationship, not normally touched upon but directly germane to the themes of this book, which can repay some fresh, if brief, consideration—which should begin, I think, with Palladio's country houses. The villas of Andrea Palladio have exerted a special fascination for modern architects from the end of the eighteenth century until today. Even before that time, their special relationship to their landscapes surely played a significant part in shaping the English gardens of the eighteenth century, out of which the predominant modern view of the relationship of suburban buildings to landscape took form.

436a. Windsor, Vero Beach, Florida. Perspective with town and golf course. Andres Duany and Elizabeth Plater-Zyberk. Scott Merrill, resident architect. 1989.

There are, I think, two basic reasons why Palladio's villas assumed such importance. First, they embodied in themselves a special tension between vernacular traditions and stylistic rhetoric. In their case, the traditions were those of the North Italian farmhouse type and the rhetoric was that of Classical architecture. All of Palladio's villas deal with that duality in various touching and expressive ways. They were working farms built for a new class of gentleman farmer, Venetian nobles who were establishing a new kind of relationship, at once practical and romantic, with the land.

Later, as for example for Thomas Jefferson, the tension was to be between Classical architecture and the building traditions of Colonial Virginia. Even later, as for Le Corbusier, it was between general European traditions of building and type and the abstraction of modern painting, out of which, as also through the work of the other modern masters, the International Style of modern architecture came into being. For that style, the villa, set in country or suburb, became the ideal building type precisely because it had few urbanistic responsibilities or constraints and so, of all building types, could be the most pictorial, the most inventive, as painters were and as the new architects wanted to be. Robert Venturi, who has done more than any other architect to bring the jealous hegemony of that pictorial style, and indeed of all styles as such, to a close, gently burlesqued that process in a number of projects. His little Classic

438. Charlottesville, Virginia. Monticello. Begun 1771. Thomas Jefferson. West and south side.

scape. Like Jefferson's Virginia, it runs from the mountains to a piedmont and on down to a tidewater plain. Some of Palladio's villas are placed on the piedmont slopes, some down in the flatlands, some even along the Brenta, itself a tidal river, if much smaller and slower than the James.

The placement of the Villa Godi at Lonedo, one of Palladio's earliest villas, is especially telling in this regard (fig. 439). It rides forward on a high slope before the mountains, with the river valley falling way below it. In massing and detail, it is also one of the most purely vernacular of the villas, with only a more or less regularized window placement and

Revival house is an example (fig. 437), where the big colonnade pushes forward but the vernacular windows open out gasping at the sides. The same duality had been explored by Jefferson at Monticello (fig. 438).

The second reason for Palladio's influence derives from the fact that his villas were mostly working farms. Because of that, they were normally set out simply among the fields and the vineyards, without the intervention of an elaborate formal garden to mediate between them and the open landscape. At most, there was an entrance courtyard, often in practice not even that. In the end, despite all its complex development, pictorial pretension, and stylistic rhetoric, this was the relationship to the landscape that the English Romantic garden of the eighteenth century was to favor and, for a number of reasons, modern country and suburban houses as well.

In general, it is one of the most fascinating studies in the history of architecture to watch Palladio's adjustment of each villa to its site and of its vernacular shell to the Classical signs with which he adorned it. The Veneto is a magical land-

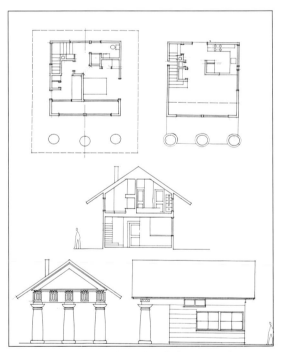

437. Eclectic House. Project. 1977. Robert Venturi. Plans, section, and elevations.

a weathered stemma above its narrow stair to assert its pretension to noble style. When, however, Palladio published the Villa Godi in his *Quattro libri dell'architettura,* of 1570 (fig. 440), he tried to dress it up a bit more properly,

439. Lonedo, Italy. Villa Godi Porto. Circa 1537–1542.
Andrea Palladio.

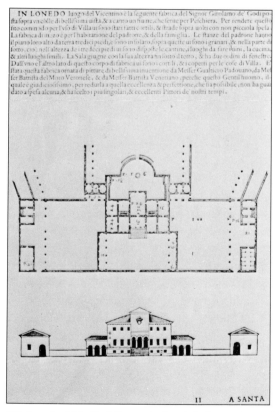

440. Lonedo. Villa Godi Porto. Andrea Palladio. Section and
plan as published in the *Quattro libri*.

with a wider stairway, a little pediment, and a bigger stemma. He also varied the sizes of the windows more rhythmically, lined them up more symmetrically, and elaborated their proportional relationship in order to render the whole thing at once more Classical and more "ideal."

That dichotomy between what he actually built and how he published it in the *Quattro libri* continues throughout Palladio's work, so that those architects in England and America who were most influenced by him but who, like Jefferson, knew his buildings only in publication, were hardly getting a true picture of them at all. But the contrast between the built building and the published drawing is a perfect one in terms of the Renaissance aesthetic, since it is between the Real and the Ideal, the realities of material practice and the immaterial perfection of the Neoplatonic world view. Hence, Palladio's villas offer a kind of controlled case history of the basic tension that has done so much to shape Western architecture from Antiquity onward.

441. Lonedo. Villa Piovene. Circa 1538 and ff. Andrea Palladio. Composite view with mountains.

As a general rule, Palladio tended to become more Classical and more Ideal with the passage of time, but there are many exceptions to that rule. For example, on the summit of the hill upon whose lower slope the Villa Godi is placed, there stands the wide-spreading Villa Piovene of the same early date (fig. 441). Its vernacular block is fenestrated much like that of the Villa Godi, but it is adorned with a generous Classical portico and pediment and extended laterally, at a later date, by more or less Classical colonnades. A major reason for the addition of these features can be read in the landscape. The higher mountains rise behind the house, and the side colonnades stretch its mass to conform to their horizontal profile, while the pediment picks up the higher pyramids that rise among them and so rushes up and forward, echoing them just above our heads. This was not the only time that Palladio was to use Classical shapes in a manner more suggestive of, for example, Amerindian practice. So in this piedmont

442. Bagnolo, Italy. Villa Pisani. After 1542. View along canal.

site, Piovene invokes the Alpine heights and Godi is inflected downriver toward the plain.

At the Villa Pisani at Bagnolo, down in the soggy depths of the flatlands, Palladio built a romantic fantasy suggestive, as is some of his work elsewhere, of Guilio Romano. The land is low and wet. A canal flows sluggishly just behind the house (fig.

444. Bagnolo. Villa Pisani. Land side.

445. Mira, Italy. Villa Foscari (La Malcontenta). 1559–1560. Andrea Palladio. River facade.

442), or just in front of it in terms of access from the water. A high wall separates the two. Behind it, an enormous fig tree grows, almost filling the space between the wall and the house. Pushed up into the tree is a daimonic face, a staring mask with goggle eyes (fig. 443). It is a rusticated portico, expressing the delicious terror of nature in the wild. The stemma of its

noble family is set in its pediment, as if stamped on an astonished brow. Towers rise alongside it, lifting the mass on that side to the height of the other, the land side of the house (fig. 444). Hence, the half-round window above the entrance of that facade—derived from Roman bath architecture and beloved by Burlington and Jefferson later—lights a high volume of space that cannot go all the way through the house, since the river side is too low to contain it. In the *Quattro libri,* Palladio was to add a pedimented portico and heighten the towers (into a curiously medieval profile), but what he would have liked to do with the rusticated frontispiece on the river side we have no way of knowing. As it stands, the two facades of the house are wholly disjointed, and the interior space is severely compromised.

It is interesting to see how Palladio was to work that all out later in a similar kind of site at the Villa Foscari, called the Malcontenta, at Mira (fig. 445). Here again is a pedimented portico on the river and a bath window on the other side. Now it is clear, as it was to be along the James, that the portico on the river marks the noble, the entrance side. But the whole facade from low base to high pediment also perfectly expresses the vaulted spaces of the interior, low and squat on the ground floor and rising on the second floor to a wonderfully high cross vault that billows up like a great cloud to shape the major living hall (fig. 446). On the land side (fig. 447), the flatly rusticated surface of the wall itself, innocent of any heraldic portico, is articulated to express that generous volume of interior space, as if, indeed, it were being stretched to contain it. It is the Villa Pisani perfected, and it is much more powerful than any of the country houses that were to be more or less modeled upon it in the New World.

446. Mira. Villa Foscari (La Malcontenta). Salon interior.

Here, vernacular considerations seem transcended, but, like the related issue of contextual design, they are never entirely absent from Palladio's work. The contexts are the farm and the place. If we travel from Bagnolo eastward toward Montagnana, we pass many farms set back from the road, with mangers that look like crèches painted by the Bassani set near the road before them. The farmhouses themselves are vernacular blocks with irregularly placed windows (fig. 448). All at once, one of the series sprouts a pediment, with a highly abstracted Classical portico set into the wall below it; the whole is suggestive of an eyed mask once more (fig. 449). It is the Villa Poiana at Poiana Maggiore, the farm made noble, idealized and classicized, but not too much so. It looks a little like an abstracted project by a Romantic-Classic, early modern architect such as Soane or Gandy. The pedi-

447. Mira. Villa Foscari (La Malcontenta). Garden facade.

448. Poiana Maggiore, Italy. Villa near Palladio's Villa Poiana.

453. Fanzolo, Italy. Villa Emo. Circa 1564. Andrea Palladio.

ment was stuffed with hay. It is one of Palladio's most rustic and intense unions of the Classical ghost and the rural body.

By way of contrast, the Villa Pisani at

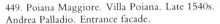

449. Poiana Maggiore. Villa Poiana. Late 1540s. Andrea Palladio. Entrance facade.

450. Montagnana. Villa Pisani. Circa 1552–1555. Andrea Palladio. Garden facade.

Montagnana is very much an urban, or perhaps suburban, building (figs. 450, 451, 452). It is set just outside the high, thin walls of that medieval town and is pressed up tight to a major intersection of roads at one of its gates. Hence, the mass

452. Montagnana. Villa Pisani. Section and plan.

451. Montagnana. Villa Pisani. Street facade.

LA SEGVENTE fabrica è appresso la porta di Montagnana Castello del Padoano, e fu edificata dal Magnifico Signor Francesco Pisani : il quale passato à miglior uita non la ha potuta finire. Le stanze maggiori sono lunghe un quadro e tre quarti : i uolti sono à schiffo, alti secondo il secondo modo delle altezze de' uolti : le mediocri sono quadre, & inuoltate a cadino : I camerini, e l'andito sono di uguale larghezza : i uolti loro sono alti due quadri : La entrata ha quattro colonne, il quinto più sottili di quelle di fuori : lequali sostentano il pauimento della Sala, e fanno l'altezza del uolto bella, e sicura. Ne i quattro nicchi, che ui si ueggono sono stati scolpiti i quattro tempi dell'anno da Messer Alessandro Vittoria Scultore eccellente : il primo ordine delle colonne e Dorico, il secondo Ionico. Le stanze di sopra sono in solaro : L'altezza della Sala giugne fin sotto il tetto. Ha questa fabrica due strade da i fianchi, doue sono due porte, sopra le quali ui sono anditi, che conducono in cucina, e luoghi per seruitori.

is high and narrow, and a two-storied loggia is pushed into it where it faces the long, narrow garden, running along the road that parallels the city wall (fig. 450). On the other side, facing the crossroad (fig. 451), there is no room for a projecting

454. Maser, Italy. Villa Barbaro. 1557–1558. Andrea Palladio.

entrance portico. That feature, therefore, is pressed flat as a signboard on the facade. Directly behind it, however, a four-columned entrance hall is contained within the volume of the house (fig. 452). The play of pressures between exterior and interior, solid and void, public and private, could hardly be developed more eloquently or with greater economy of means. As usual, Palladio dressed the design up in the *Quattro libri* to make it less directly contextual and more ideal, with projecting side pavilions and so on.

The Villa Emo at Fanzolo is one of those few projects that Palladio seems to have built as he published it (fig. 453). The site is in the midst of flat farming country. From the entrance side, no hills of any kind are visible. Hence, the building stretches wide vernacular arcades symmetrically out from its central pedimented block. The roof profiles of the wings are perfectly straight, underlining the open sky, and they induce our eyes to travel along their entire length by terminating them with solid little towers that attract our gaze and frame the expanse of sky. A broad ramp leads smoothly up to the central pavilion and carries us easily into it, along an axial line of sight and movement that leads us straight through the building to the broad central opening on the other side. Beyond, along the same axis, the view is focused by an undulating line of hills quite far off. They are the foothills of the Alps, shaping the distant horizon.

And if we could travel directly across the intervening fields and watercourses, we would come, almost exactly on that axis, to the Villa Barbaro at Maser, lying under the hills (fig. 454). Here, though it employs a central pavilion and side wings, with terminating blocks, the whole profile

of the villa is totally different from that of Emo. Now the forms all pick up those of the hills that frame them and resonate out beyond them to the higher mountains farther off. The side pavilions are especially striking in this relationship. They terminate the short wings, not widespread like those at Emo but short enough to let the pavilions rather than their own lower roof profiles dominate the form. Those pavilions crown the colonnade with pediments that are, as it were, lifted up by volutes on either side, volutes that are so abstracted and welded into the overall mass that their profiles seem fluid and continuous. They undulate, like the hills behind them.

Palladio was again using Classical elements in a way that suggests the pre-Classic, non-Greek principle of imitation. The shapes of his building echo those of the landscape as directly as do those of Teotihuacán or Taliesin West (figs. 11,

483). They also seem intended to be seen in a calculated contrast with the profiles of the Villa Emo, with which they are conceptually, visually, and even topographically linked. Emo celebrates the flatland, Barbaro the piedmont. A little like Teotihuacán, too, or even Praeneste, is the relationship of hill to plain at Maser, dramatizing as it does the movement of groundwater. In the hill directly behind the central pavilion, a richly carved grotto celebrates the emergence of a spring from the earth. The rear doors of the villa open directly upon it, while on the other side, under a pediment whose horizontal cornice is split, as by some force pushing its way out from within, the view is of open fields toward which, in fact, the groundwater is being led: touching, these relationships to the earth at once ancient and modern in conception, the house acting as temple now.

457. Vicenza. Villa Capra under the hills.

Of course, the Palladian villa that most seized the imagination of later ages, and the most like a temple of them all, was the Villa Capra, the Rotonda, at Vicenza. This is one of the very few villas by Palladio that was not originally intended to function as a working farm, though it now appears that it was soon remodeled to become one, perhaps shortly after Palladio's death. It was originally intended as a simple belvedere on the outskirts of the town, in which the client, the private man, could sit in the center of the world and look out upon its four horizons.

As it was published in the *Quattro libri,* it was, like the French gardens of the next century, an exact embodiment of the Neoplatonic aesthetic as figured in the drawing of the circle and the square (fig. 455). But where the French were to subordinate the building and to draw that figure on the earth, the Italian sensibility remains always sculptural, focusing on the building's mass in space. Still, as we see it now (fig. 456), the Villa Rotonda differs from Palladio's drawing in one significant way. Its dome is lowered, so that its profiles pick up those of the four pediments below it and so unify the building into a more solid, even chunky, mass. There is some uncertainty as to whether the change was made by Palladio himself or by someone later, perhaps Scamozzi. Archaeological evidence now seems to point toward the latter conclusion, but the modification is one that Palladio himself might well have made. It is consistent with many others we have noted elsewhere, in which the published ideal was modified by local topographic and vernacular conditions.

Whatever the case, the building, despite its ideal symmetry, has two different characters of a kind we have also seen before. It is on one side closely related to the hills behind it (fig. 457 and p. *i*). Indeed, Palladio tells us that it is to be seen against the backdrop of hills as we approach Vicenza, and on that bearing its rounded-off mass seems to fit solidly into their profiles. Seen from other perspectives, however, it seems to stand wholly free, quite vertical in form, rising above the surrounding vineyards to the open sky, as if into the very

456. Vicenza. Villa Capra. Exterior.

center of the universe (fig. 458). But we enter it from the hill side through a deep trench in the earth, while, in the reverse view (fig. 459, the columns of the portico seem to roll sculpturally out of the natural background like Titian's classical nymphs in his *Concert* in the Louvre. It is Italian; Classicism is a physical force. In the end, despite its Neoplatonic aspirations, the Villa Rotonda is sculptural, having to do with the human body standing, populating the land. And it is single, unified, and vertical enough to be experienced empathetically as such a body. It is the Greek temple revised in Italian terms (figs. 128, 458a).

That is why Palladio's most successful emulators in England, where he was most loved, were not the Palladians of the mid-eighteenth century, who invoked him in the name of correctness, but the much more physically alert Baroque architects of the previous generation, Vanbrugh and Hawksmoor most of all. Inigo Jones and

Christopher Wren had surely revered him and understood him earlier, but it was Vanbrugh and Hawksmoor who grasped the fundamental physicality hidden behind the publications and its bodily relationship to the landscape as well. The Temple (fig. 460) and the Mausoleum (fig. 461) at Castle Howard are, indeed, among the few buildings anywhere that can stand with the Villa Rotonda as powerful Classical presences on the land—the Temple more freely gesticulating than its model, the Mausoleum more passionately wrapped up in its own lonely pride. Indeed, Vanbrugh and Hawksmoor at Castle Howard seem to have understood it all, not only Palladio but France, too, with fortifications frowning in the park and shaping it, fitted with heavy-arched entrances suggesting those of Vauban. How well the Pyramid Gate goes with Vauban's gates at Gravelines and Mont-Louis, and the Carrmire bastion (fig. 462), though

458. Villa Capra against the sky.

458a. Santa Maria della Consolazione, Todi, Italy.
Circa 1508–1606.

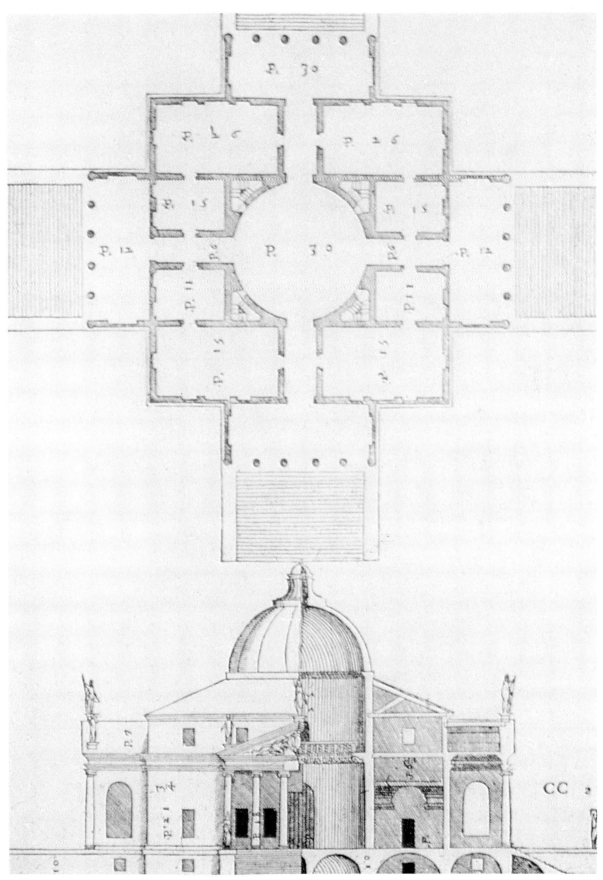

455. Vicenza, Italy. Villa Capra (La Rotonda) 1566–1570. Plan and section.

459. Vicenza, Villa Capra. View from portico to countryside.

463. Castle Howard. South facade.

464. Wiltshire, England. Stourhead. 1721–1724. Colen Campbell. East front.

Gothically machicolated, with Vauban's fort on the seacoast at Camaret (fig. 412).*

*Stephen Switzer's plan of Paston Manor, in his *The Nobleman, Gentleman and Gardener's Recreation,* 1715, expanded into the *Ichnographia Rustica,* London, 3 vols., 1718, shows a great central parterre in the form of a classic citadel, with curtains, bastions, *demi-lunes,* and a ditch. It is published in John Dixon Hunt and Peter Willis, *The Genius of the Place: The English Landscape Garden 1620–1820,* New York, 1975, p. 157. This basic anthology is essential to a study of the English garden and the Picturesque. For illustrations see also Laurence Fleming and Alan Gore, *The English Garden,* London, 1979, richly illustrated and based on a television series, tracing the development of the English garden from "the knot, the maze, and the mount" of medieval gardens (all with obvious references to earth religions) to "technicolor and technology," in the present, with some fairly ridiculous local regulations and "acres of municipal paving."

460. Yorkshire, England. Castle Howard. 1702–1714. Sir John Vanbrugh. The Temple.

Yet if the Temple and the Mausoleum at Castle Howard accord well with Palladio's villas, the main house itself cannot do so (fig. 463). One reason seems obvious. It is much too large, compared with any of Palladio's buildings, with the Villa Barbaro, for example. All Palladio's villas are, in fact, very small. They do not lord it over the landscape but are integrally linked not only to its vernacular peasant bones but also to some ancient Classical tradition of the modest country temple-shrine. Hence, the greatest English country houses, though eventually set through enclosure in what pass for open fields in the Palladian manner, are in general too overbearing to be tied to those fields in either the peasant or the Classical way. They are too large and, later, in the hands of the stricter Palladians, too hard and dry, perhaps too caught up in bookish correctness, to do so.

Colen Campbell's Stourhead (fig. 464), of the Palladian generation, also makes a good contrast with the Villa Bar-

baro, as with other Palladian villas. Its profiles are stiff compared with those drawn by Palladio. Its hard stone (as elsewhere that of red brick) is also somehow unsympathetic—assertive, when compared with Palladio's crumbling stucco in its gentle sandy tones. Palladio's buildings seem vulnerable, hence rather touchingly human, as in this sense the English examples do not seem to be. True enough, as at Stourhead, the English sheep-bearing park, like Palladio's ruder fields, comes right up to the house, but down in the valley below it, another kind of English garden is to be found, one having nothing to do with Palladian practice. It is the Poetic Garden, organized around a narrative sequence like Bomarzo. It derives from the Italian garden but tends to deal less probingly with psychological issues than does its model. It is more didactic, sometimes more directly political, and, in the softness of the English countryside, is less endowed with that awe and terror of the earth which the Italian gardens evoke so well.

461. Castle Howard. The Mausoleum.

462. Castle Howard. Carmire bastion.

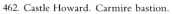

465. Claude Gellée, Le Lorrain. *Juno Confiding Io to the Care of Argus.* 1660.

467. Claude Gellée, Le Lorrain. *Landscape: Aeneas at Delos.*

It is gentler and more soothing than its Italian predecessors, and it is also more pictorial than they. Its ultimate models are the paintings of Claude Lorrain rather than the sacred sites of pagan antiquity itself (figs. 465, 466, 467). Claude's incomparably influential landscapes took the topography of Latium and recast it into what might be called the ultimate "retirement landscape," full of golden reminiscence, populated like the human brain with innumerable memories of past ages—all recollected at last in a generous golden glow, a soft nostalgia to bear us along, at home with the centuries of human culture, into the last years of our lives.

The English recreated this wholly admirable and persuasive pictorial reverie in their gardens whenever they could do so. Claude, indeed, did more than Palladio to shape models for their buildings and to set them in their landscapes. That phenomenon, creating what was rightly called the Picturesque, now seems especially relevant to the history of modern architecture, not only in these its early stirrings but also in its later phases in the twentieth century, as in that major development which produced the International Style. The architects working in that style were to be inspired by the new abstract forms that were being invented by the modern painters; they were to be obsessed by them, in fact.

And since, as we maintained in an earlier chapter, the painter was able, from the Renaissance onward, to embody more illusionistically convincing sets of environments and acts than painters and sculptors normally could create in three dimensions, it is not surprising that the painter's abstract conceptions eventually came to seem more significant to architects than the real environment itself—to its destruction when the issue became anarchic invention and aesthetic hermeticism rather than contextual urban building. Claude's effect on the English garden was an important step in that process and surely its most genial, useful, and harmless one. Like his Renaissance predecessors and, for example, Aldo Rossi later, Claude, after all, was still painting *places* and buildings in relation to places. For that reason, there was nothing destructive to architecture as an art of the environment in the emulation of his paintings by architects (figs. 465, 466, 467).

Moreover, in the English countryside, those architects of the Picturesque had a

466. Wiltshire, Britain. Stourhead. Henry Flitcroft and Henry Hoare. View of Pantheon across lake, circa 1753.

lot to build on. How wonderful even the simplest native environments of house, farm, and garden can be: probably the gentlest and most comforting setting for life ever formed by mankind. True enough, though wholly devoid of Italy's Panic terrors, some of the wildness of nature is there as well, bounding the swelling fields with stoats in the hedgerows, foxes, and the rabbit's scream. Here, the wild surrounds human beings but does not threaten them personally; it simply seems to make the picture real. In consequence, country-house culture became a rich blend of human artifice with what appeared to be on the whole a beneficent "natural" order.

It is no wonder that England's liveliest and most creative aesthetic conversation, that related to the Picturesque, had to do largely with the artful shaping of nature to make it look natural and with a deep critical interest in humanity's ways of perceiving that art and of deriving meaning from it.* Always visual and cerebral, it probed the human response to a nature become no longer a frightening force but a manmade setting in which one could live with pleasure. Embracing nature, it nevertheless moved the modern age farther than ever from the ancient view of the landscape's autonomous being and made it ever more difficult for modern humanity to view the natural order as anything other than an extension of itself.

It is not surprising, therefore, to return to the pictorial issue, that the Palladian forms filtered through Claude in England and America were simply not as sculptural—perhaps we might say not as wholly architectural, as Palladio's, which are, after all, not picturesque at all. Com-

468. Chiswick, London. Chiswick House. 1725. Lord Burlington. Facade.

469. Charlottesville, Virginia. Monticello. Begun 1771. Thomas Jefferson. West facade.

pared to the Villa Rotonda, majestic on the hill, Burlington's Chiswick (fig. 468) is an impertinence and Jefferson's Monticello looks positively tacky (fig. 469). In contrast with Palladio's serene singleness, Jefferson seems to be trying to put everything he knows into one building. Yet the tension between Classical rhetoric and vernacular traditions is clearly there, and the building expresses that attempt to expand existing boundaries, by expanding laterally, that was later to seem to become peculiarly American.

Jefferson was also influenced by the French, especially by Le Vau at Vaux-le-Vicomte (figs. 355, 357). Like Le Vau,

*As in Pope's *Epistle to Lord Burlington,* of 1731 (not to mention in a more general way his *An Essay on Criticism,* of 1409–1411), and Uvedale Price's *An Essay on the Picturesque,* of 1794.

Jefferson pulls us in at the entrance side and pushes us out to the garden, which was originally designed by him in a Late Picturesque English manner. Even the little windows that pop out in the metopes of the sides of the house are to be found at Vaux (fig. 438). Special to Monticello is the perfectly mounded hill it surmounts (fig. 470). It is like a hero's tomb in the face of the Blue Ridge, the frontier; like so many of Palladio's buildings, it is placed in the piedmont, at the foot of the high mountains and above the plain. But all around it—how American—was primeval darkness.

Finally, in Jefferson's last years, the lights of the University of Virginia came to twinkle in the valley below it (fig. 471). Here again, the model was French: Marly, by Jules Hardouin-Mansart (fig. 472), and various projects of the early nineteenth century after it. Unlike Marly, though, where the pavilions for the courtiers were evenly spaced in their rows leading away from the king's house at the head, those at Charlottesville were set at intervals that grew wider the farther away from the Rotonda they were—perhaps to echo the hilly landscape more eloquently, perhaps so that the central axis could indeed seem to extend "indefinitely," with true Cartesian expansion into space (fig. 473). *Indefinitely* was, in fact, the word Jefferson employed in his *Report to the Commissioners of the University of Virginia,* of 1818, to describe the lifelong extension of the educational process itself.*

This is not the place to describe either Monticello or the University of Virginia in detail, though perhaps it should be re-

*He says that education "must advance the knowledge and well-being of mankind, not *infinitely,* as some have said, but *indefinitely,* and to a term which no one can fix or foresee." *The Portable Thomas Jefferson,* ed. Merrill D. Peterson, New York, 1977, pp. 332–6.

471. Charlottesville. University of Virginia. 1817–1826. Thomas Jefferson. View from Lewis Mountain. Engraving by F. Sachse and Co. 1856.

472. Marly, France. Château. J. H. Mansart. Engraving by Perelle.

473. Charlottesville. University of Virginia. General view from early print.

470. Charlottesville. Monticello. Air view from the west.

marked, in connection with our basic concerns, that the columned ranges of the university (fig. 474), the product of so many centuries of development in Western architecture since the time of Greece, were in fact erected on this continent not so many centuries after the time when Teotihuacán was still in use as a sacred site (fig. 10). We remember that the Aztec kings were making ritual visits there in the early sixteenth century; the University of Virginia was built only three hundred years later. This is the curious syncopation that time wrought in the Americas, one even more mysterious when we realize that Pueblo ritual is still alive at the present day.

The contrast between Teotihuacán and the university is striking enough. They are both somehow suggestive of music, the university of the notes of piano and violin and the sounds of voices in conversation, Teotihuacán of the deep communal chant, the thunder of drums, and the pounding of thousands of feet upon the earth. Is it then so amazing that a hundred years later the masters of modern architecture had totally rejected Jefferson's music and, in America in the person of Frank Lloyd Wright, had chosen instead the primordial Amerindian image of the imitation by human beings of nature's forms? Taliesin West is, in principle, pure Teotihuacán (fig. 479). It is this that Wright turned toward during the second half of his life; the way of the old, unmoved continent, rejecting, at least in appearance, all the complexity of European urban civilization that had intervened between the pre-Columbian centuries and the present.

Wright's movement toward the primordial—it cannot and must not be called the "primitive," though Wright's generation may well have thought of it in those terms—is all the more striking because

Wright did not begin that way. Instead, he began in the suburbs with the American suburban lot. I recently heard a historian expatiating on Wright's parallel cross-axes as if he had been designing on the moon. Few critics, and almost no Europeans, least of all those who are apologists for deconstructive modernism, understand the American lot, but that is what Wright in his youth was designing for.

From the seventeenth century onward, the fundamental pattern had been the same in America, consisting of the lot, usually quadrangular, the house more or less in the middle of it, grass all around it, perhaps planted with shrubs and trees, a sidewalk, a thin grass plot with trees, and then the street with its curb. The development of the suburb simply clarified the pattern. Wright played upon it like a virtuoso, exploiting the whole unit and interweaving the building and the lot in his design (figs. 475, 476). His cross-axes divide the lot into quadrants, each one an enlargement or servant of the interior spaces. A front lawn, a garden, an entrance drive, and a garage court are all continuous extensions of the axes that cross at the fireplace mass in the center of the house.

When Wright published his work as drawings in the Wasmuth publication of 1910 and as photographs in that of 1911,* the European architects who were entranced by it had little idea of the urban context it celebrated (fig. 477) and out of which it had taken shape. (This recalls Palladio and the *Quattro libri*.) They saw the forms as spinning free in space, and this reinforced and seemed to sanction their burgeoning hatred for the traditional urban fabric which they

Frank Lloyd Wright, Ausgeführte bauten und entwürfe, Berlin, Wasmuth, 1910; and *Frank Lloyd Wright: Ausgeführte Bauten,* Berlin, 1911.

474. Charlottesville. University of Virginia. Colonnade.

475. Highland Park, Illinois. Ward W. Willitts house. 1902. Frank Lloyd Wright. View on lot.

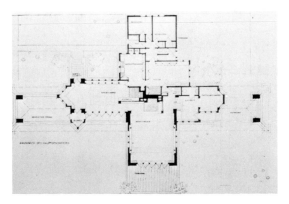

476. Ward W. Willitts house. Plan, first floor.

477. Highland Park. Ward W. Willitts house. Porte cochère, from Wasmuth.

478. Los Angeles, California. Ennis house. 1923–1924.
Frank Lloyd Wright.

were girding themselves to destroy, as indeed, paradoxically, especially in America, they were eventually in large measure to do.

Wright himself lost his suburban milieu at just that time. In a sense, he was booted out of it when he left his home and family in 1909 and, so he wrote to the newspapers, embraced free love. Then tragedy struck him and he was left alone, uprooted, to deal with the continent as a whole. In California, in those years of the early 1920s, he built four houses out of concrete blocks. All of them overtly cited the pre-Columbian architecture with which he had, indeed, flirted in his earliest work but had thereafter, until about 1914, almost completely abandoned. The Ennis house (fig. 478) surmounts its California

479. Scottsdale, Arizona. Taliesin West. Begun 1938. Frank Lloyd Wright. Distant view with mountains.

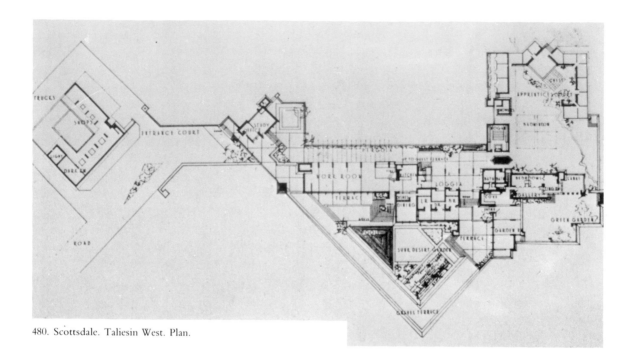

480. Scottsdale. Taliesin West. Plan.

hilltop like a temple from Tikal before the excavation of its base, and it rides across the city of Los Angeles like some avenging phantom from the pre-Columbian past.

Finally, at Taliesin West (fig. 479), Wright found his way back to the primitive mountains themselves, sacred shrouded presences far out across the continent at the desert's edge. Now that principle of imitation which Neil Levine finds in Wright's work after the abstraction of the early years discovers its proper ritual place at the mountains' feet. So Taliesin West echoes the deeply eroded striations of the so-called Superstition Mountains northeast of Phoenix; high beyond them, the reservation of the White Mountain Apache lies. The body of the building seems to grow out of the sandy slopes directly behind it. Its profiles, colors, and textures are the same as those of its surroundings. Its plan (fig. 480), like that of Hadrian's Villa (fig. 195), is an affair of intersecting diagonal axes, each of which

481. Scottsdale. Taliesin West. Masonry, overhang, and desert.

leads the eye out to dominant landscape features in the distance.

The desert itself is framed in multiple views, most of all from the climactic loggia that opens through the building next to the little suburban Usonian house with its fireplace that is hidden with its greenery behind a roughly archaic Mexican wall (fig. 481). The axis of the loggia is the open heart of the house. Along it, directed

483. Scottsdale. Taliesin West. Frank Lloyd Wright. View to mountains.

toward the mountain's most embracing form, Wright was engaged in laying out what he described as a "menhir avenue" when he died (fig. 482). Its terminus was to be a stone he called "The Madonna," which before that had stood in a pool of water on a cross-axial view toward a conical hill behind the loggia itself. Later, ill-advised building at Taliesin blocked that view; so Wright turned back toward the Superstition Mountains at last (fig. 483). He apparently understood the whole thing perfectly well. "The Mayans," he once said in an unguarded moment, "could not have done it better."

Perhaps it is not surprising that Wright should have gone this route in the end, cut off from the whole communal European urban tradition as American iconoclasm and his own egregious individuality had made him. What is amazing is that Le Corbusier, Wright's greatest contemporary and, in Wright's view, rival, was doing exactly the same thing during the same decades. He, too, was turning to the

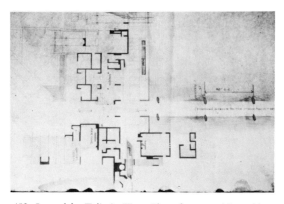

482. Scottsdale. Taliesin West. Plan of proposed "menhir avenue," 1959.

primordial and to the elemental relationships of manmade to natural forms. In Le Corbusier's case, however, the model was Greek rather than Amerindian. Nôtre-Dame de Ronchamp (fig. 487) is as much an active sculptural body as any Greek temple, but it is now a pictorially free one, free of species, bereft of fellows, writhing and, indeed, crying out—Le Corbusier called it an *acoustique paysagiste* after all—on the top of its hill in the face of the Jura.

The Monastery of La Tourette and High Court at Chandigarh (fig. 489) stand out in the landscape like Greek temples, sculptural embodiments of human action but, like Wright's forms, truly at home only in the landscape, not urban at all. Again, the fundamental relationships are those of ancient religion, but now individualized. Like Wright, Le Corbusier did not start there in his early work. We have noted his familiarity with the planning of Louis XIV, no less than that of Alphand in the Bois de Boulogne (fig. 436) and his subversion of that model to destroy the fabric of the traditional city rather than to sustain it (fig. 422).

Beyond that, like Palladio, Le Corbusier built villas; their forms expressed a

484. Poissy, France. Villa Savoie. 1929–1931. Le Corbusier.

machine aesthetic, he claimed. In fact, it was an aesthetic wholly Neoplatonic and one that the modern materials of industrial steel and reinforced concrete enabled him to carry further than Palladio had ever

485. *Ville radieuse*. Le Corbusier. Sketch "indicating human scale."

486. New Canaan, Connecticut. Glass House. 1949. Philip Johnson.

done (or apparently wanted to do) toward the dematerialization of the building itself into line drawing. His Villa Savoie (fig. 484) is stretched tight as paper, like the *bassins* of the Classic garden; its details are as thin as drawn lines, its fundamental shapes those of the circle and the square. The Man of Perfect Proportions can be imagined inside it, his outstretched limbs stretching its materials back to pure Idea. In that sense, Le Corbusier was the most completely Neoplatonic architect of all the thousands over the centuries who have subscribed to that doctrine. It is perhaps odd, then, that he did not perceive the equal triumph of Neoplatonism in Le Nôtre's parterres and so employ them in some material relationship with his villa forms. One can imagine the Villa Savoie alighting on the Parterre du Midi at Versailles like some space ship seeking its proper home.

Le Nôtre had also been admirably skillful in making small gardens seem noble and large, as in the delightful Jardin de Sylvie at Chantilly or the bishop's miter he designed for Bossuet at Meaux (fig. 426). But Le Corbusier showed no interest in the Classic parterre or, really, in any other garden form except, characteristically, the *jardin anglais* he imagined for his superblocks and, indeed, for his *Ville radieuse* as a whole (fig. 485). Again, it is the picturesque English garden, however summarily simplified, that comes through as the only garden form with which the International Style would deal as a setting for its abstract, ideal forms. It is another

486a, b. Seaside, Florida. 1980ff. Andres Duany and Elizabeth Plater-Zyberk. Robert Davis, developer. Two views.

486c. San Quentin-en-Yvelines near Versailles, France. Les Arcades du Lac. Ricardo Bofill. 1972–1975.

example of the contradictory opposites it embraced. Though perhaps, to be fair, we should see it as one of the strange condensations that created the special appeal of the International Style to the modern mind. In terms of the modern garden as such, it might be argued that Roberto Burle Marx's adaptation of the curvilinear patterns of the romantic garden according to the more intensely biomorphic curves of abstract painting is its strongest attempt

so far to achieve a new character. It is, of course, like its architecture still pictorial but, paradoxically, rather French in that, being more *drawn* than the English Picturesque has normally been (fig. 436). But most modern architects have not wanted such a garden; they have wanted their country and suburban houses to stand in what seems to be untouched nature itself. Of this, Philip Johnson's Glass House in New Canaan (fig. 486), far beyond its per-

487. London, England. Roehampton Housing Development. 1950s. London County Council.

haps more beautiful predecessor in design, Mies van der Rohe's Farnsworth House, is the ultimate expression and the logical climax of the villa mode: In it the human occupant, the liberated individual—alone, with no family, no town—is set out in nature and wholly exposed to it, precisely by being invisibly protected from it by the power and the technology of the modern day. It is the apogee of modern architecture, the Ideal realized, and there was no place to go from it until, with the revival of the vernacular and Classical traditions in the work of Venturi (figs. 315, 316, 317, 437) and others, the values of community building and of traditional urbanism could be asserted once more. One thinks especially of Duany and Plater-Zyberk at the scale of the American town, if available at present only for the affluent (figs. 486a, 486b), and of Ricardo Bofill at the scale of Versailles, for the poorest of the poor (486c).

For Le Corbusier, the city was to be all garden—Paris was already that—but it

488. Chandigarh, India. Entrance portico with sentry.

was to be an English garden with the glittering slabs of enormous buildings standing among the trees. As it worked out in practice, of course, it was only at Roehampton in England (fig. 487), after World War II, that the Corbusian superblocks ever really came to stand in an English park, handsome to look at but apparently encouraging all kinds of social problems in their total destruction of neighborhood amenities and other communal values. Le Corbusier's early villas themselves had no suburban traditional lots, like Wright's, to organize in some integral architectural manner. The relationship to the site, as at the Villa Savoie, was thus arbitrary, and, most of all, pictorial. The villas themselves were post-Cubist, "Purist," cerebral objects, standing in the contrasting Impressionist landscapes of suburban Paris. It may well be that it was, indeed, their preoccupation with doing it all themselves, like painters, that prevented the modern masters of architecture like Le Corbusier from ever coming to grips afresh with the question of the garden as a designed environment, wherein people who know and care about growing things need to take a hand. Just so, when the modern architects came to design their cities, they failed to consult anybody who knew anything about how cities were made or how people lived in them.

Much of this had to do with the appeal of primitivism to those architects: To a man, they despised the complex urban fabric of the post-Renaissance world, most especially including the Classic gardens that had grown up with it and done so much to shape it as well. Hence, no sooner had Le Corbusier announced his machine aesthetic than he abandoned it and turned in his late work to primitivistic, brutally conceived forms. The Neo-

489. Chandigarh, India. High Court Building. 1951–1956. Le Corbusier. Perspective drawing in landscape.

platonism of pure drawing was cast aside. Older Classical ideas were invoked: most of all the temple as physical body in the landscape as we noted above (figs. 488, 489). But it was now the temple seen as a kind of ruin, roughly surfaced, aggressively modeled, in general more Titanic than Olympian. So Le Corbusier developed his *beton brut* for the late work, primitivizing and brutalizing the fabric of his buildings, making them look old, primordial. Having cast out all the civilized paraphernalia of urban design, where else could he have gone but to the landscape in its most mythic form? Therefore, the columns of the High Court at Chandigarh (fig. 488) are made to leap up like those of the Temple of Athena at Paestum, with no horizontal cornice to arrest the eye (fig. 88), so causing us empathetically to experience, in both buildings, "the feelings that make the town," directly in opposition to nature's awful forms (fig. 489).

All that worked very well when it was set far out in the wild landscape, which is

491. Chandigarh. High Court Building. Facade, as painted.

490. Boston, Massachusetts. City Hall. 1963–1970. Kallman, McKinnell and Knowles.

the way Le Corbusier wanted to see Chandigarh, as his great drawings of it show (fig. 489). But it is also the main plaza of a town, and in that sense, with its vast space meagerly defined, it is in actuality much less urbanistically appropriate and effective than it ought to be. What, then, if the primitivized monsters were to invade the existing cities themselves? In fact, they did so, and by the early 1960s those Brutalist buildings had combined with Le Corbusier's cataclysmic principles of town planning to blow a good many old cities apart. The Boston City Hall, for example (fig. 490), is an uncouth monster, laying about itself with Neanderthalic roarings and tearing the very center of Boston to pieces. It evokes the ruin as well, because it has been swept clean of all those complex architectural details, developed over the centuries, like the rest of the urban fabric, that endow buildings

with a literally compromised, civilized scale.

At Chandigarh, the High Court embodies powerful physical lunges, empathetically overwhelming, like those of the American Abstract Expressionist painting of the same decades (fig. 491). It also shares that painting's ambiguity of meaning and lack of focused associations. In this, it may gain a kind of oceanic flux and ambiguity, as Abstract Expressionism surely does—and, in painting, why not and as much as possible. But a monumental public building needs to be clear in its place and its meanings, and the High Court, except in its one great and tragic gesture to the mountains, is not clear.

This is especially apparent when it is compared with one of its models, Viceroy's House at New Delhi, by Sir Edwin Lutyens (fig. 492). Both buildings span

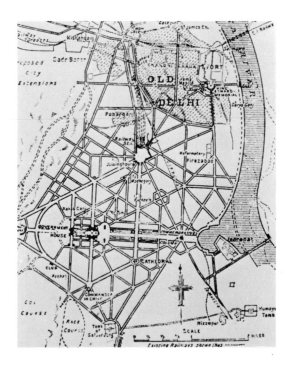

493. Old and New Delhi, India. Map. 1912.

494. New Delhi. Viceroy's House. View of Jaipur Column and All-India War Memorial Arch from dome of Viceroy's Palace.

492. New Delhi, India. Viceroy's House. 1912–1929. Sir Edwin Lutyens. East facade. Detail.

their entrances, as it were, with enormous lintels, below which the supporting columns or piers seem visually to be hung—or at least to escape from compression into pure gesture. But Viceroy's House speaks a clear, known language; it is articulate, and architecturally rather than pictorially conceived. It is also involved in a great Classic plan, that of New Delhi as a whole.

Lutyens had been a brilliant architect of country houses; his work may indeed be said to have climaxed the genre. In it, he had moved steadily toward Classical symmetry, scale, and detail, while he and Gertrude Jekyll, his mentor in garden de-

sign, soon evolved a dense condensation of the Picturesque and Classical modes to complement the house with gardens themselves richly architectural, lush, and very powerful. At New Delhi, however, the urbanistic requirements, especially those of state symbolism and monumentality, required a purely Classical scheme (fig. 493), which was in this case directly in the tradition of Versailles, perhaps recalling the plan of Washington most of all. The monumental avenue called King's Way runs straight toward Viceroy's House from the arch of the far-off War Memorial (fig. 494). The whole complex of government buildings is lifted on a vast

495. New Delhi. Viceroy's House. View from Great Place.

podium, so that upon a closer approach, Viceroy's House, dead ahead, goes almost out of sight (fig. 495).* Only its dome rises into view, an infantry pith helmet, with the column in the center of the vast square held vertically before it like a weapon presented on parade. Once upon the height, we see it all before us, the column standing on the red parade ground as upon an imperial carpet (fig. 494), the whole mass of the house stretched out laterally to wide-spreading side pavilions like a vaster version of the Villa Emo, here giving us over to a fiercer sky (fig. 497). The dome rises in the center (fig. 492). Within it the

496. New Delhi. Viceroy's House. East front and Jaipur column.

viceroy's throne was placed. High above it an oculus was set in the dome so as to direct a shaft of sunlight directly onto the throne on the day of durbar. Outside, as well, the dome and the column

*An effect not desired by Lutyens and originally resisted by him. In general, see Robert Grant Irving, *Indian Summer: Lutyens, Baker, and Imperial Delhi,* New Haven, 1981.

497. New Delhi. Viceroy's House and secretariats, with garden.

498. New Delhi. Viceroy's House. Garden and pool fountain from west facade.

screen below it embody pure authority, perhaps more than a little threat. If the whole composition was intended to magnify the power of the disciplined troops of the Raj, we should not forget that a free India has absorbed its imagery, outside and in, lock, stock, and barrel. Indeed, modern India has taken New Delhi to its heart.

On the other hand, it does not really know what to make of Chandigarh, and it treats the High Court there with small respect (fig. 491). Perhaps, in the end, this is the case because the High Court is really a private rather than a public building—as an Abstract Expressionist painting is, despite what may be its comparatively enormous size, always private in scale. Perhaps this is a higher good on an existential level; it may be the very best that the International Style could do, but a city cannot be built in this way.

New Delhi seems to serve the Indian nation even better than it did the Empire. It has certainly done so for a much longer time. The high Indian sky sails over Viceroy's House, leading us beyond it to its garden, a Mogul Versailles (fig. 497). It stretches out toward the flat horizon past lily-pad fountains (fig. 498) which Wright was not ashamed to take as models for the

499. Taos Pueblo, North House. 1976. Christmas Eve. Prepared for the Deer Dance.

little monument to his granddaughter he set up on the axis between desert and mountain at Taliesin West (fig. 483). But New Delhi is all public imagery at vast scale, designed as a symbol of the structure of the modern state, organizing and directing the activities of the hundreds of thousands of human beings whom its continental spaces can accommodate.

The capacity to identify with the modern nation still seems as far as most contemporary human beings can stretch themselves. Such surely may not be the most civilized state of affairs humanity can attain. Perhaps the very first set of man-to-nature relationships we considered in these chapters is at least potentially a more civilized one, since it brings all living things together; existence is shared equally by all. The relation of Taos to its mountain suggests the symbiotic character of that relationship (fig. 499); and Richard Falk and Claude Lévi-Strauss have told us what its relevance is to the problem of survival faced by humanity today. Falk writes: "We need to work out a whole new world view, based on a timely renewal of more primitive [*sic*] conceptions of man and nature, based on the idea of the earth as whole and limited," and he quotes Lévi-Strauss:

> It would take a spiritual revolution as great as that which led to the advent of Christianity. It would require that man, who since the Renaissance has been brought up to adore himself, acquire modesty, and that he learn the lesson of all the atrocities we have experienced for thirty or forty years. He would do well to learn that if one thinks only man is respectable among living things, well then, the frontier is placed too close to mankind and he

500. Thiepval, France. World War I Memorial. Sir Edwin Lutyens. Approach across the battlefield.

501. Thiepval. The memorial. The mask.

502. Thiepval. The sarcophagus and the scream.

503. Thiepval. From sarcophagus to French and English graveyards.

can no longer be protected. One must first consider that it is as a living being that man is worthy of respect, and hence one must extend that respect to all living beings—at that point, the frontier is pushed back, and mankind finds itself better protected.*

Surely the nation-state has come close to destroying civilization, mankind, perhaps nature itself in our time. Again, a great work of architecture by Sir Edwin Lutyens helps us perceive the character of one major part of that threat, the evil,

empty face of war. North of Amiens the land rises slowly in rolling open fields leading toward the heights of the Somme. There Lutyens built a memorial to the hundreds of thousands of British and French soldiers who were killed in this landscape, literally for nothing, throughout the summer of 1916. They were heading for the high ground. We follow their track across the open fields (fig. 500). The memorial looms indistinctly far ahead of us on the height. We move toward it. There is no cover. We imagine the machine guns sweeping the gentle slopes. We turn toward the little folds in the earth that open to left and right of the road and seem to offer a refuge from that fire; it is ap-

*Richard A. Falk, *This Endangered Planet,* New York, 1971, pp. 18–19.

parent that the infantry did exactly that before us. They are still there in many of the defilades, laid out neatly in small cemeteries where the artillery and the mortars found them. We arrive at the height, the objective (fig. 501). The monument looms over us, stepping mountainously up and back in brick and white trim like one of the American skyscrapers of the 1920s.

It is also an enormous monster; its tondi are eyes; its high arch screams. It is the open mouth of death, the ultimate "portrait" of landscape art that rises up to consume us all. The monster stands behind a carpet of grass. There is no path for us. We must violate the grass. Closer, we are enveloped by the creature's great gorge (fig. 502). One sarcophagus like a palate lies within it, under the arch. We must go left or right up diagonal stairways to approach it. The white stone panels are covered with the names of the dead, untold thousands of names.

We approach the sarcophagus; a view opens beyond it to the other side. Then we see the men (fig. 503). Out there at a measured distance from the monument two thin companies of soldiers stand silent at parade, French on the left, British on the right. It is a cemetery. National characteristics are much to the fore. The French graves of the unknown are marked by rough concrete crosses bearing little bronze plaques saying only, toughly, "*In-*

connu.'' The English graves are marked by flat limestone slabs inscribed with the words "A Soldier of the Great War, Known to God." We descend from the monument, approaching the graves. Now they seem to be facing the arch, advancing across the open space toward it (fig. 504). It should be said that everybody who visits the monument is weeping by now. It is this that does it: the terrible courage of human beings advancing in the open toward the monster, who is absolute — absolute pain and nothingness. He is emptiness, meaninglessness, insatiable war and death. There is no victory for the dead. All that courage wasted. But there they stand, the men, unbroken. It is not to be borne.

It is also touching that Lutyens clearly used the neo-Greco pilgrimage church in the town of Albert, Nôtre Dame de Brébières, just out of sight in the valley below, as the model for his memorial (fig. 505 a,b). He adopted its redbrick and stone trim and abstracted their relationship and clarified and magnified their forms. The church, after repeated bombardment, had an unintended cross vault in the side of its

504a, b. Thiepval. Names of the war dead and their graves.

505a, b. Albert, France. Nôtre Dame de Brébières, with the "Virgin of Albert."

506. Thiepval. Death rules over the dead.

510. Maya Lin. Study sketch for Vietnam Veterans' Memorial, pastel. 1981.

508. Vietnam Veteran's Memorial. View from above with Washington Monument.

509. Vietnam Veteran's Memorial. View toward the Lincoln Memorial.

tower, and Lutyens incorporated that, too, in his memorial. Most of all, Albert had been sung by all the poets in the British ranks because, as yet another fluke of bombardment, a statue of the Virgin and Child that crowned the tower (fig. 505b) hung perpendicular to the ground for many months, leaning over the street, as if the Virgin were about to dash the Savior to the ground, driven mad by compassion for the marching men below.* Now they sleep at Thiepval under the eye of death and in its silent scream (fig. 506). There is no place for the living there. It all belongs to them. The face of death is marked with their names, and men and the landscape alike lie under that last staring mask, that Aeschylean glare.

In 1980, a senior in Yale College sat in the back of a lecture room and watched a number of the same pictures of Thiepval that we have used as illustrations pass before her on the screen. She had already designed her entry in the enormous competition that was being held that year for a memorial in Washington to the veterans of the Vietnam War, but she had not yet written the statement of intention that was required to accompany it. She was Maya Lin, and as the last illustration came on the screen, she began to write:

> These names, seemingly infinite in number, carry the sense of overwhelming numbers, while unifying those individuals into a whole.
>
> Brought to a sharp awareness of such a loss, it is up to each individual to resolve or come to terms with this loss [fig. 507]. For death is in the end a personal and private mat-

ter, and the area contained within this memorial is meant for personal reflection and private reckoning.

Later she went on:

> I had an impulse to cut open the earth . . . an initial violence that in time would heal [fig. 506]. The grass would grow back, but the cut would remain. . . . I didn't visualize heavy physical objects implanted in the earth; instead it was as if the black-grown earth were polished and made into an interface between the sunny world and the quiet, dark world beyond, that we can't enter. . . . I chose black granite to make the surface reflective and peaceful. The angle was formed solely in relation to the Lincoln Memorial and Washington Monument [figs. 508, 509] to create a unity between the nation's past and present. . . . Later, when I visited, I searched out the name of a friend's father. I touched it and I cried [fig. 507]. I was another visitor and I was reacting to it as I designed it.*

Lutyens's Thiepval menaces the living, ferociously guards the dead. But in Maya Lin's memorial the ground opens for all of us. We are drawn into it, touching the cool face of death with our hand. We commune with the dead. They have a country still. The ages crowd in with us, remembering the surface of the earth and the cut into it, the Classic gesture to the horizon and to the temple and the sun. The impulse remains to respect the integrity of the earth, to find a truth in it and, beyond dying, to shape a community with it for the common good.

*Cf. Paul Fussell, *The Great War and Modern Memory,* New York and London, 1975, esp. pp. 131–5.

National Geographic, vol. 167, no. 5, May 1985, 557.

507. Washington, D.C. Vietnam Veteran's Memorial. 1980–1984. Maya Lin. The names of the dead.

CREDITS

PHOTO NO.	SOURCE
35, 36	Yale University Slide and Photograph Collection
37	Roger Wood, *Egypt in Color,* New York, McGraw-Hill, 1984
38	Yale University Slide and Photograph Collection
39, 40	Vincent Scully
41, 42	Yale University Slide and Photograph Collection
43	A. Elizabeth Chase
44	Katherine Farina
45–49	Yale University Slide and Photograph Collection
50	Vincent Scully
51	Herakleion Museum, Crete
52	Carlo Cresti, *Grecia e Mediterraneo:* "Il Palazzodi Cnosso," Sadea/Sansoni, Florence, 1967, photo by Gustavo Tomsich
53	Art Resource
54	Hoegler, *Crete and its Treasures*
55–57	Vincent Scully
58	Metropolitan Museum of Art
59–62	Vincent Scully
63	Carl W. Blegen and Marion Rawson, *Guide to the Palace of Nestor,* University of Cincinnati, 1962, reconstruction by Piet de Jong
64–68	Vincent Scully
69	Yale University Slide and Photograph Collection
70	Saskia Ltd.
71	Steven A. Seiden
72	Athens, National Museum
73, 74	Vincent Scully
75	Wycherly, *How the Greeks Built Cities*
76	Delphi Museum
77	Vincent Scully
78	Yale University Slide and Photograph Collection
79, 80	Vincent Scully
81, 82	Yale University Slide and Photograph Collection
83	Vincent Scully
84	William A. MacDonald
85a	Vincent Scully
85b	Saskia Ltd.
86	Villa Giulia Museum

PHOTO NO.	SOURCE
87–93	Vincent Scully
94	Hellenic Fine Arts Friends Society
95–104	Vincent Scully
105	Doxiadis, *Raumordnung in Greichischen Stadtbau*
106	Vincent Scully
107	Yale University Slide and Photograph Collection
108	Doxiadis, *Raumordnung in Greischischen Stadtbau*
109	Vincent Scully
110	Robert, *Die Iliupersis des Polygnot*
111	Museo Nacional del Prado
112	Yale University Slide and Photograph Collection
113	Vincent Scully
114–116	Yale University Slide and Photograph Collection
117	Vincent Scully
118	Yale University Slide and Photograph Collection
119	Rodenwaldt, *Olympia*
120	Musée du Louvre
121–122	Art Resource
123	Yale University Slide and Photograph Collection
124–126	Musée du Louvre
127	Rodenwaldt, *Olympia*
128	Vincent Scully
129–131	Yale University Slide and Photograph Collection
132	Vincent Scully
133	Schuchardt, *Archiasche Plastik Auf der Akropolis*
134, 135	Yale University Slide and Photograph Collection
136, 137	Vincent Scully
138	Saskia, Ltd.
139–144	Vincent Scully
145	Dr. Douglas Lewis
146	British Museum
147, 148	Vincent Scully
149	American School of Classical Studies
150–152	Yale University Slide and Photograph Collection
153	Allan Ludwig

PHOTO NO.	SOURCE
154	Vincent Scully
155	Steven A. Seiden
156	Vincent Scully
157	Allison Frantz
158, 159	Vincent Scully
160–164	Allan Ludwig
165–167	Vincent Scully
168	Oliver Radford
169a–170	Vincent Scully
171	Frederick Cooper
172	A. W. Lawrence, *Greek Architecture,* Pelican History of Art Series, Penguin Books, 1957, plate 81a.
173	*Hesperia* no. 29, 1960
174	von Gerkan, *Griechische Stadteanlagen*
175	Yale University Slide and Photograph Collection
176	Doxiadis, *Raumordnung in Griechischen Stadtbau*
177	Vincent Scully
178	Scheffold, *Die Griechen und ihre Nachbarn*
179, 180	Vincent Scully
181	Art Resource
182	William A. MacDonald
183, 184	Yale University Slide and Photograph Collection
185	Kahler, *Der Romische Temple*
186	*L'Afrique Romaine,* Algeria, 1949, pp. 24–25
187	Yale University Slide and Photograph Collection
188	Vincent Scully
189, 190	Yale University Slide and Photograph Collection
191	B. Michael Boyle
192	Gertrude Levy, *Gate of Horn,* London, Faber & Faber, 1948
193	Fototeca Unione
194	*Progressive Architecture,* June 1965, cover
195	Vigni, *Villa Hadriana*
196	Oliver Radford
197	Steven A. Seiden
198	William A. MacDonald

PHOTO NO.	SOURCE
199	Alinari-Anderson
200	National Gallery of Art, Washington; Samuel H. Kress Collection
201	Yale University Slide and Photograph Collection
202	*L'Architecttura*
203	Charles McClendon
204	Richard Krautheimer, *Rome, profile of a city,* Princeton University Press, c. 1980
205	Watercolor, photo courtesy William A. MacDonald
205a	Budek
206	Nikolas Pevsner, *Europaische Architecktur (An Outline of European Architecture)*
207	Sandak
208, 209	Sumner Crosby
210	Yale University Slide and Photograph Collection
211	Sandak
212	Yale University Slide and Photograph Collection
213	Rave, *Corvey*
214	P. A. Reinhardt
215	Sumner Crosby
216	Caroline Astrid Bruzelius
217	Yale University Slide and Photograph Collection
218, 219	Sumner Crosby
220	Yale University Slide and Photograph Collection
221, 222	Sumner Crosby
223, 224	Yale University Slide and Photograph Collection
225, 226	Seymour, *Nôtre Dame of Noyon*
227	Sandak
228–230	Yale University Slide and Photograph Collection
231	*Encyclopedia of World Art,* New York, McGraw-Hill, 1962, Volume VI, p. 471
232	Les Archives Photographiques
233–235	Sandak
236–240	Yale University Slide and Photograph Collection
241	Art Resource
242	Jane Hayward
243	Sandak

PHOTO NO.	SOURCE
244	Yale University Slide and Photograph Collection
245	Art Resource
246	Yale University Slide and Photograph Collection
247	Les Archives Photographiques
248	Bruno Balestrini
249, 250	Sumner Crosby
257	Photographie Giraudon
258–262	Yale University Slide and Photograph Collection
263	Vincent Scully
264	Whitman Knap
265–268a	Yale University Slide and Photograph Collection
268b	R. Thompson
269	Yale University Slide and Photograph Collection
270	Standish Lawder
271 (a,b,c)	Allan Ludwig
272, 273	Yale University Slide and Photograph Collection
274	Sandak
275	Yale University Slide and Photograph Collection
276	Vincent Scully
277	Yale University Slide and Photograph Collection
278	Steven Scher
279	Sumner Crosby
280	Art Resource
281	*Attraverso L'Italia*
282	Evelyn Hofer
283	Yale University Slide and Photograph Collection
284	Art Resource
285	Martin Trachtenberg
286	Oliver Radford
287	Art Resource
288	Sumner Crosby
289	Ellen G. Miles
290	Sumner Crosby
291	Art Resource
292, 293	Alinari-Brogi

PHOTO NO.	SOURCE
294 a,b	Art Resource
295	Gutkind, *Our World From the Air*
296	Art Resource
297	Vincent Scully
298–300	Yale University Slide and Photograph Collection
301, 302	Art Resource
303	Zevi, *Michelangelo Architectto*
304	Art Resource
305	Yale University Slide and Photograph Collection
306	Public Domain
307	Norris Smith
308	Zevi, *Michelangelo Architectto*
309	Yale University Slide and Photograph Collection
310	Oliver Radford
311	Art Resource
312	*Historic Preservation*
313	Sandak
314	*Preservation News*
315	Amy Weisser
316, 317	Venturi and Scott Brown
318	Yale University Slide and Photograph Collection
319	Walters Art Gallery, Baltimore
320	*Connaissance des Arts,* December, 1966
321	Yale University Slide and Photograph Collection
322	Vincent Scully
323	Hermann, *Die Stadt Rom im 15–16thc*
324, 325	Yale University Slide and Photograph Collection
326 a,b	Vincent Scully
327	Yale University Slide and Photograph Collection
328 a,b	Vincent Scully
329	National Gallery of Art, London
330–336	Vincent Scully
337, 338	William A. MacDonald
339–343b	Vincent Scully
344	David A. Brown

PHOTO NO.	SOURCE
345	Vincent Scully
346	Yale University Slide and Photograph Collection
347, 348	David A. Brown
349	Yale University Slide and Photograph Collection
350a, 351	Vincent Scully
352	Mitford, *The Sun King*
353	Yale University Slide and Photograph Collection
354 a,b	Vincent Scully
355	Yale University Slide and Photograph Collection
356	Bibliotheque National, Paris
357	Les Archives Photographiques
358, 359	Yale University Slide and Photograph Collection
360 a,b,c	Vincent Scully
361	Yale University Slide and Photograph Collection
362–368b	Vincent Scully
369	National Gallery of Art, London
370	Vincent Scully
371	Metropolitan Museum of Art
372 a,b	Vincent Scully
373	Saskia, Ltd.
374	Vincent Scully
375	Gemaldegalerie, Dresden
376, 377	Vincent Scully
378	Yale University Slide and Photograph Collection
379	Metropolitan Museum of Art
380a–382	Vincent Scully
383–386	Yale University Slide and Photograph Collection
387	Ernest De Ganay, *Andre Le Nostre,* Paris, Vincent, Freale et Cie, 1962
388–393	Vincent Scully
394, 395	Yale University Slide and Photograph Collection
396	Ernest De Ganay, *Andre Le Nostre,* Paris, Vincent, Freale et Cie, 1962
397	de la Croix, *Military Considerations in City Planning*
398 a,b	Vincent Scully
399	de la Croix, *Military Considerations in City Planning*
400, 401	Vincent Scully

PHOTO NO.	SOURCE
402	Rocolle, *2000 ans de fortification francaise*
403	Muller, *Treatise of Fortification*
404	Parent and Verroust, *Vauban*
405	Casa Buonarotti, Florence
406	Parent and Verroust, *Vauban*
407, 408	Casa Buonarotti, Florence
409	Parent and Verroust, *Vauban*
410 a,b,c,d	Vincent Scully
411, 412	Parent and Verroust, *Vauban*
413	Vincent Scully
414	Parent and Verroust, *Vauban*
415	Muller, *Treatise of Fortification*
416	Yale University Slide and Photograph Collection
417	de la Croix, *Military Considerations in City Planning*
418	Yale University Slide and Photograph Collection
419	Hegemann, *City Planning Housing*
420	Yale University Slide and Photograph Collection
421	Bournon, *Paris-Atlas*
422, 423	Yale University Slide and Photograph Collection
424	Steve Dunwell
425	Yale University Slide and Photograph Collection
426	De Ganay, *Andre Le Nostre,* Paris, Vincent, Freale et Cie, 1962
427	Leon Krier
428	Mitford, *The Sun King*
429, 430	Yale University Slide and Photograph Collection
431	Vincent Scully
432	Yale University Slide and Photograph Collection
433	Parent and Verroust, *Vauban*
434, 435	Vincent Scully
436a	Andres Duany
436b	Yale University Slide and Photograph Collection
437	Venturi and Scott Brown
438	Yale University Slide and Photograph Collection
439 a,b	Vincent Scully
440	Yale University Slide and Photograph Collection

PHOTO NO.	SOURCE
441a–444	Vincent Scully
445–447	Yale University Slide and Photograph Collection
448–451	Vincent Scully
452	Yale University Slide and Photograph Collection
453a–454b	Vincent Scully
455–457	Yale University Slide and Photograph Collection
458	Stephen Harby
458a	Sumner Crosby
459 a,b	Vincent Scully
460, 461	Yale University Slide and Photograph Collection
462	Kerry Downes
463	Brad Bellows
464	Yale University Slide and Photograph Collection
465	National Gallery of Ireland
466	Edwin Smith
467	National Gallery of Art, London
468, 469	Yale University Slide and Photograph Collection
470	John Troha/Black Star
471	Sandak
472, 473	Yale University Slide and Photograph Collection
474	Oliver Radford
475	Sandak
476	*Ausgeführte Bauten und Entwurfe von Frank Lloyd Wright,* Berlin, Wasmuth, 1910
477	Frank Lloyd Wright, *Ausgeführte Bauten,* Berlin, Wasmuth, 1911
478	Yale University Slide and Photograph Collection
479	Sandak
480	Taliesen Fellowship, copyright 1991 FLWright Fdn.
481	Yale University Slide and Photograph Collection
482	Taliesen Fellowship, copyright 1991 FLWright Fdn.
483	Yale University Slide and Photograph Collection
484	Yukio Futagawa
485	Yale University Slide and Photograph Collection
486a	Andres Duany
486b	Steven Brooke
486 c,d	Vincent Scully

PHOTO NO.	SOURCE
486	Robert A.M. Stern
487	British Architectural Library
488	Illustrated London News
489	Le Corbusier, *L'Oeuvre Complete,* Zurich, 1910–1965, v.5
490	Saskia Ltd.
491	Norma Evenson
492	A.S.G. Butler, *The Architecture of Sir Edward Lutyens,* New York, Scribner, 1950, v.2
493	Yale University Slide and Photograph Collection
494	Robert Grant Irving
495, 496	Robert Freson
497	Allan Greenberg
498	A.S.G. Butler, *The Architecture of Sir Edward Lutyens,* New York, Scribner, 1950, v.2
499	Ross Frank
500–506	Vincent Scully
507–510	Maya Lin

INDEX